ARA'S KNIGHTS

ARA'S KNIGHTS

ARA PARSEGHIAN AND THE GOLDEN ERA OF NOTRE DAME FOOTBALL

FRANK POMARICO AND RAY SERAFIN

ILLUSTRATIONS BY THOMAS POMARICO

Library of Congress Cataloging-in-Publication Data

Pomarico, Frank.

Ara's knights : Ara Parseghian and the golden era of Notre Dame football / Frank Pomarico, Ray Serafin ; foreword by Regis Philbin ; introduction by Gerry DiNardo.
pages cm

ISBN 978-1-62937-111-5 (paperback)
1. Parseghian, Ara, 1923- 2. Football coaches—United States—Biography.
3. University of Notre Dame—Football. 4. Notre Dame Fighting Irish (Football team) I. Serafin, Ray. II. Title.
GV939.P36P66 2015
796.332092—dc23
[B]

2015009148

This book is available in quantity at special discounts for your group or organization. For further information, contact:

Triumph Books LLC
814 North Franklin Street
Chicago, Illinois 60610
(312) 337-0747
www.triumphbooks.com

Printed in U.S.A.
ISBN: 978-1-62937-111-5
Design by Meghan Grammer

Photos courtesy of the University of Notre Dame unless otherwise indicated
Artwork courtesy of Thomas Pomerico

This book is dedicated to Ara Parseghian and to the Ara Parseghian Medical Research Foundation, an organization dedicated to finding a treatment for Niemann-Pick Disease Type C (NP-C). This dreaded disease took the lives of three of Ara's grandchildren, all of whom were children of his son, Mike, and daughter-in-law, Cindy Parseghian. Michael, Marcia, and Christa each passed away before the age of 17. The foundation is a commitment by the Parseghian family to give hope to other families whose children are threatened by NP-C and other neurodegenerative diseases. For more information, or to make a donation to the Ara Parseghian Medical Research Foundation for Niemann-Pick Type C, please visit www.parseghian.org.

Contents

Foreword

There have been football coaches at Notre Dame who will never be forgotten. Knute Rockne was the first. He was later followed by Frank Leahy, who played for Rockne and after World War II took Notre Dame to four unbeaten seasons in a row. I was fortunate enough to be at Notre Dame for that fourth straight unbeaten season. Notre Dame was at its best under his coaching. But one day Leahy had to retire. It was in 1954, and for the next 10 years, Notre Dame searched for the right replacement. It finally found him: Ara Parseghian.

Before he came to Notre Dame, Ara Parseghian coached a Northwestern University football team that was good enough to beat the Irish four years in a row. Father Theodore Hesburgh, the school president, had had enough of losing to Northwestern. His solution was to bring Ara to Notre Dame. Ara took over a team that lost seven of its nine games that previous season. Not long after he arrived on campus, on a bitter-cold February day, an entire crowd of students came out to stand in the snow and welcome him, cheering for a full 10 minutes.

His first season was a great one. After Notre Dame won its first five games, I had a feeling they were going to go all the way. I was doing a talk show in San Diego and I wrote to Ara and told him I would like to interview him after the last game of the season, in Los Angeles against Southern Cal. He said okay but wanted to do it Sunday morning instead of right after the game on Saturday, so we arranged to meet at Los Angeles Coliseum.

Every student of Notre Dame football knows how the Fighting Irish went into that final game 9–0, only to lose a heartbreaker in the final seconds. It ended the dream of a national championship, and I wondered if Ara would be in the mood to do the promised interview the next day. In fact, I told the driver who was heading to pick him up, "Look, if the coach doesn't feel like doing it, tell him I understand." But when the car came back the door opened and there was Ara. I interviewed him on the 50-yard line and I found out then and there that he was a man of class who could be counted on to honor his commitments. I have seen Ara a number of times over the years, and he really is one of the most wonderful guys I've ever met. And he was hugely successful at Notre Dame, winning two national championships and coming close several other times in his 11 years at the Golden Dome.

Frank Pomarico grew up in Queens and went to high school in Brooklyn, dreaming of the chance to play at Notre Dame for Ara Parseghian. His passion and hard work enabled him to not only realize that dream, but also to become one of the captains of one of Ara's greatest teams. For this book, he talked with many other players who shared their stories of playing football for Ara Parseghian. They tell a story of a charismatic coach who made them better men, ready to go out and make a positive difference in the world. They provide inside stories on the games that marked this exciting era of Notre Dame football, such as the 1973 Sugar Bowl against the great Bear Bryant's Alabama team, one of the greatest games in college football history. And they share their perspectives on what it took to become champions.

Let them tell you why they still remain devoted to this coach who meant so much to his team, the students, and all of the Notre Dame family.

—Regis Philbin

Introduction

This book is a historic and personal journey, an account of the lives of a group of college football players who played for the legendary coach Ara Parseghian at Notre Dame in the early 1970s. The book shares many personal experiences of author Frank Pomarico and at the same time vividly portrays a very important time in Notre Dame football history under the leadership of one of the great coaches in college football history, Ara Parseghian.

For many of us, this book allows us to relive a very special time in our lives, a time that was touched by Ara Parseghian on a daily basis. The old saying about a leader who "is in the room before he arrives" doesn't do justice to the incredible presence of Ara because for us he was always in whatever room we were in. He was a constant positive presence in our lives regardless of where we were or what we were doing. He was a leader who we always wanted to be around. Is there any greater compliment for a leader? This book tells you why life was better when you were with him and why life was better as a result of being under his leadership.

For those readers who were not personally involved, Frank clearly describes what it was like to be part of the special place that is Notre Dame. He further describes what it was like to be part of the specific group of people on campus, and that group was the Fighting Irish football team. To have had an opportunity to be part of Notre Dame and be a member of the football team coached by the great Ara Parseghian was an indescribable experience, and yet somehow this book captures it in these pages.

As the stories unfold and the past is revisited, it becomes clear that Ara was a leader in the coaching field as a strategist and motivator and was as organized as any CEO of a major company. He game-planned, he called plays, he motivated, and he did all the things coaches have done for generations and will continue to do, but that wasn't what made him special. What made him special is that he lived in all our minds and in all of our hearts—and still does to this day. This book is about the rare experience of playing for a great man, a special man at a great institution. It's rare to have had that experience and rarer still to find an accurate portrayal of it. Frank captures that experience in this book.

—Gerry DiNardo

Ara Parseghian

Prologue

The scoreboard told the game story. Two minutes, 12 seconds remaining. Notre Dame 24, Alabama 23. Third down, eight yards to go for the Fighting Irish. We were backed up on our own 3-yard line.

Two minutes, 12 seconds left in my college career. It was the kind of game I had come to Notre Dame to play in. As a tri-captain, I was keenly aware of the many hours of preparation, the commitment to excellence, and the level of resolve it had taken for us to get to this point. Our legacy had come down to this moment.

Some 85,000 fans were rocking Tulane Stadium in New Orleans for the Sugar Bowl on December 31, 1973. Two storied college football programs were meeting for the first time ever. North against South. Catholics taking on Baptists. Paul "Bear" Bryant versus Ara Parseghian, two coaches destined for the College Football Hall of Fame.

Undefeated Alabama versus undefeated Notre Dame for the national championship.

It was one of those rare games that had actually lived up to the hype. The lead had changed hands seven times, putting a premium on our ability to remain focused on the immediate task at hand. When Alabama punter Greg Gantt pinned us on our own 1-yard line with a 65-yard punt with three minutes remaining, the burden was on our offense to make a first down, or else the Crimson Tide would almost certainly get the ball back in great position to kick a winning field goal.

Two running plays against Bama's tough defense had netted five yards. Alabama called timeout, and our junior quarterback, Tommy Clements, went to the sideline to talk it over. Ara told him, "Let's go with power I, right tackle trap pass left."

Tommy asked Ara, "Are you sure about that?"

Ara said, "Yeah."

Back in the huddle, Tommy relayed the play. Since the call had come from Ara, we had no doubt in our minds that it was the right one. We just had to execute against one of the top defenses in the country.

When we lined up for the play, a false start put us back halfway to the goal line, setting up the third-and-8 situation. From the sideline Ara signaled to Tommy to stick with the call.

We came to the line in a power-I formation, with three running backs and two tight ends. One tight end was Dave Casper, an All-American, who lined up on the right side of the formation. To help sell the idea that it was a run, Ara inserted sophomore Robin Weber—who had caught only one pass all year—at the other tight end spot.

As the play started, I fired out from my left guard position as if it were a run, blocking down on the defensive nose guard. Our right tackle, Steve Sylvester, pulled to execute a trap block, again signifying to the defense that it was a running play.

Tommy Clements faked a handoff to running back Eric Penick going over the left side, then dropped back into the end zone about five yards. The play was designed for Robin to attract a defensive back and then for Dave Casper to come across the field and find the hole in the area that Robin had cleared out.

But the defensive back bit on the run fake, hard. Robin ran right past him. Tommy saw it, and let it fly.

In the trenches, engaged in a block, I heard the crowd roar.

CHAPTER 1

Playing for Royalty

Playing for Ara Parseghian at Notre Dame was like being a knight in King Arthur's court at Camelot. I felt like I was part of a special group, playing for an exceptional leader. Like Camelot, the Era of Ara would not last forever, but it would always stand out as an extraordinary time.

In writing this book, I interviewed dozens of Ara Parseghian's former players and assistant coaches in order to complement my own experiences and get a well-rounded view of the man, as well as to gain their insights on games, the Notre Dame football program, and campus life. I talked with All-Americans as well as with reserves who rarely got into games. Every single one was eager to talk about Ara's extraordinary leadership qualities and what they learned from him and his dedicated assistants.

Certain words came up again and again when former players and coaches talked about Ara's character: Intense. Disciplined. Intelligent. Prepared. Fair. Loyal. Charismatic. These traits inspired unswerving allegiance to Ara, and to each other. Ara's presence was a huge part of my own Notre Dame experience. His influence continued to shape my life long after my football playing days ended. And the men I talked with shared the same perspective on how he had changed their lives for the better.

I knew I was fortunate to be in a unique situation and that I had a responsibility not only to be a football player, but also to be an ambassador for the school. Duty and service were part of the equation. You should dedicate yourself to doing your job well, not because it would bring you applause, but because it is the right thing to do.

Under Ara, the lessons of the football field were really a first-rate education in how to live a life in which you would make a difference—to your team, your family, your community, and, eventually, to your society. He was concerned with more than just developing football talent. He was a true players coach.

With his wide-ranging intelligence, organizational skill, and charisma, he could have succeeded in business or politics. Given his power to persuade, he could have been an excellent salesman. Instead, he became a legendary coach who resurrected the fortunes of a storied football program that had fallen on lean times.

Ara's 11 seasons at Notre Dame—1964 to 1974—coincided with one of the most tumultuous times in the history of American college life. The civil rights movement, the Vietnam War, Watergate—these were events that rocked the world of student-athletes, and indeed all citizens. Unlike some coaches, Ara did not discourage his players from expressing their own views about the wider world. He understood that life was about more than football, but he demanded total dedication during the time set aside for preparation and playing the game.

Coach Parseghian put us in the best position to succeed—and achieve at a level we never realized was possible. He grasped that success depended equally on the strategic and the human elements. He was open to hearing the opinions of others but unafraid to pull the trigger and take responsibility for his decisions.

His plan was to work us hard and develop great pride. I liken it to what my father, John Pomarico, told me about his experience with the Marine Corps. He said that the pride that marines developed at boot camp in Parris Island was so strong that there wasn't anything they couldn't accomplish as a group or an individual. Ara felt that through an effort similar to the Marine Corps boot camp we would became so tight and focused that the betterment of the program was at the top of our priority list. This is what would separate us from other teams. Some of our opponents had better talent, but few had the same kind of commitment that Ara's teams had. He preached that we would have "no breaking point," that we would have faith that we could overcome any circumstance.

Looking out for one another was a high priority. If someone wasn't doing something right, we all had a responsibility to let that person know about it. If a player needed encouragement, we needed to be there for him. Ara's focus was the team, but he also was concerned about the individual player. He felt that our parents had entrusted their sons to him for four years to play football while getting an education and he was responsible to make both things happen.

He placed a high value on loyalty. Ara was extremely fair, and whenever someone is fair he gets back loyalty many times over. Fairness was something that Ara took very seriously. Every night after dinner and meetings, the head coach and his staff would talk about each player, reviewing how the individual did that day and discussing anything that had been noticed in the player's performance or life, whether positive or negative. Players knew that their efforts would be noticed, and rewarded with playing time if warranted.

"To me, Ara deserved all my blood, all my sweat, all my tears, because he cared about me, and I knew that from day one," said Eric Penick, a running back who scored one of the most memorable touchdowns in Notre Dame history. "He cared for each and every one of us. That's who he was. And he picked coaches who cared about us, too."

College athletes face plenty of potential distractions—drugs, alcohol, and the actions and opinions of family, friends, and others. It's very easy to think that accepting someone's invitation to go out and have a beer or get high on pot is harmless, but Ara made the case that in reality it would weaken the program. Listening to anyone who said you should be playing instead of someone else was a recipe for dissension. Our team was a fortress, Ara said, and if we allowed cracks in the wall, the fortress would become weaker and would eventually crumble. We are strongest when everyone is on board, he reminded us.

Ara's explanation of the program and his expectations of us—physically, mentally, and academically—gave us an understanding of how strong our commitment had to be. If we weren't driven like he and the other coaches were, we were in the wrong place. College football was physically and mentally demanding, and if we were not in on both ends, we were going to get beat up.

Coach Parseghian challenged us to show our hunger to play and be successful. That was easy for me because not only was I obsessed with playing for the man, but he also was totally clear on what he and the other coaches expected: work hard, find out everything you need to do to be successful, be fair to coaches and teammates, look out for each other like family, and stay focused on the goals of the team. Ara vowed to never criticize a player to the media, and he expected his players to do the same. This family-like focus created strong bonds.

We won a lot of football games, but there were some gut-wrenching losses, too. Ara instilled in us the need for resilience. The measure of a person was not whether he got knocked down, but rather if he had the character to get back up. And it was out of the ashes of a humiliating defeat that our team found the iron determination to rise to the greatest height.

Ara had an unbelievable ability to hold your attention when he delivered his message. I remember after one such tremendous talk that Dan Morrin, my teammate and roommate, said he was ready to run through a wall.

When Ara spoke to us at the end of practice, he often relayed inspirational words. For example, he liked to cite this quote from Horace Greeley: "Fame is a vapor, popularity an accident, riches take wings. Only one thing endures and that is character." Even though we might be worn out physically, we inevitably left the field feeling good about ourselves and being where we were. We were grateful to be around a head coach who could put things in perspective, imparting lessons not only in blocking and tackling but also in life itself.

"We were the luckiest people in the world to have Ara be a part of our life," said quarterback Joe Theismann. "Ara had a great pulse on everything and he wasn't going to allow you not to be great. He expected it of himself. Everything we became is exactly what he expected of himself. And as much as he influenced our lives, I believe every one of us is a reflection of his."

"In all my life, I have met few people that exuded such class and dignity as Ara," said offensive lineman Steve Quehl, who went on to achieve success as a business leader in the technology area. "He wore it like a well-tailored suit. It hung naturally on him and it raised the level of it in all of us."

Ara was royalty, not because he was born into a family of kings, but because he became a great leader, the kind who inspired the best in those Knights who followed him.

Ara Raoul Parseghian was born on May 21, 1923, and grew up in Akron, Ohio. He was the son of a French mother and an Armenian father who fled the genocide waged against Armenians in Turkey to come to the United States in 1915. Ara played basketball at a nearby YMCA and would later say that he had a passion for that sport similar to his love for football. In fact, his protective mother wanted him to avoid football, but Ara secretly went out for the team in his junior year at South Akron High School. After winning a spot as starting guard, he had to wear down his parents' resistance to get their written permission in order to play in games. In high school, he starred in both basketball and football, and also played on the golf team—a sport that continued to give him a great deal of pleasure as he went through life. Like many children of immigrants during that era, Ara saw sports as an avenue to success in America.

After graduating from high school in 1942, Ara enrolled at the University of Akron. But with the United States involved in World War II, he soon enlisted in the navy, which sent him for training to Great Lakes Naval Station, north of Chicago. The navy station made great use of the top-notch athletes who were sent there, and its football team competed against service academies and college programs—it even upset No. 1 Notre Dame in 1943. Under Paul Brown, who was in the early days of forging a legendary coaching career, Ara won the starting fullback position going into the 1944 season, but an ankle injury prevented him from playing at Great Lakes.

Postwar, he enrolled at Miami of Ohio, where he played football, basketball, and baseball. In football he earned All-American mention playing halfback under coach Sid Gillman, who would later helm the professional

Los Angeles Rams, San Diego Chargers, and Houston Oilers. Gillman was an innovative coach who helped change the game with an emphasis on deep downfield passing.

When the Cleveland Browns of the All-American Football Conference drafted Ara after the 1947 season, he left school and jumped at the second chance to play for Paul Brown. Ara played halfback and defensive back for the Browns but early in his second season suffered a hip injury that brought an end to his playing career. But playing for coaches like Gillman and Brown had helped prepare him to make his mark in football beyond his playing days.

Woody Hayes, then coach at Miami of Ohio, recommended him for a job as coach of the freshman team in 1950. The frosh went 4–0, and Ara was promoted the next year to succeed Hayes, who was leaving to become head coach at Ohio State.

The late Tom Pagna, who played under Ara at Miami and served on his coaching staffs for 16 years, once told me that Ara learned specific skills from his association with legendary coaches Gillman, Brown, and Hayes. Gillman was a technician who timed everything in a play and put a great value on evaluating film before that was a common thing. Paul Brown emphasized the human aspects of the game in addition to being highly organized. And Hayes had a commitment to outworking his opponents.

"Usually, great players are not great coaches," Pagna said. "What came naturally to them is difficult to communicate to a player. But if you were a great player, you could become a great coach if you lost that identity as a player and could see the whole picture. He had that ability, like few people I've ever known, to see the whole picture and be in touch with the players. Ara understood the collegiate mind better than anybody I've ever been around."

In his five years as head coach at Miami, Ara established that he could win. His teams won two Mid-American Conference championships and compiled an overall record of 39–6–1. Tirrel Burton, an outstanding running back at Miami, said Ara already was extremely organized and full of confidence. "He didn't approach coaching by yelling and screaming but from a teaching standpoint," Tirrel recalled. "As players, we wrote out the scouting report in longhand in one of those blue college test notebooks. One coach gave us the formations, another talked about the personnel, and we wrote it down instead of someone printing it and handing it out. We prepared for a game like preparing for an exam."

Miami's record during Ara's tenure included victories against two Big Ten opponents, Indiana and Northwestern. Tirrel said that in the locker room just before the 1955 game at Northwestern, Ara told his team about a conversation he had with the Wildcats coach. Ara said the opposing coach told him not to worry, that Northwestern wouldn't run up the score, he would "call off the dogs." Tirrel said, "Now, whether this was just a motivational thing or not, everybody got fired up. Our coaches had done a great job of preparing us and we felt we were as good as Northwestern." Final score: Miami 25, Northwestern 14.

That 1955 Miami team went 9–0, and the Tangerine Bowl contacted the school to assess its interest in playing in its bowl game in Orlando, Florida. Tirrel said the invitation was contingent on Miami agreeing to leave its black players at home instead of bringing them to the segregated community. "Ara and John Brickels, the athletic director, both said if we can't bring everybody on the team, we're not coming," Tirrel said. That integrity, and that concern for every player, was a basic part of Ara's character that never changed.

Ara's next coaching stop was at Northwestern, which had fallen on hard times, winning only one Big Ten game in the previous three years. In 1955, the campus newspaper went so far as to advocate that the school drop out of the conference. Instead, Northwestern hired Ara to turn its fortunes around. At 32, he was the youngest coach in the Big Ten when he took over for the 1956 season.

"His reputation was for enthusiasm, energy, excitement, for being upbeat," said Mike Stock. Stock, who also grew up in Akron, became an All-American fullback playing for Ara at Northwestern, later worked as an assistant coach for him at both Northwestern and Notre Dame, and was a longtime coach in both college and the NFL. "He was already a person everybody figured was going to be a star," Mike said.

It wasn't long before Ara brought Northwestern back to respectability, as the team went 4–4–1 in 1956. He assembled a staff that included top minds such as Pagna as well as former Miami of Ohio players Doc Urich and Bo Schembechler. Urich went on to become the head coach at the University of Buffalo and Northern Illinois, while Schembechler became head coach at Miami of Ohio and then achieved great success at Michigan.

Ara and Bo, who never coached against each other in a game, remained close and talked to each other often during their careers. According to Greg Blache, who was on Ara's staff at Notre Dame, Ara and Bo would send each other their game film for critiquing and would talk to each other every Sunday during the football season. "Those two were close for years," Blache said. "Ara wanted to be the best, but he didn't have an ego. He was always striving for perfection."

Tirrel Burton not only played for Ara at Miami, he also worked several years as an assistant coach for Bo at Michigan. "Both of those guys were forward thinkers about what football coaching is all about," he said.

Mike Parseghian, Ara's son who played as a reserve running back on the 1974 Notre Dame team before a back injury ended his playing days, confirmed that his father and Bo were friends. "If Dad got a good recruit who couldn't get admitted to Notre Dame, he would shuffle him off to Bo because [Notre Dame] didn't play Michigan back then," said Mike.

After my playing days, I found out firsthand about the relationship between Ara and Bo. I was working for a distributor of the Nautilus/Sports Medical Company. The distributor was owned by Kim Wood, the strength and conditioning coach for the Cincinnati Bengals, and Pete Brown, the Bengals' director of personnel. Pete was the son of Paul Brown, the Hall of Fame coach whom Ara had played for in the service and in the pros. My job was to answer questions and develop strong relationships with coaches at all levels—high school, college, and NFL—in my sales territory, which covered Michigan, Indiana, Ohio, and parts of Illinois.

Bo Schembechler was the first major college coach who I met. Ralph Griesser, who had attended Michigan and was a big fan of Bo, introduced us. Griesser said, "Coach Schembechler, this is Frank Pomarico, captain from Notre Dame's 1973 national championship team."

Bo's immediate, gruff response was, "Why did you bring a Notre Dame guy to deal with us?" I'm not sure why, but I told Bo that yes, I did go to Notre Dame, but that I played for Ara Parseghian. Bo paused, and said, "Son, you can stay all you want. If you're one of Ara's guys, you have to be all right."

From that moment on, it was as if I were one of his own guys. He treated me great, always saying hello to me at clinics, golf outings, and dinners for Ara. He also became a big customer—not just at the University of Michigan, but also when he became president of the Detroit Tigers—buying full lines of machines for the ballclub in Detroit; for the team's spring training site in Lakeland, Florida; and for the Tigers' top farm team, the Toledo Mud Hens. Some people who didn't know him personally may have thought that he was rude and maybe even belligerent, but at his core he conveyed many of the same qualities that Ara possesses. He was loyal, disciplined, demanding, prideful, and caring. If you were in his family, he would do everything he could to help you for your entire life. He may not have been as articulate as Ara, but he had many of the same values. He loved football and he loved to make boys into men. Bo Schembechler was a special human being.

At Northwestern, Ara's promising start in 1956 was followed by a series of close losses the following season during a winless campaign. But the team bounced back with a 5–4 record in 1958, including wins over traditional powerhouses Michigan and Ohio State. Ara's teams had a knack for taking down big-name programs. They beat Oklahoma twice, including a 1959 win over the Sooners when they were No. 2. The Wildcats' best season was 1962, when it rose to No. 1 in the AP Poll temporarily and hammered Notre Dame 35–6 en route to a 7–2 record. That was the fourth straight season that Ara's Northwestern team beat the Fighting Irish, and his 4–0 record made him the only coach to play ND for that many games and go undefeated.

Mike Stock was astounded that Ara could coach any position in all three phases of the game—offense, defense, and kicking. "No one was standing around shooting the breeze while the special teams were practicing. Everyone could see that all of the coaches were involved and they all cared," Mike said. Practices were intense, but spirited and focused. He recalled that

Northwestern practices ended with an elaborate game of tag, with certain players designated as "rabbits" according to position. Losers had to run laps.

In eight years at Northwestern, Ara's teams went 36–35–1. More significant than the won-lost record, he had restored credibility and had made the Wildcats truly competitive. But when it came to resurrecting football traditions, Ara's work had just begun.

CHAPTER 2

Ara Restores the Pride

At Notre Dame, the football team had gone five straight seasons without a winning record. Joe Kuharich, who had left the NFL to take on the head job at Notre Dame in 1959, resigned in 1962 after four seasons. Hugh Devore came in as interim coach, but the team fell to a miserable 2–7 record in 1963. This was shocking in light of the tradition of greatness established under coaches such as Knute Rockne and Frank Leahy. Ara reportedly felt he didn't have the full support of the athletic department or the campus at Northwestern, and he applied for the Notre Dame job. The 40-year-old Parseghian was hired and received a four-year contract.

The Era of Ara began with him changing the culture and building pride in the individual and in the team. "We had been beat down so bad, for so long, that by the time we were seniors we didn't have any faith in ourselves," recalled Jim Carroll, an All-American linebacker who served as captain of Ara's first Notre Dame team. "We felt guilty. We felt we had let Notre Dame down, let ourselves down and let our fellow students down. We were virtually basket cases when he came in," Jim said. "If there's one thing he did, he made us believe in ourselves. He demands respect, and in doing so he also demanded that we be a pretty damn good football team."

Linebacker Jim Lynch had just finished his freshman season when Ara took over. "There was such frustration because guys came to Notre Dame as such good athletes, so there was a real hunger and real willingness to sacrifice," said Jim, who would later earn All-American status as captain of the 1966 team. He remembers that Ara had insisted on upgrading the team's equipment as a condition of taking the job—getting rid of outdated gear like the leather football helmets still worn by the freshmen.

"You not only believed in Ara when he was talking to you in a lecture room, you believed him when you were out on the field. There was no rah-rah enthusiasm," Jim said. "Ara was not your buddy. Ara was your coach. You knew he'd go to bat for you, but he was not your buddy."

The Notre Dame student body was equally hungry for a turnaround, and one snowy, February night about 2,000 fans gathered for an impromptu pep rally outside of Sorin Hall, close to the Golden Dome. The students clamored for Ara, and he responded by giving a brief talk from the porch of Sorin, the oldest dormitory on campus. Pete Duranko, who would be a key player in the coming season, recalled the moment: "His electricity and enthusiasm got me excited. The coaches that we had [previously] were ho-hum coaches, but Ara came in and said he was going to make a winner out of this team," said Pete, who sadly passed away in 2011 after a battle with ALS.

John Huarte, a quarterback who had previously been buried on the depth chart, said the Sorin rally was the first time he heard Ara speak. "It was electrifying," he said. A bit later, Ara met with team members at O'Shaughnessy Hall, the main classroom building for the College of Arts and Letters. When the meeting ended, the players were told to leave the room single file. "I was near the front and as I went by, he mentioned my name, 'Huarte.'" When John heard Ara say the names of the next players who passed by, he became curious and stood near the door to see if Ara would continue to identify each player. "He got every player and every name in our first meeting," John marveled.

I remember that at the beginning of every season, Coach Parseghian would have a meeting with the entire team, including players, coaches, equipment managers, and medical staff. It was a welcome meeting that set the expectations for our program. His main thrust was always about the key components to his program: unity, pride, discipline, and loyalty. He would focus on these things in his talk every year in one way or another. He would explain how we would win if we listened to him and the other coaches. He wanted us to develop a sole purpose of attaining the goals set every year not just by us but also by every Notre Dame fan in the country.

In his book *Resurrection: The Miracle Season That Saved Notre Dame*, author Jim Dent quotes from Ara's talk to his team at their first gathering. It is basically the message that he would convey every year:

> You know what it takes to win. Just look at my fist. When I make a fist, it's strong and you can't tear it apart. As long as there's unity, there's strength. We must become so close with the bonds of loyalty and sacrifice, so deep with the conviction of the sole purpose, that no one, no group, no thing, can ever tear us apart. If your loyalty begins to fade, it becomes a little easier to go out and have a beer, to slack off a little in practice, to listen to someone who will tell you that you should be playing on the first string in front of someone else. If that happens, this fist becomes a limp hand.

Even though he was a Presbyterian and had not attended Notre Dame as a student, Ara understood and embraced the historical significance of his position. "You've got to remember what the head job at Notre Dame is. It's the pinnacle of college coaching," said Jim Leahy, an offensive lineman on Ara's mid-'60s teams. Jim is the son of Frank Leahy, who played at ND for Knute Rockne and then went on to coach the Irish to four national championships himself. "[Ara] really had a true appreciation and love of the school. He knew what he had inherited."

From the get-go, Ara showed an uncanny ability to identify talent and put players in the right place to succeed. Pete Duranko had been a backup fullback, but Ara shifted him to the defensive side, where he would eventually earn All-American honors as a tackle. Jack Snow had been buried on the depth chart as a running back, but Ara liked his size and sure hands and converted him to split end.

John Huarte had never won a monogram, but suddenly he was in the mix, competing to be the starting quarterback. One day during spring practice, Ara told him to go play linebacker for a series of several plays. "He probably just wanted to see if I would hit somebody like the rest of the guys do every day," John said. "A quarterback does all the pretty things, but you want to know if he'll mix it up a little bit." John did, and he won the starting job. He and Jack Snow had spent summers on the Notre Dame campus attending school and practicing routes, and it had paid off.

Notre Dame opened the 1964 campaign as an underdog on a rainy day at Wisconsin. Early in the game, at about midfield, the Irish went with a play-action pass. "Jack is deep, I throw a good ball, and it goes through his hands," John said. "It didn't bother me a bit because I knew we were going to do more of those later on, and we did." Indeed, John hit Jack with two long TD passes that day, and the receiver finished with 217 yards as the Irish thumped the Badgers 31–7. Huarte-to-Snow was on its way to becoming one of the great passing combinations in Notre Dame history. Even more important, Ara had been preaching that his team could compete, and here was the evidence that it was true.

A sleeping giant had been awakened. Confidence grew week after week, and so did the excitement around campus. It hadn't taken long for Ara to restore pride at Notre Dame, and the student body embraced the man who had awakened the echoes. When stormy weather would hit during a game, the student section would begin to chant, "Ara, stop the rain!" And so, another Notre Dame tradition was born. Fullback John Cieszkowski recalled the first time he heard it: "It was a pretty steady rain. I swear, within 30 seconds of the chant, it stopped. I wasn't surprised in the least."

Raucous pep rallies were held on Friday nights before home games. Until the late 1960s, they took place in the Old Fieldhouse, a barnlike structure built in 1898. At one end was a balcony where the team gathered. On the dirt floor, thousands of students packed together in a sweaty clutter. The marching band played the "Victory March," the sounds reverberating off the walls, ceiling, and girders. Students hurled rolls of toilet paper, formed human pyramids, and loudly cheered every speaker, typically starting with a few of the players. But the loudest screams were saved for Ara, who inevitably worked the crowd to a frenzy.

Seven games into the 1964 season, the undefeated Irish were atop the national rankings. Two weeks and two wins later—against Michigan State (34–7) and Iowa (28–0)—the team traveled to the Coliseum in Los Angeles for the finale against their longtime rival, Southern Cal.

ND took a 17–0 lead into halftime, but USC's Mike Garrett kept running for big chunks of yardage. Trailing 17–13 with less than two minutes to play, Trojans quarterback Craig Fertig hit wide receiver Rod Sherman for a TD pass on a fourth-down play from the Irish 15 for the deciding score. The pain felt by Irish partisans was compounded by the belief they were robbed of a second-half touchdown on a phantom holding call.

"It tore our guts out," Jim Carroll said of the loss. "We flew back the next day, and when we got off the plane it was dark, but they wouldn't take us to our dorms. They took us right to the Old Fieldhouse and they had a pep rally there. We were surprised the students would be there but crushed that we had let them down."

Jim added, "It showed the true Notre Dame spirit." That kind of spirit is about more than winning and losing. I would come to understand later that this spirit was the result of shared experiences and shared values. Athletes at Notre Dame did not live in dedicated dorms; they lived with other students and interacted with them in daily life. They shared a strong will to excel, and they were like a band of brothers who never wanted to let each other down.

Shortly after that amazing season ended, John Huarte's Walsh Hall roommate, George Keenan, went down the second floor hallway to answer the pay phone. A minute later, he shouted out, "John, you got it!" John Huarte had become the sixth Notre Dame player to win the Heisman Trophy. Needless to say, the award did not come with the same hoopla as it does today. But that doesn't take anything away from a remarkable accomplishment.

After the graduation of Huarte and Snow, the 1965 Irish took a step back, going 7–2–1. But the following season, Ara had two sophomores who had the potential to make a huge difference: quarterback Terry Hanratty and wide receiver Jim Seymour. The two of them worked together year-round, developing a special chemistry. In the winter, they worked on routes in the Old Fieldhouse, Terry throwing passes over the rafters. "I knew when he was going to come out of his break. I could just see his gait stiffen," Terry said.

The 1966 opener would be a home game against Bob Griese and the Purdue Boilermakers, a nationally televised matchup of two top 10 teams. "Ara called me in the day before the game and said, 'No matter what happens tomorrow, you're my quarterback. Just relax, go out there and play,'" Terry remembered.

Terry and Jim exploded on the scene. In that first game against Purdue, they connected 13 times, including three touchdown passes, to help ND to a 26–14 win. Jim's 276 receiving yards that day remain the Notre Dame record. It was a remarkable debut, but when the team gathered the next night for its film session, Ara was not about to let the sophs get too full of themselves. "We thought we were going to breeze through the film session," Terry recalled. "Then for the next two hours, Ara and [offensive coordinator] Tom Pagna were all over us for every mistake we made, every fake we didn't carry out. We walked out thinking we played a really crappy game and that the only problems the team had were the quarterback and wide receiver. Everyone else was wonderful. Ara knew quite well how to keep guys grounded."

Still, the passing combo continued to shine on the field and were soon dubbed "Mr. Fling and Mr. Cling." They developed a system for Terry to hit Jim with a quick pass if the defensive back played too far off of him. "I would just touch my face mask and Jim knew I was going to throw him the ball," Terry said. By mid-season the "super sophs" were featured on the cover of *Time* magazine, with the headline, "The Power of Talent & Teamwork."

The explosive offense was matched by a defense that would give up only 38 points all season, including a touchdown scored against the reserves and another score tallied on a blocked punt. Defensive coordinator Johnny Ray's group was led by Jim Lynch; defensive linemen Alan Page, Pete Duranko, and Kevin Hardy; and defensive back Tom Schoen, among others. After eight straight wins, ND was No. 1 and had a date in East Lansing against Duffy

Daugherty's 9–0 Michigan State Spartans, a contest that was hyped as the "Game of the Century."

"The buildup for that game was nuts," said Jim Lynch. "Everybody saw it coming after the third or fourth game [of the season]. It just kept getting bigger and bigger as the game got close. The week before the game, this was a major, major event, and you'd have 15 microphones in front of you. You'd have 15 writers that were there the whole week."

In 1966, Roger Valdiserri was just beginning a 30-year stint as Notre Dame's sports information director. He said that 600 media credentials were issued for the game, an unheard-of number for a regular-season contest. Press conferences had to be held every day in both South Bend and East Lansing.

In a strange twist of fate, Terry Hanratty had almost been the quarterback on the other side of the ball in that game. As a high school senior, he leaned toward going to Michigan State—until a lunch with Ara changed his mind. "Then I had to call Duffy up," he said. "I was 17 years old, the phone was shaking in my hands. And for the next 20 minutes, he told me I was going with a great coach to a great school, that it was a great decision. He made it easy for that 17-year-old, and to this day I have respect for Michigan State because of him."

The Notre Dame team took a train from South Bend to East Lansing, a 160-mile trip that ended badly when All-American running back Nick Eddy slipped on ice coming down the steep steps of the train, hurting his shoulder and knocking himself out of the contest.

On a cold, gray November day, two great defenses dominated, matching ferocious hit with ferocious hit. The 80,000 fans created a deafening noise, with the Spartans fans chanting, "Kill, Bubba, Kill," a rallying cry for All-American defensive lineman Bubba Smith. One writer compared the scene to a bullring in Madrid.

"You couldn't hear yourself think," said Terry Hanratty. In that loud environment, the Irish made a critical miscommunication in the first quarter. A running back came in from the sideline and relayed a play—a quarterback draw. "We hadn't run that play in weeks," Terry said. "I take my five steps back and I'm surrounded by a sea of green. I tried to go to the right and I see Bubba

[Smith] coming, out of the corner of my eye. He just leveled me, and I could feel this sharp pain in my shoulder." ND's starting quarterback had suffered a dislocated shoulder that put him out of the game. Terry recalled, "When I came to the sideline, Ara said, 'What the hell did you run that quarterback draw for?' I said, 'You called it.' He said, 'No, I called a halfback draw.'"

As a result of that injury, backup Coley O'Brien took over the Notre Dame offense. After MSU took a 10–0 lead in the first half, it was O'Brien who led the Irish back to a 10–10 tie. The Irish defense dominated the second half, never allowing Michigan State past the ND 45-yard line. In the fourth quarter, Notre Dame kicker Joe Azzaro narrowly missed a 41-year field goal that would have won the game.

When the game ended 10–10, the huge stadium went eerily silent. "It was the weirdest thing," Terry Hanratty said. "Nobody knew if a tie was good or a tie was bad." He added, "If someone would have won that game, 50 years later no one would be still talking about it." The final score left fans around the country disappointed that the issue had not been settled. That frustration led some people to criticize Ara for running the ball for six straight plays (including a fourth-and-1 gamble) to close out the game with the ball on his own end of the field.

But Ara was thinking about the big picture. The Irish had shown poise and grit in the comeback in a hostile environment despite the injuries to Eddy, Hanratty, and starting center George Goeddeke, who went down early in the game. It was not a smart strategy to heave desperation passes into a defense aligned to intercept them. And Ara knew his team had one game left to play, while Michigan State's season was done. "He took so much unjustified grief over the whole thing," Jim Lynch said of Ara's late-game decision. "All he did was play smart football."

The next week, Notre Dame went back to the Coliseum in Los Angeles, the site of bitter disappointment two years prior. This time, the Irish were going to finish the job against the Rose Bowl–bound Trojans. Coley O'Brien led the team to a 31–0 lead at the half; the final tally was 51–0, the worst defeat USC had ever suffered.

The polls were unanimous: Notre Dame was No. 1. It was the school's first national championship since 1949, when Frank Leahy's team finished on top. Ara had taken heat for his controversial end-of-game strategy in the Michigan State game, but he had led his team to its ultimate goal.

The next three seasons were solid, with Top 10 finishes, but another national title eluded Ara's Notre Dame teams during those years. Purdue, guided by quarterback Mike Phipps, was a thorn in the Irish's side, winning three in a row. Those losses came early in the season, taking the steam out of championship aspirations. Despite those disappointments, Ara's teams continued to play with pride and tenacity.

Then there was USC, which held a big grudge because of that 1966 thrashing and was gathering massive football talent. Running back O.J. Simpson helped lead the victory over Notre Dame en route to the Trojans' 1967 national championship. In the next two seasons, the Irish and Southern Cal played to ties.

In 1968, Terry Hanratty suffered an injury in practice prior to the USC game and Ara decided to start sophomore Joe Theismann in his place. Joe's first pass was intercepted by Sandy Durko, who returned it for a touchdown and a quick 7–0 lead for the Trojans. Joe recalled that, immediately after the pick, "I walked by Ara. He looked at me, and I looked at him and I said, 'Don't worry about it. I'll get it back.' Ara later shared with me that at that moment he felt he had made the right decision [in starting me]," Joe said.

The Irish tied the undefeated No. 2 USC 21–21 that day but had missed a couple of late field goals that could have won the contest. The two teams then tied at 14–14 in 1969, the only blemish on Southern Cal's record that year. Notre Dame–Southern Cal was becoming the country's best, most intense rivalry. I would get the chance to experience it firsthand in the next four seasons.

In 1969, the tie with USC and loss to Purdue left Notre Dame with an 8–1–1 regular-season record. And then the school's administration did something it hadn't done in 45 years: it gave the okay for the football team to go to a bowl game. All proceeds from bowl games were earmarked for minority student scholarships and academic programs. Notre Dame accepted a bid to the Cotton Bowl to face a top-ranked and undefeated Texas team on New Year's Day 1970. The only previous time the Irish had gone bowling was the 1925 Rose Bowl, when the Knute Rockne–coached team featuring the Four Horsemen defeated Stanford 27–10. "I don't think anybody on the team knew what to expect," said fullback John Cieszkowski, who made the trip but missed the game because of a broken collarbone. The team was asked to vote on whether to accept the bid, and Ara presented his case in favor of going to Dallas. "We didn't realize how much fun it was going to be," said linebacker Rich Thomann. "He challenged us to do something Notre Dame hadn't done since 1925. He talked about 1925 like he had been there. Ara laying out Notre Dame's history was like talking to Knute Rockne. I got so excited about this bowl game, I would have practiced a whole year because of Ara's talk."

Notre Dame's decision to go to the bowl meant that a 9–1 LSU team stayed home. In those days, there wasn't a multitude of lesser bowls for matching up teams that might have won only half of their games. As such, there was controversy because some people felt Notre Dame didn't deserve the bowl bid to play against Darrell Royal's vaunted Texas team—a team that had already been unofficially proclaimed national champion by President Richard Nixon.

But as the game moved on, it became clear that the Irish not only belonged there, but could have surely won the game. Joe Theismann drove the Texas defense frantic for much of the game and his TD passes to split end Thom Gatewood and halfback Jim Yoder put Notre Dame ahead 17–14 late in the fourth quarter. But the Longhorns rallied with a 17-play, 76-yard scoring drive that included a couple of critical fourth-down conversions. Texas withstood a last-minute drive by the Irish to win 21–17.

I believe this game surprised a lot of people. Texas had blown away their competition all year, but Notre Dame showed the country that they could line up and compete against the best in the college football world. It raised Irish fans' hopes that the next season would be special.

CHAPTER 3

The Recruits

"Frankie! Frankie! Dad's home."

My mother, Mary Pomarico, was calling me from the front door on Lahn Street in the Howard Beach neighborhood of Queens. I heard her while I was playing touch football on the street with my friends. I was excited because my dad was my best friend—the person I loved and trusted with everything in my life. John Pomarico had grown up in a poor section of Brooklyn, at the corner of 3rd Avenue and Carroll Street. At 18 he joined the marines and learned a lot about discipline and how to organize his life. He then joined the New York City Police Department and was now a sergeant, truly one of the city's finest.

When I came into the house, he was in our living room watching the Notre Dame–Michigan State football game while doing one-arm curls with a 50-pound dumbbell. He asked me if I wanted to watch the game with him. Dad said it was a huge game and that he made a friendly wager with Big Jim Williams, another sergeant in my father's precinct. Dad took Notre Dame, and Sgt. Williams had MSU.

We watched this 1966 game intently. If my Dad was rooting for Notre Dame, well then so was I. But it was easy to see that MSU had a great team and Notre Dame was hanging in there, fighting for their lives after falling behind 10–0. By the end of the game, Notre Dame tied the score despite suffering several key injuries.

But the thing I remember best is how my dad kept talking about Notre Dame coach Ara Parseghian. He was very impressed with the way the coach kept his composure during the heat of what was being called "the game of the century." Dad loved the intensity Ara showed and yet how he was under control. The game ended in a 10–10 tie, but Dad couldn't stop talking about Parseghian. I had never heard of Coach Parseghian, but I knew if my dad was impressed that I needed to find out more about this person.

After the game, Dad said, "Wouldn't it be great if you could play at Notre Dame someday?" *Wow,* I thought to myself, *if Dad really thinks so highly of this Notre Dame school, then I will set my sights on playing there.* It was a huge goal for a kid who was just a freshman in high school, but one thing I knew: it would make my Dad proud.

Many of Ara's Knights grew up hoping for that chance to get a scholarship to play for him at Notre Dame. During this time before cable TV, you could only see one or two college football games a week on a Saturday. But every Sunday morning, a one-hour edited replay of the Notre Dame game was televised nationwide. With the Irish regularly winning under Ara, these broadcasts helped solidify the Notre Dame fan base and attracted the interest of many high school players around the country who were considering college ball.

"I would watch Lindsey Nelson and Paul Hornung do those replays every Sunday morning," said Max Wasilevich, an offensive lineman from Divine Child High School in Dearborn, Michigan. "It opened up with the fans in the stands clapping to the 'Victory March.' It was awesome, even though it was in black and white in those days," said Max, who now goes by the name of Max Walsh for professional reasons, as an ophthalmologist in the Detroit area.

"I wanted to go to Notre Dame—that was a dream come true," said Tom Bolger. "I used to watch the Sunday replays and think about what it would be like to play there." An offensive lineman from Cincinnati Elder High School, Tom recalled that Ara did not have to do much persuading to get him to commit. "On my recruiting trip, he brought me into his office and started talking about Notre Dame. I was sitting there shaking my head and smiling. I think he got about a third of the way through his spiel and he said, 'You want to come here, don't you?' And I said, 'Yes, sir!'"

Not every player grew up with this dream to play at Notre Dame. Bob Neidert, for instance, had his sights set on Ohio State. "As a kid growing up in Ohio, you always think you want to play for Woody [Hayes]," said Bob, a defensive lineman. But his visit to the Notre Dame campus on a snowy winter weekend changed his thinking. "I fell in love with it right then. It wasn't the football mystique, it was the campus and the family atmosphere."

Tim Sullivan grew up in Des Moines and always thought he would go to Iowa, where some of his relatives had played. But after taking about a dozen trips to different schools (there was no NCAA limit on trips in those days), he settled on Notre Dame because of the combination of academics and athletics. "They had the highest graduation rates of athletes in the country," said Tim, who played linebacker for the Irish. He also believed that playing for the Irish would end up providing him wider opportunities. "Notre Dame was a national school, and I had no idea where I wanted to live after graduation."

Mike Townsend had decided to go to Purdue instead of following his brother, Willie, to Notre Dame. The deciding factor was that Purdue offered a major in computer science. "I went to my high school coach and told him to get the paperwork from Purdue so I could sign it," said Mike. But when he got home that afternoon, Irish assistant coach Brian Boulac was in his living room, talking to Mike's mom. "I told him point blank, the only reason I'm not choosing Notre Dame was the fact computer science wasn't a major. He said, 'Well, we can do something about that. Give me 48 hours.'"

Then Mike's girlfriend came over and she told him she favored Notre Dame. "I asked why, and she said, 'It has no women there.' She and my mom got together, and within 48 hours, Coach reassured me that I could major in computer science. So I changed my mind," said Mike, who ended up playing defensive back for the Irish and was one of the captains of the 1973 team.

Whether or not a recruit grew up rooting for Notre Dame wasn't a determining factor for Ara Parseghian. But the Irish coach put a high value on one trait in his recruits: he wanted them to be "hungry," according to Greg Blache, one of his assistants. "He liked kids that were from working-class families, who wanted something and were willing to work for it. He didn't want prima donnas," Greg said. "What we had was a group of people that he could motivate and work with and make play better as a group. He wanted tough, hardworking kids who were willing to be part of something."

I was not a naturally gifted athlete, but I fit the bill as someone who was hungry to succeed. Even before Notre Dame, I began developing something I call "the Driven Spirit," which is part physical, part spiritual, but mostly attitudinal. *It's really the way successful people live their lives. It is something that is positive, productive, motivational, creative, focused, and competitive. People that have the Driven Spirit usually have the pride, discipline, and self-confidence to become leaders. These people are accountable for their actions and try to be fair with people in their lives.*

The Catholic school system was still going strong during the '60s and helped produce many of Notre Dame's players. I attended Our Lady of Grace grade school, a typical Catholic school in that era. It was run by nuns, who were tough and loving in equal measures. They would track the competition in both the classroom and on the playground. And they would roll up their sleeves and join in our stickball games.

I played baseball at OLG, for which it was well known. My seventh grade teacher, Sister Marguerite, had two brothers who were Major League Baseball players: Frank and Joe Torre. OLG's school team played at Casino Park, at the end of Howard Beach before it connects to Broad Channel. That's where I first saw a superb baseball player named Larry DiNardo, who was an eighth grader when I was in the fifth. He could really hit the ball out of sight.

Larry's younger brother, Gerry, was in my class. He was the first guy I had a fight with at the school. I had moved from Brooklyn to Howard Beach in the fifth grade, so I was the new kid on the block and I had to establish myself. Gerry wasn't big, but he was a pretty tough kid. We had a disagreement, and he said to meet him after school at the opposite end of the school from where his Mom was the school crossing guard. We met at the appointed time and had a schoolboy scuffle that lasted about a minute and a half.

It was, as Bogart said to Claude Rains at the end of *Casablanca,* "the beginning of a beautiful friendship." We couldn't imagine it at the time, but Gerry and I would eventually follow his brother Larry to Notre Dame to play for Ara Parseghian. Gerry became an All-American guard in college; later was the head football coach at Vanderbilt, LSU, and Indiana; and then went on to become an analyst on the Big Ten Network.

We grew up during the postwar baby boom era in a neighborhood that was full of kids. There were a lot of Irish and Jewish families, and Italian Americans were well represented. The joke was that you could yell "Hey, Tony!" and enough boys would come running that you could play a baseball game.

Jack Cahill, whose dad was a fireman, grew up in the same neighborhood, and remembers that our working-class parents of that era put a huge emphasis on schooling. "Their goals were always to get us a better education. That is really what they dedicated themselves to: to making sure we were better off and had more opportunities than they had." Jack preceded me to the same high school and then attended Notre Dame before becoming a commissioned officer in the navy who served two tours of duty in Southeast Asia. He is one of those guys who has really made a difference in a lot of people's lives, helping friends and associates at the drop of a hat. Jack, like his classmate Larry DiNardo, embodies the idea of a modern "knight."

I use "knight" to describe a person who lives life with courage, honor, dignity, and selflessness. It is not a status achieved overnight, but rather the result of years of learning and acting. It is a realization of one's purpose on this earth. It is the kind of knighthood that anyone can attain if they put their heart and mind to it. My own pursuit of this path was affected by parents, grandparents, and many coaches—perhaps none more so than Ara Parseghian and also Marv Levy, another great leader who I had the good fortune to encounter in the professional ranks.

The DiNardo and Pomarico families had a great deal in common. Our mothers were both Italian, both named Mary, and both great cooks. Both of our dads also were of Italian descent, and both were New York City policemen. So as we grew up in Howard Beach, it was natural that our families started to intertwine.

Larry was a star athlete and an outstanding student, and he had a certain maturity and focus that was highly unusual for an eighth-grader. He did things the right way and he was a great example for all kinds of kids, and it was obvious that he was on track to be something special. He created a model of success that many young boys from Our Lady of Grace, and later St. Francis Prep, attempted to follow. Larry would eventually earn both undergraduate and law degrees from Notre Dame and went on to become partner in a Chicago law firm.

I began playing football in the fifth grade for the Lynvets, a Pop Warner–type league. Irv Lipschitz was our head coach, and Ronnie Grier was the line coach. They were demanding but loved us and wanted to see all of us move on to play in high school. Irv was a big Jewish guy with a booming voice that most guys were afraid of. I respected him but wasn't afraid of him and I worked very hard to be a starter on his teams.

I began developing good work habits playing for the Lynvets. It was the first time that I really started pushing myself, as I really wanted to play well for the coaches. I wanted to make my parents, coaches, and teammates proud of me. It was also a lesson in what is now called "diversity," as it was a team of Catholics, Protestants, Jews, whites, blacks, Puerto Ricans—a real American melting pot. "The huddle has no color" is what Irv taught us. We had to learn to work as a team, and if one guy screwed up, then everyone had to do push-ups or sprints. It didn't matter what your religious or ethnic stripe was, if you didn't perform right, then everyone paid the price. I would come to find out that all the best coaches shared these values.

Each year, the Lynvets players would get their football equipment in the back of a bar and grill called Ma Benny's. What I didn't know then was that Ma Benny's was a big hangout for "wiseguys," members of organized crime. But they were nice to us. As youngsters all we knew was that we were getting our football equipment, and that was fun and clean and sports keep kids out of trouble.

* * *

At the time of that 1966 Notre Dame–Michigan State game, I was a student at a high school called St. Francis Prep in the Williamsburg section of Brooklyn. Like Notre Dame at the time, St. Francis Prep was all male—in fact, 950 boys crammed into a converted grade school. It was run by the Franciscan brothers, and it seemed to me that boxing skill was a prerequisite for joining the order. At our freshman year orientation for students and parents, Brother Williams said, "Ladies and gentlemen, if we think your son is not doing the right thing, we might whack him. If you don't like that, then take your son out of school now." My Dad looked at me and said, "I like this place." I said to myself, *Wow, this is going to be a tough four years.*

The school building itself was so small that the teachers rotated classrooms, because if everyone was in the hall at the same time, nobody could move. Just to get to St. Francis, I took a subway for 45 minutes every day from Howard Beach. The trains on my line were old and always packed, so it wasn't easy to lug my books and football gear back and forth.

One of the Franciscans at St. Francis Prep was Brother Owen Capper, who would turn out to have a huge influence on me. A big German guy, Brother Owen felt that a young man who got involved in sports would have too much on his plate to get in trouble with drugs, gangs, alcohol, and girls. "Don't be part of the 2:30 club," Brother Owen would say, which was his way of urging us to take part in an extracurricular activity—such as sports, band, or the debate team. He was passionate about football as well as other sports, and he also watched over us to make sure we were staying on the right track. He taught physical education and had a paddle that he referred to as his "board of education." After football season, he wanted us to play another sport, developing a winning attitude even if we weren't great at the sport or to lift weights if we weren't competing in an organized sport.

Many of the football players were recruited to play rugby, so it was kind of our spring football. It was a very draining physical game, and I played second row and wing forward, positions that you could compare to linemen in football. We would play college teams such as Yale's seniors, a team that one season included George W. Bush. We also played West Point seniors, which was a great thrill. We held our own against the college and men's clubs that we played. The experience created a lot of camaraderie among us.

Rugby also gave me my first opportunity to travel outside of the country. My freshman year, we played in a tournament in New Brunswick, Canada. And at the end of my junior year, our team went on a tour of England, Wales, and Ireland. At that time, we were so ethnically conscious that when we filled out our passport applications, we put "Irish," or "Italian" or "German" and so on where it asked for our nationality. One of the St. Francis brothers came by and said, "What the heck are you doing? You guys are Americans!" We didn't even think in those terms.

The trip opened up a new world to us. We stayed at the homes of our positional counterparts. The food was different, the way they drove was different, and even the air seemed different.

* * *

The St. Francis Prep gym was so small that the end wall was right where the basketball floor ended underneath the basket, with just a paper-thin mat protecting you if you crashed into it. On the side, there was an extra dotted line on the floor for taking the ball out of bounds, because there wasn't room for a player to be out of bounds without standing on a spectator's feet.

The facilities may not have been up-to-date, but kids from all over the city flocked to the Prep because of its discipline, academics, and athletics. Most of the boys were from middle-class homes. Their families wanted them to come under the discipline of the brothers, to be exposed to a great education that would prepare them for college, and to be a part of a strong athletic program to keep them competitive and out of trouble.

The brothers worked as a tight-knit group, looking out for each other as if they were Navy SEALs. If one brother saw a student giving a teacher a hard time, he would pass the word around, and all of the brothers would give that kid rough treatment, such as extra homework, or a punch. Or both. Eventually the student would need to decide whether he wanted to stop being a problem or if he wanted to leave.

It was never a good idea to push one of the brothers too far, even the soft-spoken ones like Brother Andrew. Jack Cahill was classmate with one student—let's call him Jimmy—who was habitually late for Brother Andrew's class, the first one of the day. Brother Andrew never said a word until the end of the school year, when he called Jimmy up in front of the entire class and invited him to throw his best punch. Jimmy tried to refuse, but Brother said he was going to punch Jimmy for being disruptive all year, so Jimmy might as well go first. Well, Jimmy swung and hit Brother in the stomach, but Brother took it like the middleweight boxer that he looked to be. And Brother Andrew responded with one punch, which broke Jimmy's jaw. So Jimmy was wired up the whole summer. But he said the worst part was that his father would say that he must have done something really bad for Brother Andrew to punish him, and then his dad would whack him one, too.

Today, that kind of response by a teacher is probably an invitation to a lawsuit. But in the '60s in New York—and I'm sure in many major cities—parents put a lot of value on their sons going to a boys' school, in particular because of classroom discipline and the athletics. There was a great demand for admissions to Prep, so kids either conformed to the rules or they were thrown out of school.

We didn't always win, but the attitude was, if you're going to tangle with the Prep, bring your lunch pail, because we were going to give an all-out effort. Some teams were better in talent, but they couldn't stand up to our intensity, our will to win. The brothers always said it takes no talent to give 100 percent. I've lived by that motto for most of my life, and it has really made a difference.

One of the other people at the Prep who affected my life in a positive way was Brother Owen Justinian. He was my first teacher in summer school in the summer of 1966, had played at the Prep, and was a very inspiring man. He later went to Notre Dame and studied for his graduate degree during the time that I was an undergrad, giving us the opportunity to visit each other often.

Vince O'Connor was named head football coach at the Prep in 1954, and remained in that position for 61 years until he passed away in February of 2015 at age 85. He was very influential in many high school boys getting placed into college on scholarship. He really stressed the fundamentals. He was not a screamer but instead coached with the attitude that we were mature people. Like every great coach, he preached that each player had a job to do if we were going to advance the ball or stop our opponent. A football team is an intricate machine that won't run smoothly if there are a couple of misfiring pistons. Vince and his wife, Mary, have opened their hearts and home to all of the families of the boys who played for the Prep and he is truly a huge reason for the Prep's football success.

My years at the Prep were priceless. The school now has a $3 million weight room, but when I was at the Prep we did our lifting in the visitors' dressing room, which was about 12-by-10 feet. We only had a bench, some free weights, and a bunch of guys who were willing to pay the price to get better.

"Our high school was unique in a lot of the same ways Notre Dame was unique, and had a football coach who paralleled the kind of things that Ara stood for," said Gerry DiNardo. "College recruiters used to come to St. Francis and found guys sitting on the toilet doing curls because there was no room anywhere else," he recalled. The facilities might have been lacking, but the hunger for success and competition brought out the best in the players who attended the school.

* * *

During high school, I spent three summers working as a waiter and a boat boy at Camp Alvernia, which was both a sleepaway and day camp for youngsters through middle school, located on the north shore of Long Island. The camp also was run by the Franciscan brothers. It was only 40 miles from New York City, but it seemed like a different world. Fresh air, green grass, water, the beach, boating, and sports were all at our fingertips.

The opportunity to spend time outside of the inner city helped me and other high school students stay out of trouble. But I confess we weren't always model kids. We would get in trouble once in a while—like the time John Basti, Gerry DiNardo, and I bought a bottle of whiskey and chugged it down in 10 minutes. As you might guess, we got very sick. I started to throw up and lay down in a parking lot until the early morning hours. I was found by

Brother Norman and brought back to Camp Alvernia. Along with the other boys, I was docked for a month by Brother Owen Capper for doing something that was really dumb. I was sick for about three days after that, which made it tough to work out very hard. It taught me a lesson about drinking, and I didn't have another drop until I was in college.

Another time, four of us were out in the harbor in a 16-foot sailboat on a windy early evening. John Basti, Gerry DiNardo, Timmy Sockett, and I were really clipping along and decided to go over to Connecticut. It was still light when we left, but it soon began to get dark. We were in the open part of the Long Island Sound, where it is about 12 miles across. We were about halfway across when the wind died, leaving us out in the middle of the sound with no way to get to Connecticut or back to Camp Alvernia.

We were adrift the whole night. At one point a huge ocean liner came dangerously close to us, and we would all have been killed if it had run into us, but thank God it didn't. Finally the sun came up, and again Brother Norman, who was in a motorboat, found us. This was another lesson learned: don't do something that could kill you unless you are very prepared to bail yourself out. We again were docked for a month. These life lessons promoted a lot of growth in me as a person and as an athlete.

Following my junior year, Coach O'Connor invited me to attend a summer survivor course off the coast of Rockland, Maine. Coach O'Connor had been approached by Outward Bound with scholarships for inner city kids to experience the wilderness in a way that built team and leadership skills. O'Connor, who was very much like a father to us, felt that the program would not only make us better football players but would also build character that would help us for the rest of our lives.

He picked Gerry Byrnes, Gerry DiNardo, and me. The three of us had known each other since Our Lady of Grace grade school in Howard Beach and we were very good friends. We expected the experience would primarily be a training device for the upcoming football season. However, what we went through would change our lives forever, as the experience challenged us to meet both physical and mental demands.

Hurricane Island Outward Bound School was started in the mid-1960s by Peter Willauer, based on a concept developed for British sailors to help them survive if they were in a shipwreck. He wanted to put students into uncomfortable situations that would force them to grow within themselves to succeed. One goal of the program was to show you that you were not only responsible for yourself, but that you also had to do anything necessary to ensure the success of the group. The Watch consisted of 12 people. Everyone had responsibilities, and if any one person shirked his duties, then no one in the Watch could eat. This generated plenty of peer pressure to get things done.

Hurricane Island sits in the Atlantic Ocean off the beautiful coast of Maine, its water cold, clean, and deep blue. We didn't have a lot of time to enjoy all this beauty, however, because as soon as we hit the island we were met by our Watch leader and told to start running with our duffel bags over our shoulders to our camp area, which would be our base for the next month.

Order and cleanliness were priorities. Being on time for everything was mandatory. Helping one another was expected. You didn't get praised for doing extra work and you didn't get scolded if you didn't do your share. You were expected to carry your load and help someone that wasn't as able to do their share. By the end of the course, Watch members acquired a team mentality in which everyone would pull their own weight.

A typical day on Hurricane Island began with a run that was two-and-a-half miles around the island. At the end, we came to a pier and were told to jump in the ocean. If someone didn't jump in, no one in the Watch could eat. So as you can imagine, everyone would encourage those who didn't want to jump into the water.

Along with physical activities, there was time set aside for silent reflection. There would be readings designed to inspire you to think about life and what you were doing here on earth. The message that always came through is that we are here to make a difference, to make life a bit easier for others because we are all part of the greater human race. The aim of this course was to make us as spiritually fit as physically fit. We were presented the opportunity to develop a center of peace about our life by understanding that we were to love and care for one another.

Classes in the morning and afternoon were usually geared toward preparing us for our expedition or for our solo. The expedition was a five-day sailing trip by the Watch with no adults or trained personnel on board to assist us. We would have to navigate to a predetermined point and then cook our meals onshore, clean the area, and then get everything back on board and put away in order.

Solo was the part of the course that I was most interested in experiencing. It involved being put on an island by yourself for three days. It was a very different experience for someone like me, from New York City. It was a chance for three days to think about your life and what you wanted to do with it. Being 16 years old, I was done thinking about my life in about an hour. However, I knew I had to set up camp, pitch a tent, and get some food. We weren't allowed to bring any food from Hurricane Island. Each of us had to make a real effort to find food, such as dog whelks, periwinkles, snails, and certain leaves from trees or we would to lose too much weight.

On the last day of solo, I woke up about 5:45 AM thinking that the return boat would arrive any minute. But it didn't come until about noon, and for the first time during the course I had some fear, thinking I had been forgotten. Finally the boat showed up and we all were reunited at Hurricane Island. The Watch commanders told us not to eat too much to avoid getting sick, because our stomachs had shrunk. Naturally, we all ate too much anyway and got sick.

After these powerful experiences, I returned to New York City with the attitude that I could take on any challenge. Because I had been pushed to my limits, I gained a lot of confidence and I was prepared to do anything to get the job done. I developed the discipline to find out everything I needed to do in order to reach my goals in life. I also became much more passionate about life, thinking about things much deeper than just football. Hurricane Island opened my spirit, and I realized the need to reach as high as I could.

* * *

The football fields we played on at St. Francis left a lot to be desired. Before we could hold our practices at McCarren Park in the Greenpoint section of Brooklyn, we had to clean up the broken glass and cans and drug needles. The grass was long gone—McCarren was just a dirt field, seven or eight blocks from school. It was a rough area, and we used to walk to it in groups so that no one would get mugged. For kids who didn't know better, it was just one of the things we had to do in order to play.

I was a freshman when Larry DiNardo was a senior at St. Francis. I was a good size for my age at about 5'9" and 165 pounds. Brother Owen saw something in me and moved me up to junior varsity. He said, "Maybe we have another DiNardo here," which stoked my enthusiasm.

When I started at St. Francis we had face masks, but the helmets were leather. It's hard to believe now that we played in leather helmets, and I wonder how many concussions I had in those days. By the time we were seniors we were wearing the same kind of solid, state-of-the-art helmets being used at Notre Dame. I felt like I could run through a wall with those new helmets.

The spirit at the Prep was very similar to what it was like at Notre Dame—intense, passionate, and fueled by a we-will-win attitude. I played offensive and defensive tackle, moving from the JV to start on the varsity as a junior and then as a senior. We had a very good team, losing only once in each of those seasons. When I was a junior, one of our games was telecast on WPIX, Channel 11, which was the same station that carried Yankees games. At one point in the game I blocked a pass, and my buddy Gerry Byrnes quipped, "Don't worry about it, Frank. You'll get the next one." And sure enough our opponent called the same play on the next down. This time I intercepted it, which is a foreign thing for a lineman to do. I ended up being named the WPIX Player of the Game.

I weighed about 205 pounds as a junior and built myself up to 220 as a senior. Gerry DiNardo had come in as a freshman at 115 pounds and was about 185 pounds as a senior at St. Francis. Neither of us was big for a lineman, but thanks to influences like Larry DiNardo and Brother Owen, and experiences like Outward Bound, we were both developing the Driven Spirit.

Larry DiNardo became the starting guard at Notre Dame as a sophomore. He was tough and strong, but also poised, and everything he did was very mature compared with what other guys his age were doing. Larry went to Notre Dame knowing he would be playing in the most competitive athletic arena possible, as well as academically challenging. *After Larry started at Notre Dame, Gerry and I began hearing a lot more about the school and about Ara Parseghian. I honed in on the goal of following Larry there.* This was like reaching for the stars—I never thought I would get there, but I hoped, prayed, and focused every day on doing what needed to be done.

When I was a junior, Gerry and I visited Notre Dame with another friend, Ernie Razzano, to watch the Irish play Air Force. We were able to tour the beautiful campus and sit in the stands for the game, just soaking up everything we could.

My family knew Larry well, as he would come over to our house sometimes and work out with my father in our basement. Sometimes they would go to a gym that my cousin Frankie Guarino ran, which was connected to his funeral parlor on Avenue X in Brooklyn. They would lift weights in the room next to the one where bodies were being embalmed. Kind of odd, but it was a good weights gym, and if you could get past the smell of the formaldehyde, you could get a good workout.

During summer break, Gerry and I would often join Larry in running along the Belt Parkway, which links Brooklyn with Queens. It was a pretty wide-open path that was paved and stretched for about two-and-a-half miles. As we were working out with Larry, we were getting ready for our own St. Francis Prep season. We knew we were preparing a Notre Dame player for his wars and that we would be equally ready for ours.

While I was gung-ho on getting into Notre Dame, Gerry wasn't so sure. He wanted to prove to himself and his family that he could be successful on his own. After St. Francis Prep, he went on to Tabor Academy in Massachusetts for a year, where he grew to about 6'1" and 235 pounds.

"Everything Larry did was excellent and I didn't want any part of following in his footsteps," Gerry said. He initially didn't respond to Notre Dame's recruiting outreach, but at the urging of his father finally agreed to accept an invitation to visit the campus because "it was the right thing to do." It wasn't until he met Coach Parseghian that he made up his mind. This is how he described that meeting: "After five minutes sitting with Ara I said to myself, 'I'm coming here.' It wasn't all that much about what he said. He asked me if I had any reservations, and I said, 'Yes, I don't want to be following my brother.' He dispelled that worry. But it was his presence. One of the best ways to describe Ara is that he is already in the room before he gets there," Gerry said. "I went to Notre Dame because of Ara. I know it is a great school, I know it has great tradition, and I guess some of that mattered to me, but really not all that much. If I was in that room and Ara was coaching for another school, I think I would have gone to that other school."

While Gerry and I came from the big city, Notre Dame recruits came from all corners of the country. Defensive lineman George Hayduk grew up in Factoryville, Pennsylvania, with a population of about 1,000 residents. He made a verbal commitment to Penn State before getting an invitation to visit Notre Dame in April of his senior year. "I never thought they would be interested in me," George said. "I went into Ara's office. I thought, *Holy cow, this is Ara Parseghian.* He said, 'George, we want you to come to Notre Dame.' I said, 'Okay, Coach.' That's all it took. I never regretted it. Not one time."

For most players, the recruiting visit to Notre Dame was a chance to size up the school while the Irish coaches in turn continued to evaluate them. "Ara's left hand always seemed to grab your shoulder, your triceps, or your bicep to feel your body mass," said Rocky Bleier, a running back who would go on to become captain of the 1967 team. Rocky also remembered playing basketball on his recruiting visit "so the coaches could watch our athleticism."

Joe Theismann also remembered the coaches watching recruits play basketball at the Rockne Memorial building. "It was a chance for them to look at our overall skills and whether we were good enough athletes to play more than one position," said Joe, who was being recruited by about 100 schools coming out of South River High School in New Jersey. He was not Catholic and didn't grow up dreaming to play at Notre Dame. But by the end of the weekend, he was sold. When he flew home, his Dad asked him what he thought. "I said I have to go to Notre Dame. He asked why, and I said, 'Dad, I can only tell you it feels right.' It was more of a gut instinct than anything else."

The coaches had other ways to check out recruits during their visits. Pat Sarb, who played quarterback in high school, was asked by Ara to demonstrate how he held a football. "He was the only coach who asked me to do that. I guess he saw how small my hands were. When I showed up in August I had the number 25 and a defensive playbook in my locker," said Pat, who ended up playing defensive back.

The meeting with Ara was the high point of the recruiting ritual. Ara's assistant coaches made trips around the country to scout and visit prospects, but Ara met the prospects on campus himself. "He wanted kids to come to Notre Dame because they wanted to come, not because the head coach walked into their living room and laid out a beautiful plan," said assistant coach Bill Hickey, "He knew he could get kids to play hard who wanted to be there."

Ara did not believe in overpromising recruits, as Thom Gatewood found out. Thom recalled the coach telling him, "I can't guarantee you'll be a starter here. We don't know what the future will be. On your potential, we think you can make a really strong contribution to the Notre Dame football program." According to Thom, "This was a revelation for me. All these other guys, including Woody Hayes and Bo Schembechler, told me I was going to be an All-American and All-World and what a great player I was. Here was this guy telling me that maybe I'd make a contribution. It was a humbling effect, and that impressed me. Isn't that what life is really about? There are no guarantees of what happens tomorrow until you really do some work," said Thom, who went on to be a consensus All-American receiver and one of the captains of the 1971 Fighting Irish team.

Gary Potempa, a running back from Niles, Illinois, who ended up playing linebacker for the Fighting Irish, had a similar experience. "Ara said, 'Gary, we're going to offer you a scholarship, but the only thing I'm going to promise you is the chance to play.' I had been promised by these other schools that I would be a starting running back or a starting linebacker. What Ara said to me, I thought it just made a lot more sense. That just felt right to me."

Eric Penick also was highly recruited coming out of Gilmour Academy in the Cleveland area, where he was both a football running back and a state champion sprinter. Head coaches including Ohio State's Woody Hayes and Nebraska's Bob Devaney paid personal visits to his home, but Eric had to come to the Notre Dame campus to meet Ara, like everyone else. "Ara said, 'You're not guaranteed a football start here ever. But I can guarantee you one thing: you'll get a good education here and you'll graduate, because we graduate people. And from there you'll be part of the Notre Dame family.' I was impressed," Eric said.

Greg Blache said that Ara often reminded him and the other assistant coaches that they were dealing with the future of young people, and so they needed to be careful not to lie or exaggerate during the recruiting process. "At that age, whether a guy gets an education and a degree can determine the rest of his life," Greg said. "Ara told us, 'We have to understand the ramifications of our decisions when we are dealing with young people's lives. We brought them here, we're responsible for them, to see them through and help them become productive, good people.'"

Blache added, "Sometimes in a meeting, someone would comment that one of our players was not very good. Ara would say, 'Well, that's not his fault. We brought him here. We made that commitment to him. We are going to treat him like everybody else, and we are going to see that he graduates.'"

Denny Murphy, the freshman football coach at Notre Dame, was in charge of recruiting New York City and Long Island. Despite the success I had with the Prep, as my senior year went by, I thought the dream of playing for Notre Dame was slipping through my fingers.

I took a recruiting visit in February or March, when the snow was still on the ground in South Bend. When I met Ara, I was only worried about not babbling and making a fool of myself. I said, "Coach, I'd really like to come here if it's possible. I'd give you everything I can in order to be a part of this team." He said, "Frank, I know that." But he said they weren't sure yet whether I would be offered a scholarship. I knew that I was smaller than your typical college lineman.

At that time, most recruits started signing in March of senior year. March came, then April, and I had gotten no word from Notre Dame. Finally, in May, I got a letter. My parents and I opened it together, and then we all cried together. As I recall, my class had 41 recruits, and I was No. 41, the last guy to get a scholarship.

I was in and I was committed to making the most of the chance.

CHAPTER 4

Freshman Year

In the summer of 1970, football scholarship to the University of Notre Dame in hand, I spent the time excitedly getting ready for the biggest challenge of my life. I loved playing football and I was joining the most celebrated program in the country, Notre Dame. The place where Rockne, Gipp, Leahy, Lujack, Lattner, Hornung, and other legends played and went to school.

The beautiful campus sprawls over 1,250 acres in northern Indiana, and includes two lakes and wooded areas. But in 1970 the total student enrollment was only about 7,000, including graduate students, and the portion of campus devoted to living and education was relatively small. Dorms like Sorin Hall, Walsh Hall, and Dillon Hall had their own histories based on the many well-known people who had gone through them. Notre Dame is a special place, but for me the real thrill was the opportunity to play for Ara Parseghian. To me this was like playing for royalty. Ara had it all: class, charisma, character, and a commitment to the program and Notre Dame.

I devised a plan to get myself in the best possible shape before I arrived at Notre Dame, committing myself to a difficult training program that emphasized weight lifting and running. I had a chance to become one of Ara's Knights and I wasn't going to let that opportunity pass me by. I was driven to be in top shape so there would be no question that when my time came I would be someone you could count on, someone you could go to battle with.

This was my quest, and I was prepared to go all out. The mind can make people achieve great things, and my mind drove me to success. There would be no drugs to help me, no steroids, just weight training, running, games like touch football next to the Belt Parkway, handball, basketball—anything that would improve my body and sharpen my skills and my mind.

Unexpected things can happen to young people who dream and have a Driven Spirit to succeed. Peter Habeler, who was in the first group to scale Mount Everest without artificial oxygen, wrote in his book *Lonely Victory,* "You have to love the journey to the Summit as much as reaching the Summit itself."

Love of the voyage is an essential part of the Driven Spirit. Some people complained about working out, but I never did, because it meant I was taking another step on the journey. Playing for Ara was my Summit, and I loved every run, every repetition on the bench press, every squat and dead lift because it meant that I was getting stronger and faster, inching ever closer to my obsession to start at left guard for Notre Dame, to succeed Larry DiNardo, the All-American who was a candidate for the Lombardi Trophy as the country's best offensive lineman.

My mother, Mary Pomarico, provided the great Italian food that kept me fueled with plenty of energy. Often, my friends from Notre Dame would ask me what was the best Italian restaurant in New York and I would always answer that it was my mother's house, with a close second being Mary DiNardo's house. I was spoiled with great Italian dishes such as manicotti with a thick red gravy that had meatballs and Italian sausage cooking in it all day. My mother also made a great braciole, which was a piece of thin steak that was flattened, had spices added to it, and then rolled and tied with a string. The spices and juices from the meats would seep out all day and make the red gravy thick and tasty. I don't know how healthy it all was, but boy, did it taste great. I always enjoyed soaking up the gravy on the plate with about a half a loaf of Italian bread.

In the fall, after Sunday Mass at Our Lady of Grace, we would go back home and wait for the NFL game to come on. All over America, Italian boys were waiting for their mothers to put the water on the stove to get it boiling so that the spaghetti could go in. For holidays my mother would usually start meals off with an Italian salad called an antipasto. This was a real work of art: lettuce as the base, red peppers, hard-boiled eggs, anchovies, provolone cheese wrapped in prosciutto or ham, green and black olives, and Genoa salami, with a dressing of olive oil and vinegar. She also would make a great *pasta fagioli*, which was a dish made popular during the Depression. It didn't have a lot of meat, but the beans and the pasta would fill you up—and with grated Italian cheese and hot red pepper flakes it was quite a dish.

During Lent and at Easter time my mother would make a great spaghetti dish called *frutta di mare*, which meant "fruits of the sea," such as clams, mussels, and scallops. I get hungry just thinking about these dishes. One other dish I loved was *spaghetti aglio e olio* , just pasta and an oil base, but when she made it, it was heaven.

During my freshman year, I came home for a monthlong holiday break. My mom was so excited I was home that every day was like an Italian feast. Thanks to her cooking, and the feasts I had at the houses of my aunts and grandparents, I ballooned up to 258 pounds. Ara saw me the first day back on campus and said, "Turn him sideways. Maybe we can fit him through the door."

I vowed never to let myself go like that again and I got the weight off in six weeks. I worked out twice a day, playing handball with freshman teammate Gary Potempa and running and lifting as much as I could. The best way to take off the weight was to diet and work out. I did and I got back to 243 pounds for spring ball, which was my best playing weight.

My mother died in 1994, and I miss her and I miss her cooking. Gerry DiNardo's mother, also named Mary, was a very good cook as well. Many times we would eat over one another's house as we only lived five blocks from each other. Sometimes when I was visiting, Pat DiNardo (the father of Larry and Gerry) would talk about Notre Dame and what Larry was doing at the Golden Dome with Ara and the coaching staff. I would just listen and dream about the possibility that some day it could be us out there at Notre Dame playing for Ara Parseghian.

* * *

Freshmen were not eligible to play on the varsity in those days. With the other freshmen, I arrived in August about a week after the upperclassmen. We wore the same gold helmets and the same jerseys as the varsity, but with white pants so that the coaches could tell us apart from the varsity guys who wore gold pants.

Preseason meant two-a-day practices on Cartier Field on campus, along with meetings after both lunch and dinner. There was time to get in an hour's nap before the second practice. I quickly learned how hot and humid it gets in August in northern Indiana. Before the academic year began, players stayed in Flanner and Grace Halls, which were air-conditioned unlike the other dorms on campus. But once you went outdoors to walk over to the locker room in the Athletic and Convocation Center (ACC), you started sweating and found it hard to breathe. We always drank a tremendous amount of fluid after practice.

I soon began to develop some friends on the freshman team. Dan Morrin, from Bishop Egan High School in Philadelphia, was a hardworking lineman, an All-State player in Pennsylvania who had been recruited by more than 100 colleges and universities. Dan came in as a defensive tackle but would later be moved to offensive guard. We started to hang around together, going out for pizza at Louie's, a family-run restaurant that was a short walk south of campus or some nights heading to Rocco's another few blocks down on South Bend Avenue.

Another freshman teammate was Tom Devine, a linebacker from Jackson Lumen Christi High School. He had been the Michigan player of the year two years in a row, and Ara envisioned building his future defense around Tom and another linebacker in our class, Tim Sullivan, who was quick as a cat. Thank goodness he was a really nice guy because he could hurt you if he wanted to. He was the Iowa state boxing champ as well as an All-State wrestler. Tom Devine and Tim Sullivan were captains of our freshman team, but as the years went by, knee injuries stole some of their natural talent. Tom played on special teams until his knees gave out, and Tim went on to be a very productive linebacker and defensive end at Notre Dame, despite being slowed somewhat by his own injuries.

Another unbelievable athlete was Dave Casper. I was amazed that he was so strong and fast, even though he never really lifted weights. He was a naturally gifted player. Mike Townsend was another super athlete, a defensive back blessed not only with speed, but also with grace in his movement and athletic timing. Mike was fun-loving and an easy guy to get along with.

Joe Alvarado, from Bishop Knoll Institute in northern Indiana, may have been the biggest man of Mexican descent that I had ever met at 6'2" and 245 pounds. Joe was a good linebacker and center and he became our long snapper, which is one of the most difficult jobs on the field. Most people don't understand how tough that job is until there is a bad snap, and Joe never had one.

Tom Creevey was a good all-around athlete who played football, basketball, and baseball for Marian High School in Mishawaka, Indiana, not far from South Bend. Tom's dad, John, was a two-sport athlete at Notre Dame, pitching for the baseball team and playing quarterback and kicking for Frank Leahy's football teams in the 1940s. Tom was one of about six quarterbacks in our freshman class. Ara liked to recruit quarterbacks because he believed their athleticism would be valuable even if they switched positions. At one point, Tom felt he wasn't making headway on the offensive side of the ball and worked up the courage to ask for a meeting with Ara. The coach was "very approachable," Tom said. "I told him I thought I could help on the defensive side. The next practice, he gave me a tryout over there, and that's [when] my time on defense started," said Tom, who ended up playing linebacker and defensive end.

Gary Potempa, from Notre Dame High School in Niles, Illinois, was surprised to find a former prep teammate waiting for him when the school year began and we moved back into our dorms for the school year. "I was trying to get into Flanner or Grace Hall because of the air conditioning," Gary said. "But for some reason I got put into Keenan. When I went to check in, it turned out my roommate was my friend since grade school, Tim Rudnick." Gary had thought Tim was attending another school. "I said, 'Why are you coming here?' And he said, 'I'm going to play football.' He ended up doing great. He was so fast." Tim became a kick returner and starting defensive back, making him one of the most successful walk-ons in Notre Dame history.

Some of the other freshman players included Max Wasilevich, Brian Doherty, Greg Hill, Gary Diminick, Paul Sawicz, Tom Bolger, and George Hayduk, just to name a few. All these guys were not only good football players, but they were also really solid people. They were the kind of people you could depend on when the going got tough. Ara had done a great job in picking the kind of people and athletes he wanted. He often talked about the importance of chemistry and he would say over and over that he was a "people coach" first and then a football coach. That approach would prove to be very important because when the going got tough we all were willing to pull together and do what was best for the team.

Almost every guy on the freshman team was an All-American or All-State player. I was an All-City selection from New York City, and that was it. It didn't matter anyway. What mattered was that we were all going to compete to earn the right to play. All the players were eyeballing each other, trying to figure out where they stacked up against this collection of great talent. The advantage I had was that Gerry DiNardo and I had the chance, when we were still in high school, to ask his brother Larry questions and learn from him when he was home on breaks. He described in detail how his Notre Dame offensive line coach, Jerry Wampfler, taught him to block.

Basically, this is the technique: start in your stance with 70 percent of your weight on your left foot. Drive off the line on your left foot and take a step of about six inches with your right foot. Aim your face mask underneath the face mask of the defender so that you will be lower and get leverage. Your left arm starts down by your sock for two reasons. First, it helps you to balance your shoulders. Second, it puts you in a great position to cock your elbow. So when you're driving off of your left foot, you're able to deliver a blow into the defensive guy's chest with both hands. In a perfect scenario, you do that, roll your hips forward, and literally lift the defender up. Because I started learning that technique in high school, I was a little ahead of the game.

The freshmen were essentially the drill team for the varsity. You had to battle to hold your ground in practice because if you didn't, the defense, which was one of the best in the country, would run all over you. The defensive guys who we went up against in practice were tough and nasty, and they didn't want anyone to get the better of them. Assistant coach Joe Yonto would ride them hard in practice, and I would think to myself, *Coach, don't get on these guys too much because then they will take it out on me.*

In one practice, Yonto was really riding defensive tackle Greg Marx, a player who would go on to become a consensus All-American and one of the captains his senior year in 1972. I put a pretty good block on Greg, and he got pissed because Yonto was screaming at him. As I was walking back to the huddle with my back turned, Greg hauled off and punched me right in the head. There was no way I was going to let him do that to me, because if I let him get away with it, he would keep doing it to me all season. So I turned and fired a hard right to his face mask. And I put my head down and kept on swinging at him. I didn't know if I would ever play at Notre Dame, but I wasn't going to be somebody's whipping boy.

The fight was quickly broken up, which was fortunate for me as Greg had ripped off my helmet. If it went too much longer, Greg and his defensive buddies would have killed me. But something special happened when I returned to the huddle. The coaches and other players were all screaming in support, saying "Great job, Frank!" and "Don't take that crap from them!"

The only problem was that it was just halfway through practice, and I had to keep playing against Greg. I got through it, playing as hard as I could to stay above ground. But the upshot was that I earned new respect from the other freshmen, as well as some of the varsity guys. It was kind of a rite of passage to show that I was not going to quit, and that you'd have to fight every time you take a cheap shot at me. It really never happened again.

I had made a commitment that I was going to sacrifice everything I could to play for Ara. That meant getting the job done physically and academically. This wasn't easy in either case. Physically, the upperclassmen were some of the best in America. I was strong enough to compete, but I had to learn how to be a football player. It was a process that would take some time.

I continued to be inspired by Larry DiNardo, someone who was special and was driven to greatness being one of Ara's Knights. Larry was elected one of the captains in 1970, along with a hard-hitting linebacker named Tim Kelly. Guys like Larry and Tim set the example for us freshmen. Larry was a brutal offensive guard who would physically punish his opponent all game until they would submit to his blocking. Ara preached the idea that his teams had "no breaking point," and Larry adopted this attitude wholeheartedly. If you lined up against Larry, you were going to be in for a very tough day. He would never give up.

Larry had started at left guard since his sophomore year in 1968. He was really an artist with his blocking, leveraging his body in such a way that he used every inch of power from his legs and hips, followed by a tremendous blast from his arms. There was always a big collision and initial stalemate as bodies collided. As his defensive man tried to recover from the blast, Larry would keep moving his legs and would stay low, enabling him to lift the defender up and push him back, sometimes putting the player on his back.

We had good offensive line coaches at Notre Dame and we also had a master to watch every day in practice. I also watched films of other past and current Notre Dame offensive linemen, including George Kunz, Dick Swatland, and Jim Reilly. Mike Oriard and Gary Kos were also good players. But Larry was the guy I would always go back to because he was about my size and we had similar traits. I would watch his old films to learn as much as I could about my stance, about taking off from the line of scrimmage, about pass blocking, about pulling, and about staying on my block.

Larry had an X-factor, something that drove him even harder than all the other players on the team. He wasn't the biggest or the fastest, but he used everything he had to compete. What I found out was that this drive, this X-factor, could be inside of me as well. I wanted to be one of Ara's Knights, someone he could depend on when it's fourth-and-1 and we needed a touchdown in a close game. My chance would not come until the following spring, but I worked on my technique all freshman year.

The 1970 football season was a great one for Ara and Notre Dame, but one of the unfortunate occurrences was a knee injury suffered by Larry. He tried to play on the knee, but he wasn't as effective. At the end of the regular season, his knee was operated on by Dr. Leslie Bodnar, an orthopedic surgeon associated with the school's athletic department. Dr. Bodnar did a great job, and Larry was drafted by the New Orleans Saints of the National Football League. His situation made me keenly aware that football was a game that could end in a split second with an injury. Getting my education was not only important; it was very much a necessity.

The beauty of not being able to play as a freshman was that it gave me a chance to blend into the academic and social life at Notre Dame as well as mature on the field. "The fact that we spent a whole year doing nothing but practicing fundamentals made us much better football players," Jim Lynch said. "It was a time when you got yourself adjusted to college life."

Academically, I was in the fight of my life to survive that year. Math gave me difficulties, and I had struggles learning foreign languages, which is one reason I majored in business, for which a language credit was not required. There were kids from all over the country at Notre Dame who were ranked No. 1 in their high school class. So just keeping my head above water was a big thing for me.

With the help of athletic academic counselor Mike DeCicco and his assistant Eddie Brodrick, I was able to weather the storm. Mike DeCicco was from northern New Jersey and he reminded me of every Italian uncle I had back in New York—a warm, caring guy who always gave you a big hug when he saw you. He was a Notre Dame graduate himself and was an engineering professor. He wouldn't take any crap from the athletes if they weren't hitting their books like they should. He wanted us all to go to class and graduate. He doled old-school tough love, and was street smart as well.

Tom Creevey remembered the first meeting that was held for incoming freshmen players. "DeCicco gave a George Patton kind of speech. He said, 'All of you are going to graduate from this schoolhouse. We're going to have an academic advisor team to help you when you need it. But you're going to show up for class or you're going to be facing me.'" Gerry DiNardo had a similar meeting the next year. "DeCicco said, 'I just want everyone in the room to know, I make the decision on who plays, not him,' and he pointed to

Ara. And I said to myself, *Wow, I better go to class.*"

DeCicco was also the fencing coach, and his teams won five national titles—more than any other coach in Notre Dame athletic history. So he understood athletes and cared about ensuring that they received the education they would need to succeed after their college and playing days were over. When any of us would skip class or a session with a tutor, he would threaten us with one of the swords hanging on the wall of his office, describing where he was going to put it if we didn't shape up. He loved us dearly and did a great job getting many of us through his "schoolhouse," as he used to call Notre Dame. DeCicco was a major part of my experience at Notre Dame. With the help of DeCicco and the outstanding professors I had at the business school, I was able to earn a degree from a great university.

The 1970 Notre Dame football team had lost 15 monogram winners from the team that had narrowly lost to No. 1 Texas in the Cotton Bowl the previous year. Ara had some big shoes to fill at several different positions. Among those who graduated were All-American offensive tackle Jim Reilly, tackle Terry Brennan, halfback Ed Ziegler, and two tight ends, Dewey Poskon and Tom Lawson. Also graduating was cocaptain and center Mike Oriard, a walk-on who went on to start, become a captain and attain All-American status. He was a tenacious competitor, with great quickness and intelligence and he was a great example for Ara's Knights—thoughtful and alert, with a focus and purpose during his time at Notre Dame and afterward.

The Irish, however, did have some quality players with experience returning, starting with quarterback Joe Theismann. "Joe exuded confidence," said starting halfback Denny Allan. "He was very optimistic, and I loved his presence in the huddle." The backfield also featured fullback Bill Barz, a product of Mt. Carmel High School on the south side of Chicago, an all-boys Catholic school that always produced tough, hardnosed football players. The offense was well balanced with the great passing combination of a confident Theismann and wide receiver Thom Gatewood.

Thom was the feature player at split end, a class guy who excelled at two things: catching the ball and running routes. He was not your everyday football player; he was smart and creative. He was the kind of guy who would think before he would say things, and he always seemed to say the right things. The early '70s were not easy for black players at Notre Dame. There weren't many African American players at the school—or black students, for that matter. But that was changing. Ara was determined to build his team on character and athletic ability and he didn't care if a person was purple. If a person had character and the hunger to be successful, Ara wanted him. Thom was clearly a leader on the team, and that leadership would be confirmed the next year when he was elected captain of the offense in his senior season.

Bill Trapp was another split end with great hands, but he was not as fast as some other players. Willie Townsend was a young split end who had great speed and moves and great character. He and his brother, Mike Townsend, who was in my class, were not just great athletes, but were guys who would become two of Ara's great Knights. They helped make our program the class act that it was.

The running game was helped by a very strong but somewhat inexperienced offensive line. The guards were cocaptain Larry DiNardo and Gary Kos, a first-time starter who was a strong blocker like Larry, though not as quick. The center position was manned by Dan Novakov, a smart, tough player from Cincinnati's Moeller High School, where Notre Dame would get many players through the hard recruiting of Coach Brian Boulac. Tom Gasseling, a backup tackle from Washington state, was very helpful to me. He roomed in Sorin with Larry and Jack Cahill, two of my St. Francis Prep schoolmates, and Pat Mudron, a defensive lineman who was also on the wrestling team. Tom was the kind of guy who helped show you the ropes and made you feel comfortable, an attitude that really helped keep the football program close-knit.

The halfbacks and fullbacks were not blazingly fast, but could best be described as strong, tough, and athletic. They all had to block, or Ara and offensive coordinator Tom Pagna wouldn't use them. One of the halfbacks, Denny Allan, said in order to get playing time, "You had to block, you had to be able to run, and number one, you couldn't fumble very often. If you were a fumbler, you wouldn't play." Catching the ball was also a requisite for the halfbacks, because they often lined up as a flanker. Most of the backs on the 1970 team were good receivers, especially Denny and Bill Barz. A couple of other backs would give you everything they had. One was Andy Huff, a halfback who could knock you over blocking or running with the ball. John Cieszkowski, a bright guy majoring in premed, was a big fullback who was built like a Mr. Universe candidate. Other backs that made contributions were Bob Minnix, Darryll Dewan, and Bill Gallagher.

At tight end, sophomore Mike Creaney from Baltimore, had an excellent spring practice and was the leading candidate for the job. Craig Stark (naturally we nicknamed him "Naked") was a senior who gave us some depth at tight end, but Mike was the guy. He wasn't the strongest or the biggest tight end, but he had great hands and knew the offense very well. He was also a leader. Mike would embrace the younger players and help them along. He knew that all the younger players were eventually going to be his teammates and he always wanted to have a great team. He understood that if we were all pulling for each other, the chemistry for a great team would be there.

Being independent was one of the things that set Notre Dame apart. Because we weren't in a conference, our goal every year was to win the national championship. Ara looked for the right kind of players to go to war with. He was not just coaching a football team, he was also establishing a culture. Doing the right thing was what Ara wanted his players to do. In someone like Mike Creaney, he had that type of person, even though he was only a sophomore.

Defensively, the Irish were very strong with the likes of senior Bob Neidert along with juniors Walt Patulski and Fred Swendsen at defensive end. Tackles included senior Pat Mudron, Mike Kadish, Mike Zikas, and Greg Marx—all hardnosed players who could really rock your world with a forearm, which is something that I found out firsthand, scrimmaging against them every day as a freshman.

Notre Dame's linebackers in 1970 were as tough as they come. Tim Kelly, one of the captains, was the kind of player who could knock off your face mask with his forearm. Tim led on the football field with his aggressive, physical style and it rubbed off on everyone on the defense. John Raterman, a great student and good football player, was also very physical. Eric Patton from California was a great player in the middle, a combination of muscle and brains. He played hard but would never take a cheap shot at the freshmen or prep team players. I'm glad I didn't have to play against him in games because he was so good. The outside linebackers were Rick Thomann from Akron, Ohio; Jim Musuraca, also from Ohio; along with Jim O'Malley and Pat McGraw. These guys would have been starters at other colleges, but at Notre Dame they all contributed to the team even if they weren't starting.

The defensive backfield consisted of speedster Clarence Ellis; Ralph Stepaniak, who was built more like a linebacker; Mike Crotty, a small, hard-hitting safety; Chuck Zloch, and Ken Schlezes. This defense was going to be a strong part of our team. Ara always tended toward putting our best athletes on defense, because if opponents can't score then we can't do any worse than tie.

It was shaping up to be a great season ahead of us. After getting close in the Cotton Bowl against Texas, Ara and his staff felt we could make a run at winning it all. The passing and running game was there, as was a solid defense and kicking game. All we needed was a little luck and we had a chance for a special season.

CHAPTER 5

The 1970 Season

Game 1: Northwestern

The 1970 season opened on the road against a fine Northwestern Wildcats team coached by Alex Agase, a former assistant who ascended to the head position when Ara Parseghian left for Notre Dame. In 1970 Northwestern would finish second in the Big Ten and Agase would be named national Coach of the Year by the Football Writers Association of America. The Wildcats had an outstanding linebacker, John Voorhees, someone who I later got to know pretty well because he became Larry DiNardo's brother-in-law a year later.

We received the opening kickoff and wasted no time. Six plays and 75 yards later, Denny Allan carried it into the end zone from the 6-yard line. A big play of the drive was a 39-yard pass from Joe Theismann to Thom Gatewood. These two worked long hours together in practice to get to know each other and it was like they could read each other's minds. They were off to a great start to what would become a remarkable season. Later in the first quarter, Joe bootlegged nine yards into the right corner of the end zone, and the Irish lead was 14–0. Northwestern bounced back with two touchdowns in the second quarter. With the score 14–14, the Irish responded with a three-yard TD run by Denny Allan and a 17-yard scoring throw to sure-handed fullback Bill Barz.

Leading 28–14 at halftime, the Irish committed to running the ball in the second half. We scored once more in the third quarter, on Denny Allan's third touchdown of the day, a one-yard run, to make the final score 35–14. Denny wasn't the fastest runner, but had good football speed and a nose for getting tough yardage. Ara and offensive coordinator Tom Pagna liked to use several backs in order to keep them fresh.

It was a promising start. The offensive line played well as the Irish running game produced 330 yards. Joe Theismann only passed for 128 yards, but you could see the potential for a dynamic passing attack with Thom Gatewood, tight end Mike Creaney, and the backfield. The defense kept Northwestern in check, holding them to 269 yards total offense. There were a lot of juniors on the defense, but there was great leadership coming from seniors like cocaptain Tim Kelly.

Game 2: Purdue

The game against Purdue was going to say a lot about the Irish's prospects for the season. In the previous three years, Boilermakers quarterback Mike Phipps had put an early-season damper on our national championship aspirations. Purdue had a great defense coming back and dangerous offensive weapons. We played Purdue at Notre Dame Stadium, which at the time held 59,075 loud fans. It was many years before NBC televised every Notre Dame home game, so there was no chance of being overexposed. That added to the mystique of the campus, especially on football Saturdays. Since freshmen were not eligible to play, I sat in the stands with my classmates, all of us cheering fervently for the team.

Pete Schivarelli recalled that in the locker room before the game Ara relayed some remarks that had been made by Boilermakers linebacker Veno Paraskevas. "Veno had come over from Eastern Europe and he talked about how he always wanted to play football in America," Schivarelli said. "He said his real dream was to play football against Notre Dame and when he played against us at Purdue he had such great anticipation. But when the first series of plays was run, nobody hit him. He said he couldn't believe this was Notre Dame and was expecting a tough football game. He closed by saying he felt cheated."

Ara then showed the team some film from the first play of the previous season, a dive up the middle. "The guard and tackle hit [Paraskevas], knocked him on his back, and the running back stepped on him for an eight-yard gain," Pete said. "Ara was in a rage. 'He calls that not being hit! He says he was cheated. No matter what happens, when this game finishes, I want him to know he played against Notre Dame.' Then he stopped again and said, 'If anyone does any illegal play against him, he will be off this team. I want him hit hard, I want him hit clean, and I want him hit on every single play,'" the coach thundered.

Notre Dame's defense indeed came to play. The front seven in particular were keyed up to end Purdue's winning streak against us. It was a rainy day in South Bend, which was too bad for the fans. But it was the Purdue football team that really took the brunt of the bad weather. The Irish defense forced the Boilermakers to turn over the ball nine times: six fumbles and three interceptions.

Just before the half, Paraskevas pursued an Irish ball carrier near the Notre Dame sidelines. "One of our linemen hit him and he came all the way out of bounds and was right on the ground on all fours," Pete Schivarelli said. "He had this look on this face—he couldn't believe how he was getting pounded. We were all going nuts. I remember the look on his face when he was trying to get up and we were all yelling. He didn't know what the hell was going on."

The Irish running game exceeded 300 yards for the second week in a row, totaling 329 yards this time. The line was again led by Larry DiNardo, with his punishing blocking style. After Scott Hempel's 19-yard field goal, Denny Allan ran four yards for a touchdown. In the second quarter, Thom Gatewood caught a pair of TD passes from Joe Theismann, the first covering 17 yards and the second one seven yards, to put the Irish up 24–0 at the half. Thom caught his third TD pass from Joe in the third quarter, a 20-yarder. Scott kicked a 37-yard field goal, and Darryll Dewan and Larry Parker added running touchdowns to put the cap on a great victory over the Boilermakers, 48–0.

Sometimes winning in a rout gives a team the impression that it is invincible. Ara always had a plan to keep his players from getting overconfident by showing them how they could get better. At Notre Dame, you often win too big or you don't win big enough. We were 2–0, with an offense that just totaled 633 over a strong Purdue defensive team. Our stingy defense held Purdue to 144 total yards for the day. The Irish were on their way and looking for a shot at a national title.

Game 3: Michigan State

A lot of controversy still lingered from the 1966 game, when undefeateds Notre Dame and Michigan State played each other to a 10–10 tie. Some say the buildup for that contest was the greatest ever for a college game. The Irish had won home games against the Spartans in 1967 and 1969, but lost narrowly to Michigan State in East Lansing in 1968. In fact, going into the 1970 game, we hadn't won on MSU's home turf in 21 years. Spartan Stadium, which held 80,000 fans, is one of the toughest in the country for a visiting team. The crowd is loud and feisty, and the Michigan State team has a history of being very physical and giving their all. And they *really* get up to play Notre Dame.

Being a freshman, I wasn't able to travel with the team to the game. There was a closed-circuit broadcast of the game at the Athletic and Convocation Center (ACC) on the Notre Dame campus, which I attended with my freshman buddies Dan Morrin and Tom Devine. These guys were to become my roommates in our sophomore year. I always loved seeing the Irish come onto the field at away games with those crisp white jerseys and blue numbers contrasting with the beautiful gold helmets and matching pants. Ara always looked in great shape and usually wore a Notre Dame golf shirt or sweatshirt.

As it got close to game time, an interesting thing happened. The Michigan State band began playing "The Star Spangled Banner." Everyone in the ACC got up, put their hand on their heart, and sang the national anthem—even though we were 160 miles away from the game. It's important to realize that 1970 was a very turbulent time in America. Most of the students at Notre Dame were from families that were hardworking, with fathers who probably fought in World War II or in Korea. The Vietnam War was still going strong, and there were a lot of people who were very concerned about the politics of the day. However, as the anthem was played, 3,000 people stood and sang along. I loved that about Notre Dame. The words God Country Notre Dame are engraved in stone above the east door of the Basilica of the Sacred Heart. This motto pretty much says it all. We believed in God, we loved our country, and we were nuts for Notre Dame.

Football enthusiasm on the Notre Dame campus was running high after two straight wins. The game was hard fought, and the crowd at the ACC got into it as if they were at the stadium itself, cheering loudly with foot stomping, hand clapping, and a rhythmic chorus of "Go Irish, Beat Spartans!" It was like a prizefight, and our offensive line really drilled the Spartans. The Irish backs piled up 366 yards on the ground. That enabled us to control the clock and wear down the other team's defense. Besides, the best defense in the world is to keep the other team's offense on the sideline.

During the game, Joe Theismann threw an interception to Brad Van Pelt, a hardnosed, very athletic sophomore linebacker who would go on to earn All-American honors and have a great NFL career with the New York Giants. But even Van Pelt's heroics couldn't save the Spartans this day as the Irish defense manhandled its opponent, holding them to 174 total yards in a 29–0 shutout. Denny Allan and Bob Minnix both scored on one-yard runs in the first half. Late in the second quarter, walk-on running back Eddie Gulyas capped a 64-yard drive with a two-yard TD plunge off the right tackle.

Joe Theismann and Thom Gatewood were clicking beautifully, and it was apparent that this combination was becoming a key part of the offense—even though the passing game at this time wasn't needed much because of the overwhelming ground game and our stingy defense. It was a great game, and I celebrated with a victory pizza at Louie's with Dan and Tom. The Irish had dominated the Big Ten in its opening three games, outscoring opponents 112 to 14. We were on our way.

Game 4: Army

The first time I went to West Point was during my freshman year at St. Francis Prep, when we went up the Hudson to play Army's rugby team. West

Point was very impressive. There were cadets all over the place, and you could feel the tradition oozing out of the buildings. We played pretty well, and our first team actually beat them. Our first team was pretty notable as a high school team, boasting guys including Larry DiNardo, Paul Hoolahan (who won a scholarship to North Carolina), and Richie Szaro (who headed to Harvard to play), plus many other football players who would end up earning college football scholarships.

In 1970, the Army football team that came to Notre Dame Stadium was having a hard time competing against top-flight teams. They simply couldn't match up physically because of the academy's limitations on size. There was talk that West Point would loosen the strict entrance requirements so they could attract a better athlete. They never did that, and continued to have a tough time against their scheduled opponents. Years later they went to the triple-option offense, which gave them a better chance to compete against great athletic teams. They were able to use deception and their intelligence to somewhat compensate for their shortcomings in raw athletic ability.

The Irish established absolute dominance early in the 1970 game, rolling up 345 total yards in the first two quarters. With the game out of reach for Army, it gave the Irish's second- and third-team players a chance to get in the contest and show what they could do. By the end of the game, we pounded Army for 258 yards on the ground, including touchdown runs by Joe Theismann, Eddie Gulyas, Darryll Dewan, and Pat Steenberge. We also threw for 316 yards, with Thom Gatewood, Mike Creaney, and Bob Minnix all hauling in TD passes. Final score: Notre Dame 51, Army 10.

Unfortunately, one running play would haunt us for the rest of the year. The call was for a delay off the right side of the line, on which Eddie Gulyas ran for a first down. But Larry DiNardo came to the sideline, limping. He had gotten his leg tangled and tore a ligament in his knee. I watched as the guy whom I modeled my game after, a player who was having an All-American-caliber year, came off the field hurt. He would try to play a couple of more games that year, but he really wasn't able to perform to the same high level.

Ara and the coaching staff were really upset. Larry wasn't just a great football player; he was the heart of the team, a strong leader. He was one of Ara's Knights, someone who other players looked up to—especially the younger ones. He always did the right thing and was in the trenches, keeping the troops moving forward. Larry embodied the spirit of the team, someone who didn't have a breaking point—not only on the field, but also when it came to the values that Ara held so dear to his program. His injury had a deep effect on the team, and no one felt worse than Larry himself. Even though the injury was in no way his fault, I think he felt that he let down all the players on the team because this was their year and he was the main guy driving our powerful running game.

Ara often said that there was no shame in getting knocked down or hurt. The question was whether you were going to let misfortune keep you down. We had good replacements in Jim Humbert and Denny DePrimio, but they didn't quite have the experience and ability that Larry brought to the task. You wanted to go to war with someone like Larry. Ara always wanted people that were hungry to get into action, and Larry would work as hard as he could to get back in the lineup as soon as possible.

Game 5: Missouri

Missouri was coached by Dan Devine, himself a candidate for the Notre Dame job when Ara was hired in 1964. Reportedly Father Edmund Joyce, Notre Dame's executive vice president, wanted Devine in 1964, but Father Theodore Hesburgh, the university's president, really liked Ara. Father Ted (as he was known on campus) felt that Ara was the manifestation of the traits that he wanted Notre Dame to be known for: class, integrity, charisma, and work ethic. So he overruled Father Joyce, and Ara became our guy. Devine would get his chance 11 years later, becoming head coach after Ara retired.

The game was played in Columbia, Missouri. The town was full of energy for the game, and Missouri had some good talent. A capacity crowd of 64,000 very vocal fans jammed the stadium to see if the Tigers could beat the Irish. During the game, Joe Theismann had to step back from the line a number of times in an attempt to get the crowd to quiet down so he could call signals. The Missouri ticket office also pulled a surprise move by making the Notre Dame fans, who had traveled more than 500 miles to witness the game, sit scattered all over the stadium, which minimized the impact of those rooting for the Irish.

As the game started, Missouri went from its own 23 to the Irish 10-yard line, a drive that ended when quarterback Mike Farmer's pass was picked off by Tim Kelly. Even so, the fans were pretty hopped up and felt they could move the ball and score on the Irish. As it turned out, the Tigers couldn't mount much more of an attack against a very strong Irish defense. On the other side of the ball, the Irish offense was its own worst enemy, committing four first-half turnovers to lead only 3–0 at the break.

Early in the second half, Mizzou got the ball in good field position following an Irish punt, and wide receiver Mel Gray, an All-American track star, beat Clarence Ellis on an out pattern for a touchdown. The place went crazy. The pandemonium forced the ND to dig deep to find out what they were made of. The Irish scored on a five-yard pass from Joe Theismann to Thom Gatewood and then a 30-yard pass from Joe to Eddie Gulyas. A one-yard TD run by Eddie capped the scoring. Final score: Notre Dame 24, Missouri 7. The Irish amassed almost 500 yards total offense, and the defense held the Tigers to just 208 yards. We had gone into hostile territory and came out on top.

Game 6: Navy

Notre Dame traveled to Philadelphia, the "City of Brotherly Love," where the Naval Academy was hoping to pull an upset. The game site was JFK Stadium, an old facility on Broad Street. Notre Dame and Navy had been playing each other every year since 1927, a relationship that was cemented during World War II, when Navy ran many officer training classes on the Notre Dame campus. Because of the war, Notre Dame's all-male student enrollment was decimated. The navy programs literally kept the university open, and 12,000 naval officers and officer candidates came out of Notre Dame during that period. A grateful Notre Dame has pledged to keep Navy on the schedule as long as the academy wants to play. It is regarded as a debt of honor. The respect between the two institutions runs deep, and I think they will continue the series as long as both are playing football.

In the '70s, beating the struggling service academies was a no-win situation for the Irish. If you beat them too badly, you were picking on a little program. If you didn't win by enough, people wanted to know what was wrong. The truth was that when you played any academy you had to be ready because they were disciplined and they were relentless. These were the character traits they would need to defend our country. They never gave up, even when it was a lopsided score. You couldn't relax because they came to play and wanted to knock you down. In addition, the game represented a rare chance for them to play a televised game against one of the top teams in the country.

The Irish went to work that day and rolled to a 56–7 victory, racking up 600 yards of total offense: 408 on the ground and 192 through the air. The defense stopped the Navy attack, which could only muster 228 yards total offense. Navy actually scored first, with a run by Ade Dillon, and then the Irish proceeded to score 56 unanswered points. Touchdown runs by Darryll Dewan, Denny Allan, John Cieszkowski, and Bob Minnix, along with two TDs each by Bill Barz and Thom Gatewood, accounted for ND's scoring. This dominating performance brought us to 6–0 on the season.

Game 7: Pittsburgh

Pitt was a sleeping giant. There was plenty of talent in western Pennsylvania and eastern Ohio for the Panthers to draw from. In fact, Notre Dame recruited heavily in that area itself. The University of Pittsburgh was a highly regarded school with great character and history. The Panthers had their own stadium, which held about 60,000, and a strong alumni base. But their football program was searching for an identity and wouldn't find it until Johnny Majors became head coach in 1973 and really put the program on the national college football map, recruiting players such as Tony Dorsett and winning the national championship in 1976.

In 1970 the Panthers brought a 5–2 record with them to Notre Dame Stadium to play the Fighting Irish, then ranked No. 2 in the country. On a sunny afternoon, Pitt got off to a strong start, taking a 14–13 lead in the second quarter. The Irish had been on the short end of some odd plays and bad breaks, and found itself trailing for the second time in the season.

The luck of the Irish soon turned for the better. With the ball on the ND 46, Joe Theismann scrambled out of the pocket to extend the play and then threw the ball downfield toward Denny Allan—a pass that didn't seem far enough, but that sailed between two Panthers defenders and into Denny's hands for a 54-yard touchdown. A short time later, Pittsburgh's fullback fumbled, and we recovered on the Pitt 37-yard line. On the second play of the drive, the Irish lined up in a double flanker formation with Bill Barz the only back behind Joe Theismann. Pitt's secondary was playing man-to-man all day, and offensive coordinator Tom Pagna wanted to trip them up by putting Eddie Gulyas out wide and tight end Mike Creaney inside. Mike went to the flat, and Eddie took an inside route that left him all alone. Joe hit him for the score, and the dream of Pitt upsetting Notre Dame was over.

Joe hit Mike Creaney for 78 yards on the right sideline for another touchdown, and John Cieszkowski closed out the scoring with two late-game touchdowns, making the final score 46–14. The Irish rolled up 284 yards passing and 322 yards rushing, gathering 606 total yards for the day. Meanwhile, the defense held the Panthers to just 256 yards total offense. Ara felt good about his team, although he still had concerns about the turnovers.

Game 8: Georgia Tech

The Irish had opponents from all over the country, and the Yellow Jackets of Georgia Tech were the next into Notre Dame Stadium. One thing that stood out about the Yellow Jackets was their odd uniform. They wore white helmets with gold trim, jerseys that were mustard yellow with black numbers, and pants that were white with gold trim.

It was a big week for the Irish, as they were voted No. 1 in both the AP and UPI college football polls for the first time all year. Unfortunately, this euphoria was short-lived as the Yellow Jackets, who would eventually finish No. 13 in the country, almost pulled the upset of the year. The Jackets came in with a record of 7–2. They had a great defensive tackle named Rock Perdoni, who was not very big, but was quick and tough. Larry DiNardo would be playing against Rock at times. Larry was trying to come back and play as much and effectively as possible as his leadership was badly needed on the offensive line.

Tech had a very tough defense and caused us some real problems. Even though the Irish outgained the Jackets by 448 yards to 141 for the game, in the first half we couldn't get inside Tech's 20-yard line, and the game was scoreless going into halftime. In the second half, offensive coordinator Tom Pagna wanted to put some pressure on the Yellow Jackets defense, so he put the Irish in a double tight-end set. In this way the Jackets couldn't double-stack their linebackers, who had been catching the Irish backs from the backside. The Irish began to move the ball better, but after Scott Smith kicked a 34-yard field goal for us, Tech came back with a 66-yard touchdown pass from Eddie McAshan to Larry Studdard. The Irish were clearly winning the game in the statistics, but on the scoreboard, it was Tech that led, 7–3.

With 11:45 to go in the fourth quarter, the Irish appeared ready to score. Joe Theismann had directed the passing game well all game, throwing for 272 yards, but a pass intended for Denny Allan was picked off at the goal line by Tech's Rick Lewis.

Our defense held, giving the offense one more chance. Needing to drive 80 yards to pull the game out, the Irish planned to throw to Thom Gatewood on the first play of the drive. Cornerback Jeff Ford left his area for a split second to help cover Thom. As Joe Theismann scrambled, he spotted Eddie Gulyas down the sideline for a 46-yard gain to the Tech 34-yard line. Ara wanted to limit the chance for a turnover and the Irish handed off the ball five times for the final 18 yards. Denny Allan ultimately went into the end zone for the go-ahead score. After the Jackets got the ball back, Clarence Ellis made an interception with less than two minutes to play to seal the 10–7 win.

Although Notre Dame lost the No. 1 ranking, Ara wasn't too upset. The object was always to win the game, not win big or always crush the opponent. Ara felt that to have a successful team we needed to win close games like this one. And it would not be the only close game of the year.

Game 9: Louisiana State

The Southeast Conference in the late '60s and early '70s didn't have the kind of size and power that was associated with the teams up north in the Big

Ten and at Notre Dame. Because of segregationist policies, some of the SEC teams, including LSU, did not yet have any black athletes on their rosters. But SEC teams were known for quickness, toughness, and a desire to compete and win. They also had a fervent fan base.

In 1970, the Irish were going up against an LSU team that had won seven straight games and was on its way to winning the SEC championship and finishing No. 7 in the country. The Tigers came into a packed Notre Dame Stadium ready to play. The weather was sunny, windy, and cool, and the House That Rockne Built was teeming with excitement. The Tigers were led by very tough defensive tackles John Sage and Ronnie Estay. They also had a great defensive back named Tommy Casanova, who would go up against Thom Gatewood. Besides a great defense, LSU had an explosive offense that was averaging more than 500 yards per game, led by quarterback Bert Jones, wide receiver Andy Hamilton, and halfback Art Cantrelle. It was a group that had an X-factor of not wanting to be beaten.

The game came down to two rugged defenses that refused to give up a touchdown. Notre Dame held the Tigers to 165 yards of total offense, but could only amass 227 yards themselves. The Irish were really feeling the loss of Larry DiNardo in their running game as well as in leadership.

A huge key to this game was field position, which put a premium on special teams. There were two great punters in the game, Notre Dame's Jim Yoder and LSU's Wayne Dickinson. Yoder punted 10 times for an average of 43 yards per punt, each time keeping the LSU offense away from the Irish goal line. Dickinson averaged 38 yards per punt and punted 12 times.

The Irish turned the ball over a number of times, including an early fumble by Denny Allan after a pass completion on the ND 30-yard line. But the Irish defense forced the Tigers into a punting situation. ND lost the ball again when Darryll Dewan fumbled on the Tigers 3-yard line as we were about to score. With 14:21 to play in the game, a Joe Theismann pass bounced out of the hands of Bill Barz and into the arms of LSU safety Bill Norsworthy, who raced to the Irish 34-yard line.

Cantrelle, a real workhorse back for the Tigers, got the ball down to the 18-yard line. On third-and-4, Clarence Ellis came up with a great defensive play, shooting through and tackling Cantrelle's sweep short of a first down. Then it was LSU's chance to go ahead with a field goal. The Bengals kicker Mark Lumpkin was well within his range, but Rich Thomann and Bob Neidert schemed a way to get to the kick. Here is how Rich recalled it: "Our field goal rush called for Neidert to take in the upback so I could rush from the outside and block the kick, but almost no one ever gets there fast enough to do that. I told Bob that I'd pull the upback out so he could rush underneath, which is a shorter distance to the ball. It worked beautifully, and Bob laid out vertically and blocked it. My linebacker coach, George Kelly, was mad at me because he said I didn't make enough of an effort to block it. I just ignored him. I got 'the look' from Ara. That's all I needed."

It would be LSU's last opportunity; the Irish would have more. Notre Dame was forced to punt, and Yoder rolled one down to the 1-yard line. The chance for something big to happen was close. The Tigers were forced to punt to Ellis, who returned it to the LSU 36-yard line with just under five minutes to play.

An interference call at the LSU 17-yard line put the Irish in business. Joe Theismann rolled wide on second-and-goal and threw a pass intended for Thom Gatewood—but it was almost intercepted by Casanova, who dropped the pass. With the Irish given a reprieve, Scott Hempel came in to kick a 24-yard field goal. He did his job, and the game ended Notre Dame 3, a tough-as-nails LSU 0.

There was a lot of joy in the Notre Dame locker room, but there were concerns about how the team had two tough wins in a row against teams that were not supposed to be as big and strong. Up next we had to travel to Southern California to play an always difficult Trojans team.

Game 10: Southern California

There was a song that came out in the early '70s called "It Never Rains in Southern California." Well, in 1970 it rained heavily throughout the ND-USC game in Los Angeles. The Trojans had a record of just 5–4–1 going into the game with the Irish. These guys weren't having a great season, but they were big, fast, and talented. And Notre Dame seemed to be jinxed out in Los Angeles against John McKay's teams. The Irish hadn't won at USC since 1966, when it routed the Trojans 51–0 and claimed the national championship. McKay vowed after that game that the Irish would never again beat his team in the Los Angeles Coliseum. Interestingly, McKay was an Irish Catholic from West Virginia and a big Notre Dame fan growing up. So competing against the Irish was a top priority for him.

The game started out nicely for the Irish with an 80-yard drive, mostly on the arm of Joe Theismann. It was the beginning of a record-setting game for Joe despite the rain and muddy field. The drive ended with him running 25 yards for the score, putting the Irish on the board first.

But the Trojans had a fantastic back, Clarence Davis. He was great at following his blocking and grinding out positive yardage, talents that would allow him to go on to have a fine NFL career. On this day he scored two touchdowns in the first quarter to help the Trojans to a 21–7 lead. USC quarterback Jimmy Jones also had a great day, going 7-for-7 in the first quarter behind solid protection against a defense that had not given up more than 14 points in a game all year.

In the second quarter, John Cieszkowski caught a nine-yard pass from Joe Theismann, and the halftime score was 24–14. Then the third quarter proved to be a humbling one for the Irish. Fumbles and interceptions hurt its chances of making a comeback as the rain continued and the muddy field became worse. The Trojans marched down to the Irish goal line and tailback Mike Berry fumbled the ball. One of the Irish defensive players had the ball between his legs but USC offensive tackle Pete Adams fell on the ball for a touchdown to make the score 31–14.

The Irish received the kickoff and took over near their own goal line. Joe Theismann faded back to pass, and the wet ball slipped out of his hand and landed in the end zone. The Trojans defense, which was labeled "the Wild Bunch," fell on it for a touchdown—the second one in 42 seconds. It was then 38–14, and the dream of a national championship was drowning in the mud and rain of Southern California.

"We were standing on the sidelines with our shoes almost underwater," said Joe Theismann. "The second half, it just poured and poured." Still, Joe kept slinging the ball in an effort to rally the team. He threw a 46-yard scoring strike to Larry Parker and ran another score into the end zone himself. The final score was 38–28. The Irish only mounted 31 yards rushing that day, but Joe threw for an unbelievable 526 yards, which is still the Notre Dame single-game record. USC's Jones threw for 226 yards, nowhere near Joe's totals, but in critical times he had the Irish's number this day.

It was a humbling and disappointing loss, but the 1970 team would have a chance to redeem its season as it was invited to go up against the No. 1 team in the country, Texas, in the Cotton Bowl. It would be a rematch of the previous year's hard-fought bowl game, in which the Longhorns squeezed out a 21–17 victory. Texas had a 30-game winning streak going, the longest in the country. It would be a tremendous challenge for Ara and his team against one of the most explosive teams college football had ever seen.

The Cotton Bowl

There was a big buildup for the Cotton Bowl on New Year's Day of 1971, based on the closeness of the previous year's Cotton Bowl, the long Texas winning streak, and the perception that this 9–1 Notre Dame squad was better than the Irish team that had come to Dallas the year before. The national sports commentators were calling it the main matchup of the bowl season. In that era, Notre Dame didn't take along the freshmen players since they were ineligible to play, so I watched the game at home with my father during my Christmas break back in New York.

The disappointment of the previous year's loss to Texas fueled Ara's competitive fire. Pete Schivarelli, a reserve defensive tackle, recounted how the players were excited to learn that they had been invited to attend a Dallas Cowboys playoff game at the Cotton Bowl. "We were in a team meeting at the hotel, and someone brought up the Cowboys game," Pete said. "Ara got that look in his eye. He said, 'We came here to play a game, not to watch one.'" The team did get to attend the game, but after it ended, the Irish went through a full-equipment practice on the same field. "People were leaving the stadium, and we were going into practice. Ara set the tone that night. It was all business. When the game came, there wasn't anyone with any doubts."

Much of the Longhorns' success was the result of the innovative wishbone offense that coach Darrell Royal unveiled in the 1968 season. In this formation, the quarterback took the snap from under center with a fullback close behind him. Two halfbacks were set farther back—one to the left and the other to the right. The alignment was designed to run triple-option running plays, and the way Texas executed this offense, it was nearly unstoppable.

In the previous year's Cotton Bowl, the Longhorns had rushed for 331 yards and passed for 107 against a pretty stout Notre Dame defense. The Irish played a traditional defense that day, using a 4-4 front. Against this scheme, the Texas fullback was able to run for big yardage because the outside linebacker was put in a bind: he would either have to take the fullback or the quarterback. If he went to stop the fullback, the quarterback would keep the ball and edge down the line of scrimmage, then turn upfield or pitch the ball back to the trailing halfback. The offensive tackle would block down with the guard on the defensive tackle and then scrape off and block the inside linebacker. Having put the outside linebacker in this situation, Texas was headed for significant yardage if the quarterback made the right read, as the next defender to have a chance at the ball carrier was the safety.

The Longhorns executed the wishbone offense to perfection and often won by big margins, enabling their backups to get a lot of experience, too. The 1970 team rushed for 340 yards and averaged 41 points per game, while giving up only about 12 points per game. The offense was led by running backs Steve Worster and Jim Bertelsen, and quarterback Eddie Phillips was also a dangerous runner.

Ara went to work developing a plan to put his defense in position to stop the wishbone. He grasped the need to defend the wishbone both vertically and horizontally, taking away each progression—the dive, the quarterback keeper, the option pitch, the vertical pass. And so he devised a strategy that would turn out to be the blueprint that changed college football, giving defenses a fighting chance against the wishbone.

Ara's new defensive alignment put 10 men in the box, the area from the tight end to the tackle on the other side of the offense line. It was a non-penetrating defense that put defensive back Clarence Ellis one-on-one with the best Texas receiver, a worthwhile gamble since Texas was not a great throwing team.

Ara called his scheme the "mirror defense," because linebackers would line up in an inverted *Y*, mirroring the lineup of the offensive backfield. On each side, the defensive end was responsible for taking the outside pitch man. The outside linebacker lined up on the outside shoulder of the offensive tackle. As the offensive tackle came off of the line to block the defensive tackle, the linebacker would head straight for the fullback. This disrupted the entire rhythm of the precise Texas offense. As soon as the Texas quarterback gave the ball to Worster, the fullback would get blasted by a linebacker. Worster fumbled four times in the game with the Irish claiming the ball three times. In total, the Irish forced nine fumbles during the Cotton Bowl and recovered five of them.

Texas actually was the first to get on the scoreboard. The quarterback, Phillips, ran for 63 yards on the first play from scrimmage, leading to a 23-yard field goal by Happy Feller. Texas fans put up their "Hook 'em Horns" hand signal—confident that their team would prevail as it had the year before. Then Joe Theismann went to work, leading the Irish to three scores in the game's first 16½ minutes. He capped an 80-yard drive by hitting Thom Gatewood on a 26-yard strike to give the Irish a 7–3 lead. Thom unfortunately pulled his hamstring as he went into the end zone on the scoring pass, which sidelined him for the rest of the day.

John Cieszkowski also had three key rushes on the drive. Overall he had an outstanding day, running from his fullback position with great determination for 52 yards on 13 carries. "Our attitude was, 'We've been here before and we're going to own these guys,'" John said. "Physically, we dominated that game and that team man for man. There was nobody on that field who did not literally dominate his opponent."

This first touchdown created a psychological shift. The Longhorns, who were used to dominating the opposition, then had to play from behind. Texas fumbled the ensuing kickoff, and Notre Dame's Tom Eaton recovered on the Texas 13-yard line. After a nine-yard run by John Cieszkowski, Joe Theismann went the final three yards on a keeper as the Irish went up 14–3. Things were not going well for the Longhorns; they were struggling with everything they had done so well during their long winning streak.

Early in the second quarter, the Irish got the ball back on their own 47 following a punt and drove to the Texas 15-yard line. "They blitzed the line-backer, and Theismann read it perfectly," John said. "I was taking the handoff from him and he decided to pull it out and keep the ball at the last second." Joe raced down the right sideline to the end zone to up the score to 21–3.

The Longhorns responded with their best drive of the day, seven minutes and 84 yards, finished off by Bertelesen's two-yard scoring sprint around right end. They added a two-point conversion pass from Phillips to Danny Lester. Although it was a successful drive, Texas had been forced into relying on something they weren't used to doing: passing the ball. The big plays in this drive were three passes from Phillips to tight end Deryl Comer for 8, 36, and 10 yards.

Joe Theismann hurt the ulnar neve in his arm in the second quarter, and Ara called on backup quarterback Pat Steenberge. "Our coaches had picked up on film that their nose guard made a little adjustment with his hands as to which way they were slanting," Pat said. "We would read the nose guard at the line, and it tipped off whether they were slanting left or right. We'd run the trap into the slant. All day, whenever we needed yardage, we'd run that trap play."

With the half winding down, Ara then turned to another reserve quarter-back, Jim Bulger, who had a cannon arm. Jim could throw the ball 80 yards in the air, something that only a few NFL quarterbacks could match. Ara told him to drop back and just throw the ball deep and let Clarence Ellis run under it. Clarence, normally a defensive back, caught it for a 37-yard gain. Irish kicker Scott Hempel then booted a 36-yard field goal just before halftime to make it 24–11 at the break. Scott, like the vast majority of place-kickers in that era, used a straight-on style, not the soccer style that dominates now.

Joe Theismann returned in the second half. "I had no feeling in the last two fingers of my right hand the entire second half," he remembered. "I wish I had been able to throw the ball around the way we wanted to." The Irish game plan turned conservative; meanwhile, the Longhorns offense kept committing turnovers. The result was no more scoring, and the 24–11 score stood up. It was a stunning upset for Notre Dame.

The final seconds set the scene for an interesting footnote. George Kelly, an assistant coach on defense, told some of the reserves to stand near Ara to make him realize that we had a safe lead and to consider putting them into the game for a few plays. Pete Schivarelli was one of those reserves and he recalls Ara saying he would make the substitutions on the next timeout. "I remember watching that clock, and my heart began to sink as it kept running. There never was a timeout," Pete said. "I would have loved to get into that game. But the game ended, and all we cared about was that we won and we wanted to lift Ara across the field, and that's how it came about that I was right next to him."

A news photographer captured the moment of celebration. The picture of Pete and teammates Mike Creaney and John Dampeer hoisting Ara on their shoulders appeared the next day on the front page of the *New York Times* and in other newspapers across the country. "To have that picture with Ara—if you said you could have only one photo, other than your family, that's the photo I would take," Pete said.

That scene was later selected as the basis for the bronze statue inside Gate D at Notre Dame Stadium that honors Ara—a statue that was funded by contributions from his former players. Ara, who always made it a point to share credit, objected to the whole idea of a statue but finally agreed to it when the Cotton Bowl scene was suggested because it wasn't just him who would be represented but his players as well.

* * *

When you are a champion and you get beat in a convincing manner, it's tough to take. I've been on that end of the result, and it sticks with you. You never want to feel that way again. It was difficult on the Texas team and on their fans, but they were very gracious in defeat, congratulating the Irish for the victory.

The Irish hoped the win would propel them to the top of the polls, but when Nebraska won the Orange Bowl that evening, the 11–0–1 Cornhuskers got the nod instead. Notre Dame finished No. 2, with thoughts of what could have been if not for that loss in the rain to USC.

It was an amazing season in many ways. The offense averaged 510 yards a game, still the season record at Notre Dame. Perhaps even more remarkable was the balance—279 yards per game on the ground and 253 yards a game passing. Joe Theismann, who set a school passing yardage record that stood for 29 years, finished second in the Heisman Trophy voting to Jim Plunkett of Stanford. As for the defense, it really stepped up in the November wins against Georgia Tech and LSU as well as in the upset of Texas.

A lot of key players, including starting guards Larry DiNardo and Gary Kos, were graduating. The players behind them had some experience, but it was my goal to be bigger, stronger, and more determined than anyone else. It was my chance to realize my dream and make the starting lineup. I was driven to make it happen.

CHAPTER 6

Lifetime Bonds

Wintertime at Notre Dame can be brutal. The temperature usually hovers between minus-5 and 20 degrees, and with the wind blowing off nearby Lake Michigan, wind chills can dip to 30 below. Frequent cloud cover and high humidity add to the bone-chilling reality of walking to class. The temperatures are similar to those in Chicago, but because of lake effect, snowfall averages between 72 inches and 90 inches annually at Notre Dame compared with 30 to 40 inches in Chicago. The campus joke is that Edward Sorin, who founded the school in the winter of 1842, originally meant to camp only temporarily on the site, saying "Let's just stay here until it stops snowing." But it never did, and so the school remains.

In this environment of snow, wind, and cold, certain places at Notre Dame became very meaningful. These included your dorm, your dining hall, the Rockne Memorial (with its swimming pool and basketball and handball courts), the library, your classroom buildings, and the LaFortune Student Center and Huddle snack bar. Student life also centered around religious places such as the Grotto, Sacred Heart Church (which now has the status of a basilica), and the Golden Dome on top of the Main Administration Building with its statue of the Virgin Mary.

Rich Thomann lived in Holy Cross Hall, originally built on the hill overlooking St. Mary's Lake as a seminary for the priesthood but later converted to a residence hall for students. "Winter was so bad, but we had fun playing in the snow," he said. "I walked to breakfast every morning across a frozen lake, below zero degrees on many a dark morning, stopping to pray at the Grotto for one of those damn tests I had to pass." The Grotto, located in a secluded spot between the Golden Dome and St. Mary's Lake, is a smaller-scale replica of the famous grotto near Lourdes, France. It is a place for quiet reflection, and students, alumni and visitors often come here to pray and light a votive candle for a special request.

Moreau Seminary, which serves the Congregation of Holy Cross, is situated on the far side of St. Joseph's Lake, the other lake located behind the Golden Dome. It is where the football team stayed the night before home games. Some other places that we visited often were the Morris Inn, the Notre Dame Bookstore (with its outdoor basketball courts behind it), and Gilbert's men's clothing store.

Gilbert's could supply the wardrobe for every Notre Dame man—well, almost everyone. Jim Leahy recalled the time Mike McCoy arrived for a road trip not wearing a sport coat, professing to not own one. Ara Parseghian told McCoy, a defensive tackle who weighed close to 300 pounds, to go over to Gilbert's and get one. "McCoy said, 'I tried, sir. They don't have my size,'" Leahy recounted. "Ara said, 'What size do you wear? They have every size in the world.'" McCoy answered that he wore size 56, double extra long. "The whole room of coaches broke out laughing. Ara told him, 'You can wear your sweater on this one trip, Mike.'"

As you would imagine, some things have evolved over the years, but the campus has the same kind of effect on those who are there today. There is something that links all Notre Dame students, past and present. The common bond is similar to a military experience, but different in that it is more spiritual. By spiritual, I don't necessarily mean religious, even though the majority of students are Catholic. You could be Protestant, Jewish, or Muslim and still fit into the Notre Dame spirit, which is a deep appreciation of life's journey and our underlying purpose to make a positive difference in this world of which we are a part. It is a recognition that we need to pass down to the next generation what we have learned about life.

Notre Dame has never had athletic dorms. Football players live on the same floors and often in the same room with nonathletes. Just about every former player looks back positively on that experience and on the close lifetime bonds that were developed with other students.

"When you're an 18-year-old high school senior you think there might be something special about an athletic dorm," said Rocky Bleier, a running back who after graduation was wounded as an infantryman in Vietnam and then defied the odds to play football again and become an integral part of four Super Bowl–winning teams in Pittsburgh. "At Notre Dame you were a student first and an athlete second. It was better. You don't become a number, you become a person."

Quarterback Joe Theismann said that the biggest thing he took away from Notre Dame was the feeling of being part of a family. "We have a great fraternity of graduates around the world who will never allow you to sleep out in the cold," he said.

Dorm life is very much like family life, especially in winter when the options outside are not great. We got to know our hall mates very well. We learned their likes and dislikes, their strengths and weaknesses, and how to be sympathetic when they were hurting because of a family issue or a girlfriend problem. I became a better-rounded person from the long hours of just sharing stories and getting to understand dorm mates who came from various backgrounds, different parts of America, and even other countries. I became exposed to some pretty sharp young men.

As Tom Creevey put it, "The dorm became your fraternity. We felt a great camaraderie, doing things together and getting to know each other through the four years." Dorm mates ate together, formed teams for the annual Bookstore Basketball intramural tournament, put together their own bowling leagues, and just generally hung out. Notre Dame even has its own tackle football program, which pitted hall teams against each other, drawing players from the many high school athletes who go to school there. (Today, Notre Dame women have their own intramural flag football league, too.)

I lived in Sorin Hall, and as the oldest dorm on campus, it had great tradition. But what I liked the best was the way the older guys in Sorin would take the time to show newcomers the ropes. There wasn't any tradition of hazing. It was more an attitude of, "Hey, guys, this is the real deal if you want to enjoy what Notre Dame has to offer." They really acted like older brothers. We would do some wild things that only those guys would know about. A large majority of Notre Dame students live on campus, so dorm life was a big part of the journey through the university. I think that's why the reunions are so special. They rekindle all those experiences and feelings of our youth.

Dan Morrin, my teammate and Sorin roommate, said, "I loved eating lunch with 20 guys every day with something to talk about. Guys on our floor were from Los Angeles, Chicago, Wisconsin, New York, Pennsylvania. They weren't all athletes, but they felt they were part of the team because they knew you and me and Gerry DiNardo and Tom Clements and Pete Demmerle and Tom Devine. The 200 people in the dorm would root for us because we were their guys."

Dorm mates were always around to lend support. Gary Potempa, who lived in Keenan Hall, remembers being scheduled to give a brief speech as part of an upcoming pep rally. "I was sitting with the guys in the dorm, and they all started throwing out ideas for what I should say at the pep rally. It was extremely cool," he said. "I got to be good friends with a bunch of them. It was a way to get away from football and hang out with regular students."

My residence hall, Sorin, opened in 1889. It is located just southwest of Sacred Heart and the Main Building with its Golden Dome, right in the heart of campus. It was a great location; you were close to everything. Even when it was snowing like crazy we could get anywhere in 10 minutes or less—the North Dining Hall, classrooms, Rockne Memorial, Notre Dame Stadium, and the Athletic and Convocation Center (ACC), which housed football training and locker rooms and contained an arena for basketball and concerts.

It was a two-minute walk once a week to Badin Hall, where the Notre Dame laundry was located. Every Tuesday morning we would fill our large laundry bag and throw it from our floor down to the first level of Sorin, where it was picked up by the laundry service. Every item in that bag had a tag with a number sewn on it. My number was 01316. Every shirt, every piece of underwear, every pair of pants that was mine had that number, which I still remember more than four decades later. It's burned into my brain, like my first telephone number, UL-4-9261. On Friday morning we would go to Badin Hall and pick up our wrapped bundles of laundry, everything pressed and folded neatly. Even our jeans had a nice crease in them. The women who worked there really took pride in their job.

Another unusual aspect of Notre Dame dorm life was the maid service. Every Monday through Friday, maids would start about 8:00 AM and go to every room. These were usually older women who would remind us of our moms back at home. They would vacuum, clean sinks, make the beds, and generally tidy up. They would pick up the clothes we had left on the floor, which is more than our moms would do. Our moms wouldn't let us get away with the messes we had in our dorms like our maids did. They were kind to us, and I don't remember anyone ever disrespecting any of the maids. We loved them and considered them as part of our hall family.

Each dorm also had a worker assigned to go to the main campus post office and get the mail. Getting a letter or a package was a big deal in those days before e-mail, texts, or Facebook. Phone calls were not cheap, so we would pick a day and time when the price was discounted. On Sundays at 2:00 PM I would call my house in Queens and ask to speak person-to-person to Mr. Anthony Pomarico. There was no Anthony Pomarico, but that was the signal for my Mom to decline the call and then dial me back in a minute or two. We would talk for about 30 minutes about how things were going with school and football. I was the first one in my neighborhood to go away to college, so a lot of people wanted to know how Frankie was doing.

* * *

I began working out the day we got back from Thanksgiving break in 1970. I was in the weight room—bench pressing, squatting, and deadlifting. Those were my three main lifts. I would run on the off days and play handball or basketball. I quickly realized I couldn't measure up to some of guys who had been all-league or All-State in high school basketball, so I stuck to what I did best and that was lifting and running.

Other freshmen football players, including Dan Morrin and Gary Potempa, were ready to start training, too. But the guys who really liked to lift were the track-and-field athletes, including Paul Gill and Emilio Postelli. They were intelligent, had a great work ethic, and loved to improve their strength. I learned a lot from them about lifting and the history of Fr. Lange's weightlifting gym behind the Main Building. Fr. Lange had a passion for lifting weights himself and was recognized as one of the strongest men in the world when he was in his twenties. It was reported that, even at age 65, he could deadlift 600 pounds. He fervently spread the word about the benefits of weight lifting. Over the course of three decades, he trained many athletes and other students. I was never in his original gym, but a lot of his home-designed equipment was still in the ACC.

Weight training was helping me get stronger and bigger, and I saw a chance to compete for the starting job at left guard. Larry DiNardo and Gary Kos were graduating, leaving both guard spots open. I was bench-pressing 370 pounds, and both my squat and my deadlift were just more than 500 pounds. That was great, but I had to be able to move as well. I ran the lakes three times a week if the weather allowed, and played handball. My body responded. My chest got thicker, my back started to fill out, and my legs and buttocks were as strong as I could get them.

Dan Morrin and I would start our workouts at about 3:30 PM and lift until 5:30 PM three times a week. When someone would ask why we were working out so hard in January, my response was always, "If we're going to beat Southern California, we are going to have to outwork them." Our winter that year was cold and snowy for about four months. It seemed like every morning the wind would be howling and the snow was coming down sideways. To go to breakfast or class, we would bundle up from head to toe—boots, heavy jeans or corduroy pants, sweatshirts, jackets, and stocking hats. Dan and I would kid each other about the weather, saying that we were glad we weren't in Southern California because they didn't really appreciate 70-degree weather like we did.

Kidding aside, we loved being at Notre Dame and playing for Ara Parseghian. We were becoming aware of how special of a leader he was and how competitive he was in everything he did. It was rubbing off on us. So being in the middle of winter in South Bend wasn't a problem. As Peter

Habeler writes in his book, *Lonely Victory,* "The physical prerequisites alone will not get you to the summit. It's got to be a burning desire and it must be the right desire. You must want the challenge as much or as more than the glory of the victory." The point is that you have to love every aspect of your journey to your goal in order to achieve it with a wholeness or completeness. Nothing about playing for Ara felt like work because the end goal was to achieve greatness. Our ultimate goal was not to just play, but to play for a national championship.

Some of the upperclassmen assumed their experience would be enough to earn them a starting position in 1971. But by the time we got to March, they could see how strong I had become and they started to realize they needed to catch up in order to compete. They were all good guys and good football players. They had just finished their season, they were recovering from injuries, and they felt it was their turn. But I was driven by a force that refused to be denied.

Even though I would only be a sophomore, I knew that I would have a fair chance to compete against the veteran players. With Ara, you had to earn your spot every day. In fact, the coaching staff reviewed the performance of every single player after every practice. "Sometimes it would just be a sentence or two, but we went through every player," said assistant coach Greg Blache. "Ara would always say, 'The depth chart is not etched in stone. If you want to be the starter, earn the right to be the starter.'"

Ara's staff ran a six-week program beginning in March to get us ready for spring practice. I was in shape when the workouts began, and by the end I was hungry for spring practice to commence. As freshmen, we were put up against the first team in spring to see if we could hold our own. It was not only difficult physically, but we also had to learn the whole varsity playbook.

I dedicated myself to learning the plays, and with the physical ability I had developed I was soon running on the first team in spring practices. I had developed quickness and power, and my blocking style was based on Larry DiNardo's. On top of that, it was the Driven Spirit—the obsession with reaching my goal—that enabled me to go toe-to-toe every day with some of the best defensive players in the country. For me, the goal was like climbing

Mount Everest. I wanted to be the starting left guard at Notre Dame as badly as I needed to breathe. It may sound extreme, but that's the way I felt. That is the way you need to feel you you want to reach your goals in life. By the end of spring ball, I was the starting left guard for Ara Parseghian's Notre Dame team. I also won the Herring Award that year as the top freshman lineman.

Meanwhile, I was thrilled to find out that two of my teammates from St. Francis Prep would be coming to Notre Dame in the fall. One was John O'Donnell, a hardnosed Irishman who would become a linebacker for the Irish. The other was my longtime friend, Gerry DiNardo. I couldn't wait for the 1971 season to come around, when I could welcome my friend as a Domer and get my chance to play for Ara's Fighting Irish team.

East Door of Sacred Heart Church

The Art of TP Thomas Pomarico

CHAPTER 7

Sophomore Year

When freshman year ended, it was great to get back to Howard Beach. I usually carpooled to the East Coast, catching a ride with my teammate Dan Morrin to Philadelphia. Then my dad would pick me up from there, or Dan's father would drive me the rest of the way. With the highway speed limit at 75 mph in those days, it was about a 12-hour trip. Gas at that time was 32 cents a gallon, if you can believe it.

I had not been home since Christmas, and my mom, aunts, and Mrs. DiNardo prepared a lot of delicious food to eat. I didn't want to make the same mistake I had made at Christmas break and gain 15 pounds, but I did enjoy myself. I loved seeing my family. It felt like I wasn't going through Notre Dame alone, that everyone in my family was experiencing the journey through me. I was very close to my brother Johnny Boy, who was about 12 years old at the time. He loved talking about Notre Dame, Ara Parseghian, and the team's players. He shared the information he got from me with his own group of friends. It was as if I had found the Holy Grail, and everyone wanted to know what it was all about.

My mom surprised me one day with a full-size poster of me in a "huck 'n' buck" pose, which was the name given to photos of football players in a posed action stance. A photographer would take this shot every year with our uniforms and shoulder pads on, but without a helmet. I was excited to see the poster and asked my Mom where the original photo was. She said that I couldn't get it back because the guy who made the poster was a bookie, and he wanted the original as part of the deal to make the poster. I thought, *Holy smokes, I hope the law never breaks into his office and finds that picture. They might think I had some kind of connection to gambling.* Fortunately, that never happened. Ara would warn us every year about the NCAA rules against associating with gamblers, and I took that seriously. I told my mom that next time we'd go to a legit photo studio to get the poster made.

I developed a summer workout program with Gerry DiNardo. Gerry had spent a year at Tabor Academy under Coach Mike Silipo, a guy from the neighborhood who became a head coach and worked out with us in the summer. Mike really took care of Gerry, helping him to expand himself physically and academically. Gerry had grown to 6'1" and 240 pounds from about 200 pounds. After all his bulking up, he was just about my size (243 pounds). When Ara offered Gerry a scholarship, the Notre Dame coach wondered out loud if Coach Vince O'Connor and Brother Owen Capper were breeding guards at St. Francis Prep.

Gerry and I inspired each other as we each tried to outdo the other lifting in my basement or running on the Belt Parkway. My dad had bought me an Olympic barbell set and a bench press, and Gerry and I would lock ourselves in the basement for hours doing ungodly workouts in order to get bigger and stronger. We pushed each other, rep for rep, pound for pound weight lifting. I would tell Gerry that I was going to aim for bench-pressing 350 pounds that summer, and he would answer that he would match me. The two of us did that with every exercise, as well as the runs that we did three times a week. The runs always turned out to be extreme efforts to the very end, each of us pushing the other; sometimes we would even vomit at the end.

Gerry and I knew we had a once-in-a-lifetime shot to play major college football and be part of the national scene. We threw ourselves at the challenge. We never took drugs, never did anything illegal to compete—it was just hardnosed, all-out training.

Ara often reminded his players that everyone has the will to compete on Saturday, when the band is playing and the cheerleaders are jumping and the fans are going wild. The question was whether you have the dedication to prepare to win in January when the wind is blowing and you have to trudge to the Athletic and Convocation Center (ACC) to lift or play handball, or in the summer when it's hot and you are on the Belt Parkway with traffic and mosquitoes all over the place. That's when champions are made.

Before my freshman year, I had gotten a job as an ironworker along with Larry DiNardo. Larry took me into the union shop to see if we could get work. The general manager of the shop was Jerry Place, a big Irishman who you didn't want to cross. As I was waiting to see if I could get a job, he would throw guys out of his office, yelling and telling them, "Don't come back if you are going to screw up." He saw me and said, "Hey you, come on in here." When I got in, his whole attitude changed. He loved the fact that local guys were getting a chance to play big-time college football and he would ask questions about how the upcoming season was looking. Jerry would say, "We are all rooting for you guys. We watch every game that's on TV." In the summer of 1970 I worked in the south end of Manhattan, close to the World Trade Center. They were just topping off the second tower at that time. When the towers came down in 2001, the memory of the WTC opening up added to my sense of sadness.

The ironworkers took tremendous pride in their work. It was physically hard, and it was scary to be up high walking on just the metal beams. I was scared stiff. Larry told me, "Don't worry, you won't fall." I didn't, but it took me some time before I was comfortable with the beams. We made great money for the time and I made enough that my parents didn't have to give me any spending money the whole year. I had enough pizza and beer money to last all of freshman year.

Gerry joined me on the job that summer of 1971. "When we were ironworkers in Manhattan, we'd go home at crazy hours and work out," he recalled. "We woke up in the morning, got on the subway by 6:00 AM and worked eight hours on the 42nd story of the AT&T Building on 47th Street. We took the train back home, worked out, had dinner, and got to bed at midnight. We didn't think it was anything extraordinary at the time."

At the beginning of August, we received a box from Notre Dame containing our football shoes for the season. We got them early so that we could break them in and avoid blisters during camp. The box also signified that your butt better be ready for the start of football. Gerry and I wound down our jobs as ironworkers and took off a couple of weeks to just train for the season. We were in good running shape, which was very important. If you couldn't run and had to take some time off because you got sick or dehydrated, that would seriously hurt your chances to compete for a starting position. Gerry and I were flying down the Belt Parkway at this time of the summer. It was like the first *Rocky* movie, when Sylvester Stallone's character started out in bad shape and at the end he was sprinting up the steps of the Philadelphia Museum of Art. That was what we were like in August: big, powerful, and we could go all day.

Gerry would have to wait another year because he was a freshman. (In fact, 1971 was the last season that freshmen couldn't play varsity.) I was and still am in favor of freshman not playing. There is too much of an adjustment from high school physically, socially, and most importantly, academically. In terms of football, there is a big difference between 18-year-old freshmen and seniors who are three or four years older, both physically and confidence-wise. When freshmen return to their hometowns and get asked if they are starting, they sometimes feel like they are a failure if they are not. That is the furthest from the truth. They need time, experience, and maturity.

There was always a feeling of excitement returning to Notre Dame for another year. The sight of the Golden Dome shining in the sun represented a proud tradition and spirit of excellence. It also meant reconnecting with teammates and friends who came from all around the country. The Midwest was well represented on the team, but we also had players from California, Texas, Florida, and New England. Students often wanted to talk to me to hear my New York accent, sometimes commenting that they thought it sounded like something out of the movies. The good part was that some girls liked the accent, and it helped break the ice with them, which was very helpful to someone like me who came from an all-boys high school. In truth, though, I wanted to fit in rather than feel different because of my accent, so I worked hard to shed as much of it as I could.

Once we were back on campus, the team gathered for dinner. Ara welcomed us after the meal, setting the tone for the season ahead. He conveyed his great expectations for us, not just in academics and football, but also in behavior. We were to be a credit to our parents, alumni, and teammates. He talked about being a champion every day. It wasn't something you did once in a while; it was the way you lived.

The next day we received our equipment, including new helmets. We had a couple of days of working without pads in the heat and humidity of August to start. At that time, weight lifting was not a big priority for Ara. He preferred that his athletes played handball rather than get too tight with weights, but I had a hand in eventually changing his mind about the value of a weight program.

The ACC was only three years old at the time, and our locker room there gave us plenty of space, even though it wasn't fancy. The locker room in Notre Dame Stadium was a different story. The lockers were the same ones that had been used when Knute Rockne's team opened the stadium in 1930. It didn't bother me, because the small green metal lockers were the ones used by Johnny Lujack, Leon Hart, Paul Hornung, Nick Buoniconti, Johnny Lattner, Jerry Groom, John Huarte, Jim Lynch, Terry Hanratty, Larry DiNardo, and legions of other stars who played for Notre Dame. There was a sense that their ghosts were cheering us on.

So for me, it wasn't about fancy lockers and plush facilities; it was about the chance to build on a great heritage. Ara emphasized that the tradition at Notre Dame is great, but not one of those guys who played here in the past is going to throw a block, catch a pass, or make a tackle for us. We can't live off of a tradition of excellence, but we have the chance to add to it, he encouraged. (Those same thoughts about building on a winning tradition were shared by some other coaches I've been around, in particular Herb Brogan, Michigan High School Hall of Fame coach at Lumen Christi in Jackson, Michigan, where my son Tommy had a great career before becoming a three-year starter at the University of Michigan.)

I loved that Notre Dame did not do things showily. Some people wanted to put stripes on the uniform or on the gold helmets. Linebacker Tim Sullivan responded by saying we have plain uniforms and we just plain win ballgames. We don't need any fancy stuff. We appreciated the tradition, and we wanted to create our own heritage so that guys just being born would come in one day and say, "This is where Ara's teams dressed."

Notre Dame has remodeled the locker rooms several times since the early '70s. Like many other schools, they are in an arms race to have the best facilities in the country. The training areas have been updated with the best weight room, medical facilities, and indoor football fields. The guys nowadays can't beef about practicing in the cold because every time the temperature drops too low, they go into the indoor facility.

The food has also been significantly upgraded. The South Dining Hall, built in 1927, is a beautiful building, with high ceilings and long tables. Its Gothic style has inspired recent students to suggest it could have served as the Hall of Hogwarts in the *Harry Potter* movies. The North Dining Hall opened in 1957. That's where we had our training table, along with meetings every night after dinner. The meal was usually the same food that other students received, kept warm until practice was over. It was typically beef, chicken, or sometimes fish—and it wasn't great, except the game-day steaks, which were the best meal of the week.

During the hot, humid summer, players had a tendency to gulp their liquid as soon as they sat down to eat. One day, Ara watched as guys guzzled down their milk along with their fruit punch and soda. "The Man," as Ara was known to us, asked for our attention, and you could hear a pin drop. He said, "I've been watching you guys gulp your milk as if it were water." He paused and then said, "Milk is a food. You're not supposed to gulp it, you take a sip and let it fill your mouth, and then you swallow. Don't gulp your milk. You are going to get a sick stomach and then you won't be able to practice. If that happens, you are going to have to answer to me and you are going to get your ass kicked by me."

Everyone just sat there and thought, *You know, the Man is right*. It showed the command he had over us. Our mothers would have said that a million times, and it wouldn't have stuck, but after just one comment by Ara we never gulped our milk again.

* * *

The first days of summer camp were devoted to conditioning. We would weigh in and weigh out of practice every day to see how much water weight we might be losing. It was also a way the medical staff could determine if something more serious was going on with a player. There was a big chart next to the scale, which was the biggest one I had ever seen. It looked like a scale to weigh livestock.

On one of the first days, Ara would have us do a 12-minute run. He wanted the backs to be able to get close to two miles, while anything over one-and-a-half miles was pretty good for the linemen. I did okay, almost a mile and three-quarters. The upperclassmen were old hands at the conditioning stuff and knew how to pace themselves to hit an acceptable length. They understood that you weren't going to win a starting job with this run; it was just designed for the coaches to determine if you had been working out on your own.

Excitement about the coming season was running high, given our victory in January over the No. 1 Texas team in the Cotton Bowl. We had a lot of work to do, however, as graduation had left big holes to fill. Only three defensive starters had graduated, but they were core players—linebackers Tim Kelly and Jim Wright and a very quick defensive end, Bob Neidert. The defensive backfield was strong and experienced, with All-American Clarence Ellis, along with Ralph Stepaniak and Mike Crotty. Sophomore Mike Townsend, a safety who had the athleticism and speed to keep up with top receivers, had looked great in the spring.

At linebacker were Rich Thomann and Eric Patton, both back from outstanding junior years. Other linebackers were Jim Musuraca, Jim O'Malley, the fierce-hitting Gary Potempa, and a couple of great athletes, Tom Devine and Tim Sullivan. John Raterman, a senior who had played a lot in his sophomore year, had since been slowed by injuries to his knees but could still contribute because of his experience.

The defensive line may have been Ara's strongest yet. Walt Patulski, an All- American, and Fred Swendsen played the ends. These two were not loud guys, but they had the size, range, and strength to play against any offensive line in the country. At tackle were Mike Kadish and Greg Marx. Mike was a quiet guy with tremendous natural strength. He never lifted weights, but at 6'5" and 270 pounds, he was a bear to move. On the other hand, Greg was very animated when he played football and he would say all sorts of things to his opponents to get into their heads. He would go on to be a captain the next season and earn All-American status.

Among the good backups was Tom Ross, a sophomore from Pennsylvania, who had a lot of potential but ended up not seeing much action at Notre Dame because of injuries. And then there was Mike Zikas, who ended up being drafted by the New York Giants. He was a tough defensive tackle who had this habit of putting a finger in one nostril and blowing out the other to clear his head of snot. And of course it would usually land on someone's shoe, sock, or shin. If you got hit, someone would joke that you got "Zikased." Mike was a very good, tough football player, and a good guy who sadly passed away in 2004.

The offense had lost quarterback Joe Theismann and starting guards Larry DiNardo and Gary Kos to graduation. There were four guys vying to win the QB job, with Joe's backup, Bill Etter, considered to have the inside track. During the 1969 Notre Dame–Army game, Bill made a run for about 60 yards. As a high school senior, I was able to go to that contest because it was played in Yankee Stadium. Bill was a good athlete and a great competitor, but he was having issues with migraine headaches, and there was a chance he wouldn't be able to play.

Next in line was Pat Steenberge, a Pennsylvania native who was a heady quarterback, able to throw well and to run enough to keep the offense moving. Pat had gained 40 minutes of playing time the year before, which isn't a lot, but it was more experience than Jim Bulger had. Jim had shown off his strong arm with his deep throw to Clarence Ellis near the end of the second quarter in the 1971 Cotton Bowl to set us up for a field goal. He was big for a quarterback, about 6'5" and 225 pounds. He could run the offense if he had to, but he was short of overall experience.

One other contender was sophomore Cliff Brown, the first African American quarterback recruit to come to Notre Dame. At that time, when many Southern teams had not yet integrated their rosters, there were only a handful of black quarterbacks at colleges anywhere. Another product of Pennsylvania, he could throw a great, tight spiral that was beautiful to watch. He carried a lot of pressure on him, but he handled it very well. He was a solid teammate and a good student of the game. Cliff would get his chance to play and break a kind of color barrier for Notre Dame quarterbacks, blazing a trail for future players including Tony Rice, Kevin McDougal, Jarious Jackson, Everett Golson, and others. Cliff eventually had a good career at Notre Dame and earned his degree but sadly passed away in 2012 at age 60.

On the offensive line, five years of starting experience had vanished with the graduation of Larry DiNardo and Gary Kos. They were going to be tough to replace, not just because of their size, mobility, and experience, but also because of their leadership. They had been mentored by Jerry Wampfler, a very good offensive line coach who taught them how to be aggressive and punish defensive players. Wampfler had gone on to be the head coach at Colorado State University, but I had learned those blocking techniques by talking with Larry and watching film for hours on end until I got a great feel for the craft.

There are about 70 to 75 offensive plays per game. If we could control the line of scrimmage and run the ball, we would control the clock, put points on the board, and grind down the other team. To do that, it was important to have a well schooled offensive line. Among the guys competing for the guard positions were seniors Denny DiPrimio and Jim Humbert. Both knew the offense very well and had gained experience as backups the year before. Jim had a masterful blocking technique, but knee injuries slowed him a bit. Denny wasn't as big as Larry DiNardo or Gary Kos, but he had good football knowledge and could use all the tricks in the book.

Tom Bolger and I were two sophomores working to win one of the positions. Tom had played for Elder High School in Cincinnati. Tom's dad had played Major League Baseball, and Tom was also an excellent baseball player. Ara always felt that it was difficult for an underclassman to play offensive line. Not only was it hard physically, but learning the offense and maintaining mental maturity was a lot to ask of an 18- or 19-year-old player. At the end of spring practice, I had been working with the first team, but I was going to have to prove myself every day in order to hold on to that position.

During August camp, Ara wanted to see who could do it physically and mentally. He was looking to see who was hungry and had the competitive spirit. That was the guy he wanted to go to war with. Playing for Ara was like going into battle for a righteous king. You wanted to do well for him because you believed in him. I always felt I was playing for someone who was like a father to me. I had a father that I loved and respected, but then I felt like a knight playing for a king.

Before practice we would get dressed in the ACC, and the trainers would tape our legs. One of the athletic trainers was Gene Paszkiet, a Notre Dame grad who started as a student trainer during the days of Frank Leahy. He stayed with the program, one year rolled into another, and he became part of the Fighting Irish story. When he retired and then passed away, it was like a piece of Notre Dame went with him.

Gene cared deeply about the players, though some of them had a hard time communicating with him because he was very much of the old school. A lot of the guys talked to another trainer, Big John Whitmer, a Western Michigan graduate who was close to our age. Big John came off as a really tough guy, but when you got to know him, it turned out he was a real puppy dog who related well to the athletes. If Gene said you were healthy enough to practice, sometimes we would ask John for his opinion because we knew he was looking out for our best interest. Not that we didn't believe in Gene; it was just that with John it was more like talking to a teammate instead of a coach.

Ara was the most organized coach I've ever been around. (Marv Levy, my coach later with the Montreal Alouettes of the Canadian Football League, was pretty close.) Ara had his practices down to a science in order to prepare us for the upcoming opponent. In the spring or preseason, with no game immediately ahead of us, he had us working on new techniques and plays that he would possibly use in games. Tommy Clements, who came on board as a freshman in 1971 and began to make his mark at quarterback the next season, said, "Ara was very organized, and he could also communicate effectively with the players. He knew exactly what he wanted you to do, and if you weren't doing it, he would correct you and make sure you were doing it the right way."

Before the start of practice, players would warm up for about 15 minutes. Receivers ran routes and took throws from quarterbacks, the specialists did their kicking and snapping, and linemen went through their drills. Wally Moore, our offensive line coach, would update us on our assignments and we would usually go over the plays we would run during practice.

When the whistle blew for the start of practice, the team would take a lap from one end of the field around the goal posts and back to the opposite end of the field. This would warm up our legs. Then we would line up for calisthenics—seniors in the front, then juniors, sophomores, and freshmen. The captains would face the team, with Ara in between them. When he said, "Set Two!" every person on the field knew it was the formal start of practice. I bet if any of us heard "Set Two" even today, we would all start our series of exercises.

Ara would lead cals every day except game day. I think it gave him a chance to be active and stay in touch with the players as an athlete. Ara was extremely active and competitive as an individual. He played handball three or four times per week with the other coaches. The coaches always were playing games like basketball, racquetball, and volleyball with each other. Ara not only wanted his players to be hungry to compete, but he also wanted his staff to be the same way. "If it was not football season, Ara liked to play handball at noon," said assistant coach Mike Stock. "Ara was a fierce competitor—capital letters on the word 'fierce.'"

After cals and stretching, the team would do a series of three 30-yard sprints. The first one was at about three-quarter speed. After the sprint we would get into another line and do an all-four crabwalk, two rolls, and then jump up and sprint to the next line. The second and third sprints were all-out, followed by two rolls after the second sprint and then a carioca drill, which involved twisting the hips and cross-stepping in order to improve agility. By this time our bodies were very warm and we went right to special teams.

Ara believed in the importance of special teams, and we worked on some aspect of them every day of the week. Because of this emphasis, we rarely got beat on special teams. Every coach had an assignment during the special teams practice. They were on us and wanted us to take this part of the game very seriously. After 15 minutes the horn would blow and we were off to individual drills, linemen with linemen and backs and receivers together.

Offensive coordinator Tom Pagna recalled the emphasis on fundamentals. "Ara used to say to me, 'Tom, it's not today's work that is going to do it. It's every day for seven minutes. Every day for five minutes.' He was absolutely right. You have to do your work every day until it becomes a habit. If something does not simulate what we do in a game, why bother?" As Dan Morrin put it, "We practiced what we played and when we got to the games we played what we practiced."

During practices, assistant coaches ran drills and plays while Ara observed the goings-on from a platform tower situated between the defensive and offensive fields. We were convinced that he could see both sides at the same time as he never seemed to miss anything.

"One day in practice I didn't make a particularly good play against a sweep," said linebacker Rich Thomann. "I hoped Ara didn't see my lack of effort, but after the play everything stopped and here he came, down the ladder. He walked over to the huddle and stood right behind me and whispered so no one else could hear. He told me they were going to run that same play again, and this time I would stop it or his shoe was going to be inserted in my rear. I made the play, and he went back up the ladder. He was pretty tough when he had to be."

Ara also knew how to teach when the situation called for it. "Some coaches would yell, 'You missed a block!' Well, no kidding," said offensive tackle John Dampeer. "Ara didn't do that. He would tell you from a technical point of view what you could do to improve. He knew the details, like if your stance was off a little bit."

In some ways, practices were harder than the games. "You had guys behind you that were going to take your job if you weren't at your best," said

Tom Bolger. "When you got into the game, you were so well prepared and the guys you practiced against were so tough, sometimes it didn't seem like a major challenge. After games, scout team guys would come up to you and ask, 'How was the team you played compared to us?' And in most cases, our scout team was better."

We might not have always had the best athletes on the field, but with Ara and his staff, we were always confident that we were better prepared than the guys on the other side of the line of scrimmage.

CHAPTER 8

Game Week

The Sunday night before the opening game of the 1971 season, the team gathered at the North Dining Hall following practice and dinner. Coach Ara Parseghian used these Sunday night meetings to review our upcoming opponent, Northwestern in this case. I was going to be the starting left guard at the University of Notre Dame as a sophomore. I felt I had taken a big step toward becoming one of Ara's Knights. I was on cloud nine, the only sophomore starting the 1971 opener (although other classmates would also start later in the year). We had other sophs who were much better athletes than I was—such as Dave Casper, Mike Townsend, Cliff Brown, Tim Sullivan, Tom Devine, and Gary Potempa—but I was in a spot where the opportunity presented itself since last year's starting guards had both graduated.

Ara always stressed the best qualities of the other team and warned us that if we didn't play the way we should that we could get our ass beat. "He'd build up our opponent with all they had accomplished," said Rocky Bleier. "By Friday, even if that opponent had a losing record, it seemed like you were playing the national champs."

On the Sunday night before the start of the 1971 season, Ara gave us a scouting report on every player on Northwestern's team, explaining his strengths and weaknesses. When he came to the defensive line, he said their best player was Jim Anderson. "Pomarico, you'll be playing against him," he said. He looked at me with those piercing eyes and said, "You will be ready."

It was game week, and all the hard work, the weight training, the running on the Belt Parkway, playing handball…it all came down to this point in time. I kept asking myself if I was ready, and the answer I would come up with was *Yes I am. Bring it on. I'm going to give the best effort I possibly can. I'm going to use all the things in my toolbox to compete.* A lot of those tools were put there by Ara Parseghian, Larry DiNardo, assistant coaches Tom Pagna and Wally Moore, my father, Brother Owen Capper, and my high school coach Vince O'Connor. I had one week to go, and the arena was waiting: Notre Dame Stadium.

Practices leading up to game day were scripted down to the minute. Ara was involved with developing the game plan on both sides of the ball, according to assistant coach Bill Hickey. "He would sit with the defensive staff on Monday and Tuesday mornings and set the defensive game plan with them," Bill said. From Tuesday afternoon through Thursday, Ara would work with the coaches on the offensive end to develop the strategy for that side of the ball. "Not many coaches are that detailed or that totally into the game," he said.

Monday of game week involved a "time up" of some offensive and defensive plays. Time up involved running through plays at about three-quarter speed. Once the season began, Ara also used Mondays to give out awards from the previous week. Some Mondays during the season also involved what we called the "Toilet Bowl," which was a scrimmage between the freshmen team and varsity players who had not gotten into the game the previous Saturday. We practiced for about one-and-a-half hours on Monday.

On Tuesday, we would do our normal practice with drills and individual work on our position. Practice was about 2 hours and 10 minutes. We worked hard timing up our plays on offense and on defense working on recognition of the opposing team's offense. Most of the time we didn't do full contact at practice, but we would run some live goal line in the early part of the year to get ready for the schedule. As the season went on, the risk of injuries became more significant, so our live practice work was kept to a minimum.

Wednesday was also a full-pads practice of about 2 hours and 10 minutes involving special teams, individual work, and team time up. On Thursday, practice was only about one-and-a-half hours, consisting of special teams and time up with no individual drills. The tempo was quick, but the contact eased off a bit.

"One of my most vivid memories is how Ara would get us all together after practice, and he knew exactly what to say," said defensive lineman George Hayduk. "If we had a tough practice where things weren't going good, he knew how to get us back up again. He was very insightful about what young people were living through."

Ara liked to have some fun with the team on Thursdays and Fridays. With game preparation winding down, he would have a competition with different parts of the team involving what he called "cheers." The offense, defense, and prep teams were challenged to make up a jingle or act out a skit about the upcoming game. The friendly competition would get some great laughs. "Ara would go to each group and listen," said Bill Hickey. "He would take a few seconds to ponder, then he would point to the winners, and the kids would go out of their minds. It was a tremendous thing to loosen up the players two days before the game."

Then Ara would talk to us about the significance of the upcoming game and remind us to keep our noses clean and do our schoolwork, because if we weren't eligible, we couldn't play. We would then break practice and go to training table. There would be short meetings after dinner, then back to the dorm to do our schoolwork or attend whatever social event we had planned.

Friday practice was short, about one hour, concentrating on special teams and time up of our offense and defense. We would do another set of cheers and then we were ready.

The Phantom Letters were a motivational tool that assistant coach Tom Pagna came up with. He would write weekly inspirational letters and post them on players' lockers. They were signed "The Phantom," though we pretty much figured out he was the author. Here is the letter he posted before the opener against Northwestern in 1971:

> Most people have the Will to Win. Only Winners have the Will to prepare to win. This day and this week are the beginning—They are pages in the book of your life. How will the 1971 Irish book read? Will it state?
> 1.) They are hard nose and hitters!
> 2.) They had no breaking point behind or ahead
> 3.) They played the game for the full 60 minutes.
> 4.) They played with a full heart.
> 5.) They were not individuals, but an intricate weave of many talents dedicated to one final result.
> 6.) They had Class-Polish-Pride.
>
> If it states these things, it is naturally acceptable they can be champions. You play a game on a given day with a given opponent. Saturday the 18th, Northwestern, is the day and the opponent. No game will be as important as that game that day.

Pep rallies were held Friday evenings before every home game. The marching band would go through campus playing the "Victory March," and students would run alongside and behind them, whooping it up. For many years the rallies had been held in the Old Fieldhouse in the middle of campus, but by 1971 they moved to the newer Stepan Center on the north end. It was a nicer venue, though nothing could match the intensity of the Fieldhouse scene of swarms of sweaty, feverish students hanging from the rafters. These days, the rallies are held in the Athletic and Convocation Center (ACC), and they seem to be more scripted and more Hollywood than ever before.

Denny Murphy, our freshmen coach and a former player at Notre Dame, told me about a tradition passed down by generations of Irish players: they'd visit the Grotto the night before a game to say a little prayer that we would do our best in the game ahead of us. Dan Morrin and I always held up that tradition for home games. For some reason I always thought it helped and felt I always had special help when we went out and played at Notre Dame Stadium.

After stopping at the Grotto, we made our way to Moreau Seminary for the night. Ara liked the idea that we were away from the campus and its football-weekend party atmosphere. At the time, *Playboy* magazine had a poll on party schools. Notre Dame didn't make the list, and when *Playboy* was asked why not, someone answered that the magazine didn't want to lump the pro partiers at Notre Dame with the amateurs at other colleges.

Moreau Seminary housed young men who were studying to be priests in the Holy Cross order. They would give up their room for Friday night so that the football players could stay there. It was much better than staying at a hotel. There was a movie theater in the seminary, and we would see a western or a war movie with a lot of action—often a John Wayne film.

After the movie and light snack, we went back to our rooms for the night. The first night I stayed at Moreau, I got to my room and was getting ready for bed when all of a sudden there was a noise, the closet door opened, and out jumped Dan Novakov, our senior center. It scared the bejesus out of me. I almost started swinging at him as I thought it was some nut job who had gotten into the seminary somehow.

When I finally realized it was Dan, the guy who would play next to me the following day, in came our captain Thom Gatewood, laughing at how scared I was and welcoming me to the starting lineup for the Northwestern game. It turns out that it was somewhat of a Notre Dame tradition to scare the new guy in the starting lineup. Dan and Thom told me how they were put through the same rite of passage before their own first start. It kind of settled me down after that and I wasn't as nervous about the game—but I did sleep with one eye open.

Game day. I hadn't slept well the night before the Northwestern game, but I woke up with a lot of enthusiasm. My mom and dad had come in from Howard Beach and I was going to play football in front of 59,075 people, about 58,075 more than ever attended any of my high school games. It seemed like every sports radio station around the country was carrying the Notre Dame broadcast.

The team attended morning Mass in the chapel at Moreau. Father Touhey was the team priest and he always gave a great talk to fit in with the Gospel, usually related to how God wants us to reach deep inside of ourselves to do our best. When we played on the road, the Mass was usually held in a banquet room in our team hotel. At the end of Mass, we lined up and walked up to the altar, where Father Touhey gave each of us a holy medal, usually a representation of one of the saints. I saved all those medals and today I still have them in a little pouch. It's something I don't often talk about, but the medals were very special to me. I always put that game medal in my right kneepad, and in the left leg kneepad I put a Sacred Heart scapular that was given to me by my Aunt Elizabeth. I never hurt my knees playing for Notre Dame. I can't say for sure that it had anything to do with the religious objects, but I couldn't help thinking that the Big Guy upstairs helped.

After Mass we would walk around Saint Mary's Lake to the North Dining Hall for our pregame meal and final meetings before the game. I loved the pregame meal. It was a chance to have really good food, prepared to our liking. And second, it was the last chance to relax with the guys before we really would focus on the coming game. The food consisted of steaks, eggs, baked potatoes, pancakes, bacon, sausage, toast, and cereal. Those steaks were the best you could get.

Following the meal, Ara gave a short talk to get our focus on the game. Then we broke up into our individual position meetings. Offensive line coach Wally Moore went over everything he could to help us prepare for what to expect. As a first-time starter, I was extra-focused; I wanted to make sure I didn't mess up any assignments. Northwestern was well coached by Alex Agase, a good coach who had an excellent career in the Big Ten conference. (Many years later I met him when he was a volunteer coach at the University of Michigan, and I was amazed he remembered me and how I played that day against their best defensive tackle, Jim Anderson.)

We were ready as a team and we were told to be at the stadium by noon, about 90 minutes before kickoff. Dan Morrin, Tom Devine, and I headed back to our dorm, Sorin College. You could feel the positive energy on campus and I savored every minute of it. On our walk, students who recognized us wished us good luck. When we reached Sorin, all the guys on the front porch started to cheer as we entered the dorm. The halls were filled with parents and students who offered encouragement. Dorm mates asked us to stop and meet their family and friends. It was a very festive atmosphere.

My parents were waiting for us in our third-floor room. They had supported me in my journey, and they were excited and proud. My mother couldn't believe it was all happening, and my father had a smile from ear to ear. They would come to many of my games during my time at Notre Dame—in fact, my father made every game I played in 1971. Also in the room were Dan's father, Joe, and his uncles from Philadelphia, as well as Tom Devine's friends from Lumen Christi High School.

At 11:45 AM, Dan, Tom, and I headed to the stadium. The campus was alive with fans and the smells of tailgating wafted through the air. Various dorms and clubs would raise funds by grilling burgers and hot dogs, and the lines were especially long for the grilled steak sandwiches served up outside the Knights of Columbus building. As we walked, people who recognized us cheered as we entered the stadium.

The locker room was quiet when I arrived at just about noon. It almost seemed like a church, with everyone talking very low as they got taped up and mentally ready for the game. Notre Dame Stadium at that time was basically unchanged from when Rockne and Leahy had coached. There were the old lockers and a small open area where Ara would gather the team and give final instructions. The showers had brick walls and stone floors. The locker room was nothing like the open and plush one that exists today. We didn't mind. We weren't there to be pampered; we were there to play for Ara Parseghian and Notre Dame. As far as I was concerned, the only thing that really mattered was how good of a team we were and how high we could reach.

I went to Big John Whitmer to get my ankles taped and then just sat in front of my locker watching everyone else. It was a very cool experience to watch some great athletes get ready for competition. I then took some time to think about what had happened to me in the last couple of years. What I had dreamed of, passionately believed in, pursued with the Driven Spirit was just about to come true.

Larry DiNardo was then a graduate assistant for the team and about 15 minutes before we went out of the locker room he came by to offer me support and advice. Larry said, "You want to warm up hard and be ready as soon as the game starts. Don't think you can get warm during the game. The harder you warm up the better you'll play. The first series or two you might feel sluggish, but keep working hard. You will get through that. Then things will start slowing down, and you'll be doing your job just like you have been practicing it."

Larry went on to become a high-profile lawyer, but he would have been a great college football coach if he had chosen to do that as a career. He was the best technique line coach I ever had. I was filled with emotion looking at my blue Notre Dame jersey with No. 56 on it, the same number Larry had worn. I wanted to live up to the standard of excellence of that great number. To me, it represented the values of pride, discipline, and loyalty—especially to Ara and Larry.

Ara gathered us in the small, open area of the locker room. He didn't give any rah-rah speech, he just asked us to give our best for 60 minutes and play what he called "the interval." The interval was from the snap of the ball to the whistle. If you time a play, it usually takes only about five or six seconds, and if you add it up any individual is only playing about five or six minutes per game. We were all pepped up after Ara talked to us and we all tapped a sign just before going down the stairs from the locker room. It was not the PLAY LIKE A CHAMPION sign that is touched today; that didn't come until the Lou Holtz era. The bronze sign we tapped had George Gipp's deathbed speech on it, as recounted by Knute Rockne:

> I'VE GOT TO GO, ROCK. IT'S ALL RIGHT. I'M NOT AFRAID. SOME TIME, ROCK, WHEN THE TEAM'S UP AGAINST IT, WHEN THINGS ARE WRONG AND THE BREAKS ARE BEATING THE BOYS . . . TELL THEM TO GO IN THERE WITH ALL THEY'VE GOT AND WIN JUST ONE FOR THE GIPPER. I DON'T KNOW WHERE I'LL BE THEN, ROCK. BUT I'LL KNOW ABOUT IT, AND I'LL BE HAPPY.

As we went down the stairs you could hear the cleats clicking and the sound of the crowd getting louder and louder. When we came out the door, there was always this little old man standing at the door cheering us on. I never knew who he was, but you could tell it was something this man lived for.

Then we were there at the tunnel. I could see the famous stadium filled with zealous fans waiting for Ara's Knights to come onto the field. I looked for my mother and father in the stands, spotted them, and gave a big wave. I was filled with pride. As a kid from Brooklyn, I felt that every New York City nun, every New York City cop, and all the stockbrokers who worked with my Mom were rooting for me. My teammates were slapping me on the back, and guys like Eddie Gulyas, Rich Thomann, and Dan Novakov told me if I could hold my own against the guys on our defense in practice, I would do great against Northwestern.

Led by Ara Parseghian, the Notre Dame Fighting Irish 1971 football team ran out on to the field. We felt we were ready, and soon the whole country would find out what we had.

The Grotto

CHAPTER 9

The 1971 Season

Game 1: Northwestern

Running onto the field for the first time as a player for Notre Dame, I could hardly feel anything but a huge rush of excitement. I waved one more time to my mom and dad in the stands. I was ready, and the team was ready. And we were wholeheartedly behind Ara Parseghian. He had a light within him that would brighten the room.

The Notre Dame defense that had been so great against Texas in the Cotton Bowl was even better in 1971 and dominated Northwestern in the opener. The defense scored 12 points itself and repeatedly gave the offense great field position. A blocked punt by Walt Patulski gave us the ball on the Wildcats 32-yard line, and quarterback Bill Etter guided the rushing game into the end zone in five plays. The final play of the drive was a buck trap play off of my left guard position. I nailed my block and so did left tackle Jim Humbert as Eddie Gulyas scored on a three-yard run. I was excited about the touchdown because I wanted Ara to feel confident that he could call a run to our side if there was an important short-yardage play. I wanted that responsibility. I was full of confidence at that time (though before too long I would find out there were many ballplayers in the country who would be difficult to block).

The Wildcats came back to tie the score at 7–7, but it was all Irish after that. In the second quarter we scored 23 points on a four-yard run by Bob Minnix, a Thom Gatewood eight-yard TD pass from Pat Steenberge, a 36-yard field goal by Bob Thomas, and a four-yard run by John Cieszkowski. The defense scored twice on interception returns in the second half: 40 yards by Ralph Stepaniak and 65 yards by Mike Crotty. Sophomore Greg Hill ran four yards for the final TD to cap a 50–7 win.

My first game was in the books. After the game, Ara gave me some encouraging words that made me feel like a million bucks. I went out for dinner with my parents after the game, and the Pomaricos celebrated both the victory and the beginning of my college playing career. We felt part of something unique and special: we were now part of Ara's Army.

Game 2: Purdue

We knew we had our work cut out for us traveling to West Lafayette, Indiana, to play Purdue at Ross-Ade Stadium. They had three standouts on the offensive side of the ball, starting with quarterback Gary Danielson, who came from Dearborn Divine Child High School in Michigan, the same school that produced my Irish teammate, Max Wasilevich. Danielson was tall and had a great arm, which also served him well during a solid NFL career. Otis Armstrong, from Chicago, was a terrific running back who was eventually elected to the College Football Hall of Fame and who once led the NFL in rushing as a member of the Denver Broncos. The other superb talent was wide receiver Darryl Stingley, who was later a first-round draft choice of the New England Patriots. Sadly, Stingley's pro career is best remembered for the play in which he suffered an on-field spinal cord injury that left him paralyzed.

Defensively they had hardnosed linebackers Rich Schavietello from Chicago and Jim Teal from North Carolina. These guys could run and tattoo your head with hard forearms. At middle guard was an All-American, Gregg Bingham. At 6'1", 235 pounds, he was not the biggest guy, but he could run from sideline to sideline like a defensive back. He would go on to play pro ball for 12 years for the Houston Oilers.

The bus ride from South Bend to West Lafayette is an uneventful journey through small towns and cornfields. We stayed at the Student Union Hotel on Friday night and ate the same Friday night meal we would always have on the road: prime rib, baked potato, vegetables, salad, ice cream, and two cookies. I never tired of the meal. We went to the movies the night before games even if we were on the road; it was a great way to unwind. Still, it was hard for me to put the Purdue defense out of mind. They looked great on film, and we knew the Boilermakers wanted to get us back for the 48–0 thrashing we had given them in 1970.

On game day, it rained heavily. It was obviously going to be hard to run and pass the ball in the mud. Our away uniforms, white and gold, were muddy by the end of warm-ups. I didn't have to catch a ball or hold on to one, but it was going to be really tough for all of us to get our footing and stay on our blocks. The Boilermakers took a 7–0 lead in the second quarter on a 26-yard screen pass from Danielson to Armstrong. Bob Thomas, our sophomore kicker, missed two field goals, one after a bad snap. (Bob would have better days with us, would go on to kick for the Chicago Bears and other NFL teams for 12 years, and then begin a legal career in which he became a member of the Illinois Supreme Court.)

It seemed at halftime the rain stopped so that the Purdue marching band could perform along with the featured twirler they called the Golden Girl. When the teams came back on the field, the sky opened up again, and it poured. Ara was showing confidence in Pat Steenberge under center, but the Irish couldn't run or pass with any consistency in the bad conditions.

Late in the game, we got the first of two big breaks. Purdue shanked a punt and we took over on the Boilermakers 42-yard line. Pat Steenberge moved the Irish to the Purdue 5-yard line, but on second-and-goal, Pat lost control of the slick ball, and safety Chuck Piebes fell on it to seemingly put the game away for Purdue. However, the weather would once more play a role.

The Irish dug in and forced Purdue to punt from their own end zone. The snap to punter Scott Lougheed was low, and he had trouble fielding the ball. He finally grabbed it and stepped to his right to kick it. Just as he made his drop to punt, Irish defensive back Clarence Ellis gave him a shot and the ball came free. Defensive lineman Fred Swendsen fell on the ball for a touchdown. The Irish celebrated—defensive tackle Mike Zikas did his version of a rain dance. Behind only 7–6, and with the game down to its final two minutes, Ara elected to go for the two-point conversion and the win.

Tight end Mike Creaney remembers that Ara turned to offensive coordinator Tom Pagna on the sideline and asked him: "'What have you got?' Pagna looks right at me and says, 'We're going to run that genuflect play.'" It was a goal-line play that had just been put in at Thursday's practice. "Ara looks right at me and says, 'What do you think, Mike?' I said, 'We got it, Coach.' I have a feeling if I said, 'God, it's really raining,' he would have called a sweep or something else. I could see it all flash across his face."

The play called for Pat Steenberge to fake a handoff for a sweep right and then turn around and throw back to the left to Mike Creaney. It was called the genuflect play because Mike's role was to first fall to his knees as if he had missed a block, then get up, and go to the far left of the end zone. As the play unfolded, Pat faked the handoff but then found himself under heavy pressure. He just lofted the ball over the outstretched arms of a rushing defender toward the vicinity of where he figured Mike would be.

"I was open and open and open and open and fearful that someone was going to recover in time because it took so long for the ball to come down," Mike said. Finally, the football nestled in the receiver's waiting arms. Notre Dame 8, Purdue 7—we were ahead for the first time, the score held, and the genuflect play became part of Notre Dame lore. We felt very lucky to win, and it made us understand that we couldn't just throw our helmets out on the field and expect to win.

Game 3: Michigan State

The day after each game, Ara wanted us to run a mile and do some stretching to get the soreness out of our bodies. An alternative was to do something like play handball, a game that Ara himself enjoyed. I would sometimes get a hold of Gary Potempa, and we would play some handball, a very taxing game that gave us a tremendous sweat.

I got a surprise at the Sunday-night meeting: I was being moved to left tackle for the Michigan State game. I thought maybe it was because I hadn't played well against Purdue, but it turned out that it was because Jim Humbert, our regular left tackle, had injured his knee. The staff thought I would have a better chance against Michigan State's defensive line that helped make Duffy Daugherty's team one of the toughest in the Big Ten. All week, I practiced firing out of my stance and slugging our prep team guys as hard as I could in preparation of Saturday's game. In football, you take things personally. The guy on the other side of the line wants to make you look bad, so you work as hard as you can to win on every play.

On one particular play, a run up the middle, I fired out and continued to block until the whistle blew. The Spartan lineman didn't like that and proceeded to give me an elbow to the head. It was quite a blow. I reacted and threw a short punch to the head. Of course, you can punch all you want and not do much damage to a guy wearing pads and a helmet. But it set off a big fight, with guys on both teams throwing major meat hooks trying to get the best of each other. I was pulled from the pile by MSU coach Duffy Daugherty himself, who grabbed me by the collar. He said, "You two stop this fighting and play football." I'll never forget this 5'6" Irishman holding us two big linemen.

The game was played on a steamy, mid-80s day at Notre Dame Stadium. There was still a lot of emotion left from the teams' 10–10 tie in 1966. Five years had passed, but the head coaches were the same. We scored two touchdowns in the first quarter on short runs by Bob Minnix, which turned out to be enough. Michigan State got its only two points on a safety when we fumbled in our own end zone. We won our third game of the year, 14–2, as our defense held Michigan State to 136 yards and no touchdowns.

Game 4: Miami

I watched film on Miami's All-American defensive lineman Tony Cristiani and thought he was a guy who seemed to know both the play and snap count. I found out he came from a family of trapeze artists and that he had learned to walk the tightrope at an early age. He was lightning quick, and all week our coaches were concerned about the speed of the Miami defense overall. The Hurricanes had a lot of talent and quite a few older players, as some of them had been in the military and entered the college program at 22 or 23 years old.

I was happy to move back to guard as tackle Jim Humbert returned to the lineup, even though he was still hurting from his knee injury. I loved playing next to Jim because he helped me a great deal with his knowledge and experience. On the other side of me was center Dan Novakov, who had started a number of games in 1970 and played in the Cotton Bowl. Jim and Dan, who were both from Cincinnati, knew my game still had to be fine-tuned, but that I was ready to take a spot in the foxhole. Both helped me tremendously, and we cemented friendships for life.

Early in the second quarter of a scoreless tie, Irish quarterback Bill Etter injured his knee after throwing a pass to Thom Gatewood. Ara turned to sophomore Cliff Brown, who slipped on the Orange Bowl's artificial turf a couple times before changing shoes and changing his fortune. He did a good job leading us to victory, 17–0. Our defense had another stellar game, holding Miami to 111 yards.

One thing Miami's Tony Cristiani had a habit of doing was raising his arms in the air in triumph whenever he made a sack. This was years before this kind of showmanship became somewhat commonplace in football, and our guys didn't like it. We felt it was a hotdog move to show up the other team. So when Andy Huff ran for his score, I ran right up to Cristiani and raised my arms in the air, not to crow, but just to remind him that we had scored in his area and that we were going to press him all night. And we did, dominating the line of scrimmage and rushing for 257 yards. We were deep in running backs that year with Eddie Gulyas, Andy Huff, John Cieszkowski, Bill Gallagher, Bob Minnix, and Darryll Dewan—all hardnosed guys who could block as well as run.

We were 4–0 and feeling pretty good about ourselves, even though we had not put up big scores against our opponents the previous three weeks.

Game 5: North Carolina

I was very familiar with North Carolina, coach Bill Dooley, and his staff since I had been strongly recruited by them two years earlier. The school had a beautiful campus, great weather, lots of pretty girls, and a good football team. Dooley had offered me a full scholarship and was disappointed I didn't accept it, but he understood my decision to go to Notre Dame. Like a lot of Southern teams, the Tar Heels were quick and mobile, but not as strong as the Big Ten–type teams. Dooley's teams were very scrappy. They wouldn't hesitate to take a shot at you on a punt or kickoff, especially if you weren't looking. It's all part of the game, but payback can be pretty tough.

Phil Bracco, a buddy of mine from St. Francis Prep who played for North Carolina, told me that Dooley gave a pregame speech reminding his team that Notre Dame players put their pants on the same way the Tar Heels do. The pants are bigger, but they put them on the same way, he joked. Speaking of uniforms, Carolina's light blue color looked crisp and clean at game's beginning but appeared quite muddied by the end of the game.

We scored the first three times we had the ball on Bob Thomas field goals, putting us up 9–0 at the half. The Tar Heels tried all kinds of gadget plays, one of them on a kickoff return when Lewis Jolley started to run up the middle and then threw a lateral to Earle Bethea going up the left sideline with a host of blockers. The only player who could stop him was Clarence Ellis, and he broke through to stop Bethea on the Irish 43. For good measure, Clarence then intercepted a Carolina pass on the next play to stop the scoring threat.

In the second half, an Irish fumble gave North Carolina the ball on our 33, and two pass completions brought them to the 4-yard line. The stingy Irish defense was put to the test and it responded, stuffing three straight running plays. On fourth down, Mike Kadish crashed through and deflected a field goal attempt and the Irish took over on downs. Thom Gatewood caught his second touchdown pass of the season in the fourth quarter and the Irish went on to win 16–0 against a really scrappy Carolina team.

It was the second straight shutout—a big point of pride for the defense. In fact, it would have been the third in a row had it not been for the safety scored by Michigan State against our offense.

The fans were getting restless, however, with the grind-it-out offense. They had gotten used to Irish quarterbacks John Huarte, Terry Hanratty, and Joe Theismann—guys who could fling the ball around the field for big chunks of yardage. Many thought that Cliff Brown could be that quarterback, but I believe Ara and his staff did not want to put too much on him too soon. Not only was he only a sophomore, but he was also carrying a big load as Notre Dame's first black quarterback. He had a really strong arm, but he wasn't the most accurate passer, a lot of that having to do with inexperience. He also had a strong leg and handled a lot of our kickoff duties.

Linebacker Tim Sullivan was impressed by how well Cliff handled the pressure: "Cliff was like a brother to me," he said. "It bothered me when I heard comments from the crowd [about Cliff's race], but I felt he handled it very well. He had to hear it. But I never heard him make any bad comments." He added, "Cliff showed what a Christian is all about. To me, he was real Notre Dame guy."

Game 6: Southern California

After years of watching USC with their great athletes including Mike Garrett, O.J. Simpson, and Clarence Davis, I couldn't wait to play USC. It was quite possibly the greatest intersectional rivalry in all of college football. "There was respect for them, but they had that Southern California mystique about them that they were great athletes and they came from an area that was nice to live in," said defensive lineman Tom Creevey. "Many of our players came from the Midwest or East Coast, where it wasn't always sunshine. We kind of felt it was the hardhats against those who had the weather and the beach."

This year, USC was coming to South Bend. No Hollywood, no beaches, and no sunshine, just clouds on a cool day. Coming out of the tunnel for the game, I saw the contrasting cardinal and gold colors of the Southern Cal uniforms. They just looked fast, strong, and athletic. They had stars like fullback Sam "the Bam" Cunningham, who had ripped through the vaunted Alabama defense a year before—a factor that reportedly convinced Alabama fans that they should allow Bear Bryant's team to become racially integrated. Other stars were wide receiver speedsters Edesel Garrison, a track champion in the 440-yard dash, and Lynn Swann, who became one of the all-time greats in both college and the NFL. They had two quarterbacks,

Jimmy Jones and Mike Rae, who both could put the ball on your front porch. Jimmy could run as well, putting extra pressure on the defense. I later played with him for two years in the Canadian Football League and found out he was a classy guy.

The 1966 Trojans had been humiliated on their home field 51–0 by Notre Dame, but coach John McKay's teams had given the Irish fits after that. On this day in 1971, USC made it look easy, using their speed to hit big plays. The Trojans had practiced throwing deep to Garrison all week, and it worked in the game. Garrison caught TD passes of 31 and 24 yards, snared another 42-yard pass to set up a one-yard scoring run by Cunningham. Bruce Dyer raced 53 yards to pay dirt with an interception. It was 28–7 USC by the half, our only score coming on a one-yard run by Andy Huff.

The Irish tried to make a game of it in the second half, scoring on a four-yard run by John Cieszkowski. But a fumble in the fourth quarter stopped the comeback momentum. Tempers were starting to wear pretty thin, and on a play when USC fumbled and recovered, their offensive tackle John Vella came firing into the pile. Greg Marx, who had been battling with him all day, took exception and a donnybrook started. "Almost everyone was in there," John Cieszkowski said. "I grew up as a boxer and maybe a little street fighter, so I was doing my little part behind the scenes." Punches flew all over the place. I didn't want to get thrown out so I didn't leave the bench area to get involved. Neither coach wanted it to come to this, as it took away from the game being played.

The final score of 28–14 was a blow to the great pride of the Notre Dame defense. We still had four big games to go and a chance at a bowl game. But the loss gave our national championship quest a big hit. We had come to the realization that we were a team with a top-notch defense but an offense that struggled, particularly in the passing game. Thom Gatewood, our talented wide receiver, had caught 77 passes in 1970 but would only catch 33 passes in 1971. John Dampeer summed up the situation: "The year before we had Joe Theismann, a second-year starter, and the offense was really sophisticated. A guy like Gatewood, who was a senior, knew how much had been taken away from the offense [in 1971] to make the adjustment for our quarterback. It was really frustrating."

Thom Gatewood recalled the frustration he felt that season. "It was a difficult situation. I was going from a very productive position generating a lot of momentum to producing a very flat season," he said. "It was difficult for me to just gear up, knowing I was not primarily an offensive receiving weapon but instead was primarily in a support role."

Cliff Brown, the third quarterback we had used that year, had struggled in the USC game, and Ara and Tom Pagna were trying to find a scheme to fit the talent we had. We ran the wishbone at times and other times would run out of a pro set, always trying to keep the quarterback position from being the make-or-break position for the offense. That was very hard to do against the very talented teams. After USC, Ara not only had to be a football coach, but he had to become a psychiatrist and mend the broken spirit of the defense and convince the offense that it could still score points against the best defenses in the country.

Game 7: Navy

A home game against Navy was up next, and they were a scrambling bunch of football players that would sell out on every play. The Midshipmen wanted to define their season by beating the Irish. Their uniforms were very similar to ours: gold helmets and blue numbers on their white jerseys. The Navy players were not as big and not as fast as we were, but they were going to give it their best shot and force us to earn the victory.

We had a decent day offensively with 281 yards rushing and 20 first downs, though we only threw for 45 yards. Ara wanted to control the clock and the game. We scored all our points in the first half with a one-yard run by Eddie Gulyas over the right side and two rushing touchdowns by Bob Minnix in the second quarter. Bob was a fast and hard runner, could catch the ball pretty well, could block, and was getting an increased amount of playing time.

We won 21–0, and we were back on the winning track. Life was always better around Notre Dame when we won. Then again, as my roommate Dan Morrin would say, we were expected to win every week.

Game 8: Pittsburgh

There were a lot of Notre Dame fans in Pittsburgh. We stayed downtown at a very nice hotel right on the riverfront. In the hotel lobby the night before the game, I saw the biggest guy I had ever seen in my life. He was over seven feet tall and looked like he weighed more than 400 pounds. One of our coaches told me the guy was Pittsburgh's defensive tackle, and I said to myself that I was going to be in for a long day. It turned out the coach was kidding, it was really Andre the Giant of World Wrestling Federation fame. I was relieved, to say the least.

The other thing that stands out in my mind was our pregame meal. I was sitting at a table of eight players and we started to get silly, laughing and telling jokes. We didn't notice that the coaches and other players were looking at us, thinking we better shut up and start thinking about the game. Someone in the group, I think it was Tom Devine, told a joke that cracked everyone up, and we were clearly out of control. Ara came over to our table and said there was way too much levity at this table and that we were going to get our ass kicked on the field. Immediately we all shut up and finished the rest of our meal in silence.

Ara was clearly upset that we would be so cavalier about the game. He always conveyed to us that we had an opportunity to do something great at Notre Dame and that every game was important. We needed to take advantage of each opportunity. He wanted us to have fun, but when it was time to be serious, it was important to be focused.

The game against Pittsburgh went very well for us. We scored 14 points in each quarter and rolled to a 56–7 win. Larry Parker, a speedy halfback, ran for two touchdowns, and Eddie Gulyas ran for three more. Thom Gatewood caught an eight-yard pass from Cliff Brown, and Willie Townsend and Darryll Dewan added TD runs late in the game. Our defense was led by Eric Patton, Rich Thomann, and Jim Musuraca at linebacker; Ralph Stepaniak, Mike Crotty, and Clarence Ellis in the defensive backfield, and Walt Patulski, Mike Kadish, Fred Swensen, and Greg Marx on the front line. They did an awesome job holding the Panthers to just 113 yards.

Coach Parseghian always tried to include on the travel team guys from the area we were playing. We had a number of players from western Pennsylvania, and with the big lead we amassed they got a chance to play in front of their friends and families. Even though it was lopsided, Ara really didn't run up the score; we kept the ball mostly on the ground.

After the game, I went up to Ara in the locker room of the old Pitt Stadium. I told him I was sorry for my behavior at the pregame meal. He told me that was fine, just don't let that kind of thing happen again. I'm glad we won by 49 points. It made it a lot easier to apologize to the head coach.

Game 9: Tulane

We were 7–1 when Tulane came in to Notre Dame Stadium. This was the last home game for the seniors, and they had been a great class. Ara wanted to prepare us well so that we could send off the seniors with good memories of their final game at Notre Dame. I didn't fully understand how important Senior Day was until I became a senior myself. Four years of hard work would be coming to a close, and players would be moving on with their lives, in many cases never to play a competitive team sport again.

Tulane had a stout defense that gave the Irish a hard time in the first half. One of our drives stalled when Eddie Gulyas was stopped just inches short on fourth-and-2 from the Green Wave 17-yard line. Then a field goal attempt by Bob Thomas late in the second quarter was blocked by Tulane's tough linebacker Mike Mullen. Underdog Tulane scored on a 14-yard pass from Rusty Lachaussee to flanker Steve Barrios and led 7–0 at the half.

In the second half, our offense began to click. Cliff Brown directed a 68-yard march and snuck in from the 1-yard line for a score that tied the game. Then Cliff and John Cieszkowski made key plays to sustain a 72-yard scoring drive that ended when Mike Creaney took an eight-yard pass from Cliff and carried a Green Wave defender into the end zone for the go-ahead score. In the fourth quarter, another long drive culminated in Cliff running around left end for a five-yard score. Final score, Notre Dame 21, Tulane 7.

During the game, I twisted my ankle, and it hurt like hell. However, there was no way I was going to sit out. I earned my position, and unless I was being wheeled off on a stretcher, I was not coming out of the game. I didn't play my best game, but Tulane had some very good players. The Notre Dame offense rushed for 241 yards and passed for 154, as Cliff Brown had his best game. Our defense held Tulane to 189 total yards. We were 8–1, and with one game to go we had a chance to become Ara's third team to win nine games.

Game 10 - Louisiana State

In 1970, we beat Louisiana State 3–0 in South Bend. This time the game would be in Baton Rouge, and the Tigers were really gunning for us, as Tim Sullivan found out the previous summer when he was visiting a friend's brother at a basketball camp and ran into "Pistol" Pete Maravich, LSU's star hoopster. "Maravich said, 'You can't believe how much they are looking forward to playing you. They don't care if they lose all the other games this season as long as they beat Notre Dame,'" Tim recalled. In case there was any doubt, the billboards in Baton Rouge that read GO TO HELL, NOTRE DAME confirmed that we were in hostile territory.

Like many schools below the Mason-Dixon Line, LSU had not yet integrated its football team. The night before our game, our team went to a movie theater. "Our black teammates were with us," Tim said. "When they sat down, people from about three rows in front and three in back got up and walked out. Being a northern, Catholic school, it was clear that we were in their country now."

Besides the reception, we were going to have a tough time against an LSU team that featured a good defense and explosive offense. Their weapons included quarterback Bert Jones, who would go on to a good NFL career; Art Cantrelle, a determined runner; and receiver Andy Hamilton, who had good speed and great hands. The defense included All-SEC lineman Ron Estay, strong and fast. (I later played against him in the CFL, and he was All-League every year.) Linebacker Warren Capone was fast and smart—he was only a sophomore but called their defenses. All-American Tommy Casanova played defensive back and returned kicks; he went on to become an All-Pro safety for the Cincinnati Bengals and after football he became a dentist.

As for me, I needed a dentist in the week leading up to the game. My tooth was aching horribly, and I went to Dr. Stinger, our team dentist, who told me I needed a root canal. He performed one on me, but it didn't feel good afterward. After trying to live with the pain for a day, I went back and told Doc Stinger to pull the sucker out. He tried to convince me to hang in there with the pain, but I said I had to be ready for the game, pull it. He did and later gave me a bridge that lasted about 30 years. Before he pulled it, my weight had dropped from 245 pounds to 238; I couldn't afford to lose any more.

LSU's stadium held almost 70,000 fanatics and was nicknamed Death Valley because of its intimidation factor. The fans weren't all nuts; there were those who appreciated the tradition of Notre Dame and were there to see a good football game. But there were some who did crazy stuff like throw full cans of beer and half-filled liquor bottles at us.

LSU also had a Bengal tiger in a cage just outside the locker room, with microphones all around it. Shortly after we got to our locker room, Tim Sullivan decided to go up and take a look at the field even before getting into uniform. "The field was all lit up, but the tunnel wasn't. As you walked out the door, there was a huge cage with a Bengal tiger in there, sitting up on a little step and looking the other way," he said. "I had never been close to a tiger, growing up on a farm in Iowa. Before I knew it, the tiger sprang. He hit that cage and he sunk his teeth in right where my face was, and I'm looking down his throat, with the hot breath and the growl that sounded like a T-Rex. I must have jumped four feet backward." He continued, "I went back in the locker room and sat in my stool and I thought, *You dummy. Why do you think they put that tiger there?* It was for guys like me to go out there and something like that to happen."

As soon as the visiting team came out of the locker room for the game, someone started poking the tiger with a stick. The microphones picked up the sound, and there were speakers right outside the door, so we got hit with a roar as soon as we came out.

We received the opening kickoff, and from the beginning, I believed we could move the ball on the ground. In the first quarter, I really felt we had scored when Andy Huff drove off the right side, but officials said he was stopped short of the goal line. That call, and several other incidences in the game, left many of us thinking we got homered by the referees.

Three times in the first half we were inside the LSU 10-yard line but got turned away. The Tigers began gaining momentum each quarter and by halftime they were up 14–0. We still felt that we could score on their defense, but it didn't happen until the fourth quarter, on a short pass from Cliff Brown to Thom Gatewood. We went for two, and Bob Minnix caught a conversion pass from Cliff, but we still trailed 21–8 at that point. Andy Hamilton then caught his third TD pass of the game, and the LSU Tigers finished on top, 28–8.

Many things went wrong that night in Baton Rouge. The tale of the game was that we had outgained the Tigers in yardage and first downs. But if you can't put the ball in the end zone you don't win the game. We could have beaten them, and I wished for the chance to play them again. But it never happened. Ara and the coaches were very disappointed—not so much in our effort, but in the outcome of the game.

Ara let us go down to New Orleans for the night, and it was a great experience to be on Bourbon Street for the first time. The guys had a ball and we blew off steam. We stayed out all night and returned to the hotel as the sun was coming up. The flight home to Notre Dame was a short one, as most of the guys slept.

Aftermath

Within a day or two of returning to campus, Ara called a meeting and presented an opportunity for us to play in the Gator Bowl. It would mean spending about a week in Jacksonville, Florida. Ara tried to explain the advantages—a chance to be in good weather during the wintertime, and to have an experience that we would remember for a lifetime.

I personally was all for it. But Ara put it up for a vote as many of the seniors weren't really excited about the trip. "He took a big chance," said Thom Gatewood. "He left it totally up to the players. He could have dictated and bullied us on that." Thom said the players had gone to the Cotton Bowl the previous two years because the team wanted the challenge of playing the top-ranked team and a shot at a national championship. "It was hard to be sold on why we were supposed to go [to the Gator Bowl] my senior year. It was like a jury: we were debating the pros and cons. Nowhere in the equation did we see a shot at a national title."

I was crushed when the vote was to turn down the game. I saw an opportunity slip away. That was the last time the Fighting Irish players had a chance to vote whether to go to a bowl. If invited, we were going to go in the future, because the money was so big it would help fund all the other sports at Notre Dame.

With that, my sophomore season was over, and it was back to the weight room and the handball courts for me. Going home for Christmas was fun, but perhaps not as much fun as going to the Gator Bowl, which I watched at home with my father and brother. I had two more years to go, however. There would be other chances to regain our pride.

CHAPTER 10

Changing Times

Ara Parseghian's tenure as head coach at Notre Dame coincided with a period of immense social change in America. Issues including the Vietnam War and the Civil Rights movement created tensions across the country and were reflected in campus life. The times they were a-changing. The Notre Dame campus is very self-contained, which in some ways isolates students from the goings-on in the rest of the world. But the students, including football players, were not totally immune.

Ara himself had an avid interest in the world beyond the lines of the football field. He rose early and went to Milt's Grill, a hole-in-the-wall South Bend restaurant, where he met regularly with Joe Doyle, the sports editor of the *South Bend Tribune*, who never betrayed anything the coach told him in confidence. Ara also took time to scan newspapers such as the *Chicago Sun-Times*, *Chicago Tribune*, the *Wall Street Journal*, and the *New York Times*.

"When we arrived at the office for our 7 AM meeting, Ara didn't want to talk football. He wanted to talk world events," said assistant coach Bill Hickey. "He understood from the start the effects of Watergate. He almost called it," said Bill, referring to the break-in at the Watergate Hotel in Washington that eventually led to the resignation of President Richard Nixon. Another assistant, Greg Blache, said he was "utterly amazed" at Ara's wide knowledge. "The scope of his intelligence went far past football. It was mindboggling, the insights he had into economics and politics."

"It was fun to be around Ara because you could have great discussions with him about so many things," said Roger Valdiserri, longtime Notre Dame sports information director. "Ara could argue about anything Nixon did or said."

In 1970, the Notre Dame coach publicly endorsed the candidacy of local congressman John Brademas, an antiwar Democrat. Theodore Hesburgh, Notre Dame president, spoke out against continued U.S. involvement in Vietnam. Fr. Ted agreed with many of the goals of student protesters, but he adamantly opposed any tactics that became violent or disrupted order. Ara and Fr. Ted had very similar attitudes in that way.

For some players, the effects of the war hit very close to home. "You had buddies that maybe didn't go to college, and when you got the home, newspapers read that one or two of your friends were dead," said Jim Leahy. "That's when it really hit me."

Individual football players were divided in their opinions on the war, while some said they were basically too busy with practices and studies to get involved. Some, like offensive lineman Steve Quehl, felt pulled in different directions between their student and athlete roles. "I was a walking contradiction," Steve said. As an English major playing football, he found he was "regarded with some suspicion" by both groups. "I had to make a concerted effort to connect with contemporaries—almost overcompensate—depending on which environment I found myself operating in at any given moment."

Offensive lineman Mike Oriard was opposed to the war and was excited when Joseph Heller, author of the classic antiwar novel *Catch-22*, visited campus as part of the Sophomore Literary Festival in 1968. But Oriard did not feel any personal disconnect in playing football, even though he knew some critics saw the game as a symbol of violence in America. "There is no time where I felt conflicted about playing football," said Mike, who, after playing four years for the NFL's Kansas City Chiefs, went on to become an English professor and an associate dean at Oregon State. He also authored *The End of Autumn*, a critically acclaimed book about life in the NFL, and wrote four other books about the role of football in American culture. "For me, it was an intensely personal thing. Football was where I worked through my adolescence. Going to the Grotto, doing the whole Notre Dame thing, it was an intensely personal, private crusade whose meaning was only personal. It was me proving things, discovering things about myself."

Many of the football coaches around the country at that time had conservative outlooks. "The football coach was the quintessential figure of male authority," he said. "I think that Ara was taken by surprise, and he got through the period where he might have stumbled and done something foolish that would have blown up on him. I think he figured things out and adjusted." He added, "To acknowledge that his players were people—young men who were trying to figure out how to live in an increasingly complex world—that's impressive."

Defensive lineman Mike McCoy said Ara kept players focused on the goal of winning a national championship: "He said, 'The only way you're going to accomplish that is to work together on and off the field. You can think different things and you can disagree, but you have to work together as one." Mike believed that politics "shackled our guys and didn't give them a chance to do what they had to do" in Vietnam. After the 1970 Cotton Bowl game that Notre Dame narrowly lost to Texas, McCoy and linebacker Bob Olson were sitting in the training room—"with just our jock straps on," as he put it—when former president Lyndon B. Johnson walked in. LBJ was the president who initially escalated the conflict in Vietnam. "He was the last guy I wanted to see," Mike said. "I had no respect for that guy at all. You talk about conflicting things, that was a conflicting thing for me."

In the spring of 1970, the National Guard shot and killed four students, including two bystanders, during an antiwar rally at Kent State University in Ohio. The result was a nationwide student strike. A number of rallies and speeches took place on the Notre Dame campus, and some football players skipped spring practice to attend one of them.

"There were about 11 of us who thought, *This is more important than spring football, we're not going to practice*," said quarterback Bill Etter, a two-game starter in 1971 whose college career was cut short by injury. Bill said he wasn't impressed by the speaker. "By the time we got home, all we could think was, 'What did we do? Why did we not tell somebody?' I thought I was going to lose my scholarship."

The players who missed practice were called into Ara's office the next morning. As Etter tells it: "We were sweating it. We're trying to be real small because his eyes were piercing. Those eyes could kill. But I'll never forget that he didn't have a hard look, he had a concerned look. He said, 'You have responsibilities as teammates. I understand that this is an important time and there are a lot of concerns out there for young people.' So instead of a tirade, he starts talking about the concerns of young people."

Bill said that Ara pointed out to the group that more than 90 teammates had attended practice and that he needed to institute some punishment. "He told us that we had to show up early before the spring game to help get the field ready. And another thing—he said, 'This is the end of it. We win as a team, we lose as a team.'" Summing it up, Bill said Ara handled the situation "like a father." Many of Ara's Knights came to have that feeling about their coach, that he was like a father away from home.

One of the changes unique to Notre Dame was the transition to accepting women students, in 1972 for the first time in its 130-year history. Notre Dame was still an all-male school when I entered in 1970. St. Mary's College, an all-women's school that was much smaller than Notre Dame, was located just across the highway and students at both ND and St. Mary's were allowed to take some courses on each other's campus. There were talks that Notre Dame and St. Mary's came close to merging, but when that fell through, Notre Dame decided to begin directly admitting women. This was a huge shift in campus culture, and many students and alumni reacted strongly, one way or another.

Offensive lineman Max Wasilevich, like me, was a junior when the change occurred. Even a few years after graduation, he found that the coeducation was a sore spot for some. As a student at the Wayne State University School of Medicine, Max was spending time one day with a neuro-ophthalmologist at the Kresge Eye Institute in Detroit. The doctor called Max into a private room. "He closes the door, he gives me this look, and he says, 'Why did you let Notre Dame go coed?' Like I was responsible for it," Max said. "I guess he was just trying to say he was a Notre Dame grad and he was not happy. I said I think it made us respect women more and respect ourselves more."

Tom Creevey, a defensive lineman, thought it was a "welcome sight" to have women students at the school. "It gets old looking at guys. I thought it brought a lot of excitement to the campus." Mike Townsend, the defensive back, observed the biggest change in the classroom, bringing in a calming effect. "Even the professors acted differently," he said. "I think it was the best thing that could have happened. My girlfriend didn't like it. But what could I say?"

About 400 women began attending Notre Dame in 1972, and they moved into Badin and Walsh Halls. That was tough on the guys who lived in those dorms, as it disrupted relationships they had formed with hall mates. Many of the new women students were transfers from Saint Mary's, and one of them, Beth Kennedy, ended up marrying Tim Sullivan. "She graduated in 1973, one of the first women graduates of Notre Dame," said the Irish linebacker. "I was sure glad for it. We've been married 30 years."

Personally, coming from an all-boys high school, I liked the all-male atmosphere at Notre Dame. When the school began admitting women, I was against it. I thought it might negatively affect the camaraderie and spirit of the place. A lot of guys didn't want girls at Notre Dame until they had their own daughters. That was the case with me. I changed my mind when my daughter, Lisa Ann Pomarico, applied and was accepted to Notre Dame in the fall of 1999. She graduated with honors from St. Joseph High School in South Bend and went on to graduate from Notre Dame in 2003. I am proud of her academic achievements. The family joke is that she got into Notre Dame as a thinker, while I got in as a stinker.

Racial integration came slowly to Notre Dame. The first African American, Frazier Thompson, enrolled in 1944. In 1953, Wayne Edmonds became the first black player to win a letter in football, helping Frank Leahy's team go undefeated. When Ara Parseghian started at Notre Dame, the number of black students, including athletes, was still low. At the 1966 "Game of the Century" between the Irish and Michigan State, the Spartans had 12 black starters. For several years, Spartans Coach Duffy Daugherty had actively recruited Southern black players who could not play elsewhere. Notre Dame's Alan Page, an All-Pro in the NFL, earned a law degree and eventually served as an associate justice of the Minnesota Supreme Court after his All-American collegiate career.

Fr. Hesburgh served as chairman of the U.S. Civil Rights Commission and he marched arm in arm with Martin Luther King Jr. in 1964. But even under his leadership, there was a scarcity of blacks on campus for many years. In the fall of 1970, 58 minority students enrolled, more than double the previous year.

Ara's staff had also begun recruiting more black student-athletes, including Clarence Ellis, Bob Minnix, and Thom Gatewood, and a few others who came to Notre Dame in 1968. Thom said Bear Bryant recruited him for the University of Alabama and he could have been the first black football player in the Southeastern Conference. "I didn't think Alabama was going to take care of my academic needs," he said. "I didn't want to be a sacrificial lamb that way. If I was going to make a social statement and make a stand, I wanted to come away with something. I decided I wanted to be a well-educated black man going forth in America, whether or not I played a down of football." He went on to become owner and president of a promotional products distributor in New Jersey and co-owner of an award-winning video television production company.

As a college player, he earned honors as both an All-American wide receiver and also an Academic All-American, and in 2015 he was elected to the College Football Hall of Fame. At Notre Dame, he found that many of his teammates had never played with an African American player in high school. "We were breaking new ground. We were exchanging ideas that were totally foreign, and yet I don't really sense that there was ever any real hostility on the field or in the locker room. When we hit the field, we had an instant bond," he said. "My groin pull hurts as much as yours. When the crowd cheered, I sensed it was cheering for all of us. There were families in South

Bend that invited me into their homes of different colors. I still have relationships with those families. The Notre Dame experience is a long-lasting one, not three downs and you're out."

But there were some difficult moments for him. Once, walking back from town, "someone in a car yelled out some racial statements and fired what I thought was a gun overhead. I dove down and that car took off." Some hate mail and phone calls also arrived when he was named a captain in his senior year, the first black player to win that status at Notre Dame. And one night on campus, he was hit on the head from behind and had to spend a night at the infirmary. "A lot of the teammates rallied around me at that point," he said.

Tight end Mike Creaney was one of the white guys who enjoyed comparing experiences with Thom. "Thom introduced me to Magic Shave," a razorless hair removal cream marketed to black men. "We used that as a cultural bridge. I don't know about Magic Shave or how to cook collard greens, but we got into a variety of conversations."

Creaney recounted arriving at the airport in Baton Rouge when the Irish went down to play LSU in 1971. "Thom turned to me and said, 'I'd be a little careful coming off this plane if I was you.'" That puzzled Mike, who asked for an explanation. "Thom said, 'Mike, there's only one thing worse than being a white, northern, Catholic Irish Democrat from Notre Dame playing football down here. That's being a black, northern, Catholic Irish Democrat from Notre Dame playing football down here. They're liable to shoot at me and hit you, so I'd be real careful.'"

Mike Townsend arrived at Notre Dame in 1970, the same year I started. He was part of a group of 118 African American freshmen students in our class, the largest ever at the school, but still found social life difficult, especially because freshmen were not allowed to have a car at school. He said the team's black players would meet after practice at the Student Center and share their frustrations.

"Cliff Brown was the leader of the pack. He felt he needed to go back home, and we all said 'Yeah, but why come back?' We all conjured up where we were going to go." The players went to see Ara, who sensed that Cliff was the leader of the group and invited him into his office to speak privately. "Coach Parseghian reduced that fever. He got Cliff to go back home one weekend when we weren't playing. He got a bellyful of his mom's cooking and she told him, 'You don't need to be going to another school.'" Mike said. After Cliff returned, "He led the charge for us to stay on campus.

"We were drawn to express ourselves, and yet we knew Notre Dame was an excellent school. It afforded us a lot of academic and athletic opportunities, so we knew we really had to think about what we were going to do." He went on to become one of our captains and make consensus All-American in 1973. And, he said, the social atmosphere improved somewhat after both Notre Dame and Saint Mary's College brought in more African American students and after he became an upperclassman who could drive a car into town and make new friends.

Eric Penick, who enrolled at Notre Dame in 1971, said that campus security guard Ernie Rice befriended many of the black athletes. "He played football at [South Bend] Central High School and he was the first black detective in South Bend," Eric said. "He took us to his house—all the black players in our class, like Wayne Bullock, Ron Goodman, Al Samuel, Reggie Barnett. He made sure we weren't homesick. When his wife died during our senior year, we were the pallbearers."

Eric said his Mom and Ara gave him similar advice about how to handle any obstacles he faced as a black student-athlete. "My mother used to say if you know the rules of the game, son, you can play the game. Don't worry about what they're not allowing you to do. Find out how it works so you can get to where you need to be. It might be harder for you, but don't allow that to stop you," he said. "Cultural differences are everywhere. It's not what's important. It's how you handle those situations. That's what Ara was telling me about character. How you handle negative situations is what makes a stronger person and determines what you are at the end."

Luther Bradley, who arrived on campus in 1973, said one of the issues that concerned black players was the absence of African American cheerleaders. "We wondered why, and somebody went to Fr. Hesburgh," Luther said. The issue was quickly resolved with the addition of a black female cheerleader.

Coach Parseghian guides his knights on the field, though—just as importantly—he prepared them off the field as well.

Coach Parseghian demonstrates the proper technique involved in handing the ball off.

Ara Parseghian, who won 95 games at Notre Dame, readies himself prior to a contest.

If Notre Dame was considered to be Camelot under Ara, quarterback Tom Clements was his Lancelot.

I block for our great quarterback, Tom Clements, against Navy in 1973.

Gerry DiNardo (72) prepares to block for his first-team All-American quarterback, Tom Clements.

Tight end Dave Casper, a tri-captain, displays his 4.6-second 40-yard dash speed while running past the Michigan State defense.

The 6'3", 245-pound Dave Casper was Notre Dame's 1973 Offensive MVP before going on to a Hall of Fame career in the NFL.

Ballhawking defensive back Luther Bradley skies for an interception against Alabama.

Starting guard Larry DiNardo provided inspiration, and after he left, I would wear his number with pride.

I bulked myself up to 243 pounds by the time I was a senior, but I could still fire off the ball quickly.

Three members of the Notre Dame team in 1972 and 1973—(from left) me, Gerry DiNardo, and linebacker John O'Donnell—hailed from St. Francis Prep in Brooklyn.

Speedy wideout Willie Townsend was the older brother of Mike Townsend.

Mike Townsend, who led the country in interceptions in 1972, was a fun-loving guy and easy to get along with.

Paul Sawicz, Pete Hartman, myself, Ara, Sherm Smith, and Steve Sylvester pose with the game ball after defeating Army.

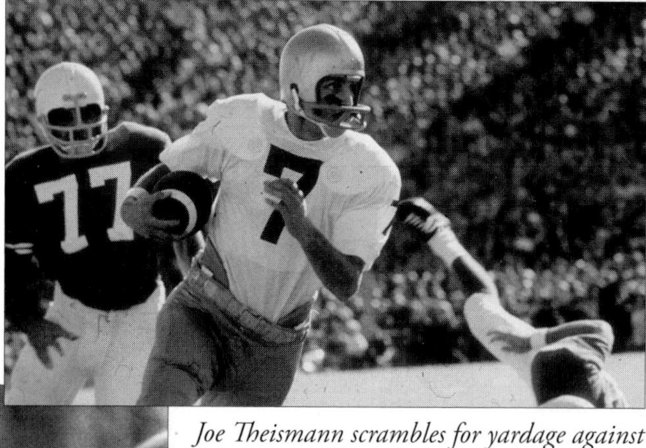

Joe Theismann scrambles for yardage against the Texas Longhorns, who Notre Dame played in 1970 and 1971.

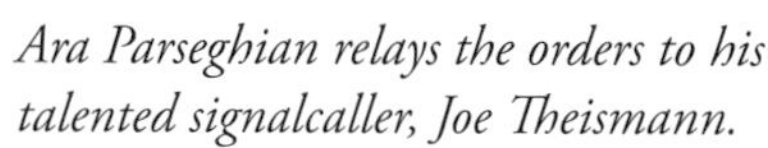

Ara Parseghian relays the orders to his talented signalcaller, Joe Theismann.

Eric Penick rushes for an 85-yard touchdown during Notre Dame's 23–14 victory against USC in 1973.

After defeating Alabama in the Sugar Bowl, we celebrate our national championship.

Ara Parseghian raises the 1973 Sugar Bowl trophy after we defeated Alabama 24–23.

Gerry DiNardo (left) remains a great friend of mine to this day. (Courtesy Frank Pomarico)

Tri-captains of the 1973 Notre Dame national championship team (from left) Mike Townsend, Dave Casper, and I get together at the team's 30-year reunion in 2003. (Lighthouse Imaging)

With his wife, Katie, by his side, Ara Parseghian, presents the colors to the Irish Guard prior to the 2012 Michigan-Notre Dame game while surrounded by former captains (from left) Walt Patulski, Larry DiNardo, John Dampeer, Phil Sheridan, Jim Carroll, Heisman winner John Huarte, Mike Townsend, and me. (Lighthouse Imaging)

As a black assistant coach, Greg Blache was sometimes involved in listening to and communicating with minority players. Greg was a walk-on as a freshman in 1967, but a leg injury cut short his playing career. Ara invited him, as a sophomore, to help coach the freshman team. He stayed at Notre Dame through the rest of Ara's tenure, which launched his long career as a college and NFL assistant coach.

During the late 1960s, black athletes faced pressures from student groups and outsiders to stage protests to draw attention to issues of discrimination. Greg recalled being in a meeting in which a black student organization tried to convince Notre Dame's African American players to boycott a game. "I argued it was unfair to ask these players to risk their scholarships. It was a tough room to be in, and I was defending an unpopular viewpoint. My argument was, don't force these players into a position you don't understand." In the end, one player who was injured took part in a picket line, but the other players took the field.

When Notre Dame played Alabama in the Sugar Bowl at the end of the 1973 season, the local NAACP tried to convince African American players to boycott the game in support of striking sanitation workers in New Orleans, according to Eric Penick. "I told them I was not going to boycott. We came as a team, we play as a team. That's who we are," he said. "Bottom line, if you want to prove that white and blacks can play together, then you need to watch how we play. We're going to beat Alabama because we are united as a people and as a team."

Within the team, white and black players acknowledged there were some tensions about playing time. Black running back Larry Parker became a lightning rod, becoming vocally upset when he lost his starting job. Larry and his younger brother, Mike, who was a defensive back, got in a fight with another player, and Ara suspended them from the team for a year. We had a meeting in which we all thought Ara was going to tell us that he removed the players from the team because of the fight, but it turned out it was the straw that broke the camel's back. The coach had a whole list of offenses, including insubordination during a game. By the time he got through the list, we were all pretty mad at those guys, as we were working hard to keep our heads above water. But Ara was someone who believed in second chances, and he gave them a chance to come back.

The overwhelming consensus among players was that Ara made playing decisions based on merit, not color. "Ara's attitude was that everyone is a man, and you treat everyone the same, no matter if you were number one or number 118," said Mike Townsend. Luther Bradley agreed. "I never felt Ara didn't play someone because of race or color. I always felt he played the best guys to give us the best opportunity to win a ballgame."

Greg Blache summed it up. "Ara was colorblind. He had a feel for people that weren't necessarily treated like everyone else. I don't know if it was his own experience growing up Armenian, but he just had a specialness about him that immediately put me at comfort with him."

CHAPTER 11

Becoming a Knight

I have compared playing for Ara Parseghian to being a knight playing for royalty. Let me explain what I mean a little more. The medieval legend of King Arthur helped establish the model of a knight. From Camelot, Arthur ruled his kingdom with right being right instead of might being right. Arthur met with his knights at the Round Table to discuss the issues of the kingdom and to plan adventures, such as the quest for the Holy Grail, the cup from which Jesus drank at the Last Supper. The table was round to make sure all understood that every one of the knights had equal status and authority.

Arthur's knights followed a code of chivalry:

Never do outrage or murder.
Respect life at all levels.
Have patience and humility.
Do not commit treason, a crime against country or King.
Do not be cruel. Grant mercy to those who ask, even in combat.
A Knight must help women if they need it.
Never harm a woman.
Don't join in on fights over anything less than God or country.
Search for self-knowledge, your purpose in life.
Understand that the Kingdom of Camelot is a great place, but the Kingdom of Heaven is inside of us and all around us.

> Make a positive difference for all the people you have contact with.
> Be a center of peace for all and pass it on to the young.

It has been many centuries since knights dressed in armor and roamed the countryside on horseback. But the ideal of knighthood remains relevant because the world still needs capable, committed people who follow a code of honor. Even in today's England, the monarchy continues to award knighthood to recognize major contributions to the country. Aaron Sorkin, creator of the series *The Newsroom*, described his intent for the series on HBO: "What the show says is you don't need a suit of armor. You can act like a knight even if you don't have a horse. We can all just be a little bit better than we are." When George Lucas created *Star Wars*, he called his heroes Jedi Knights, men who used their training and power for the common good. It was another example of how the world still yearns for the qualities that knights stand for.

King Arthur's ideals were pure and fair and earned him great loyalty. It is not a stretch to say that Ara Parseghian stood for similar values. For those of us lucky enough to be under his leadership, Notre Dame was our Camelot.

Ara wanted his players to be a cut above, not only on the football field but also in the rest of their lives. He sought to develop men with good moral judgment who could become leaders because they had core values that were decent, honest, and respectful of others. Consistent with Notre Dame's mission, Ara tried to cultivate young people who would grow to serve the community and contribute to a better world. "A part of the legacy of the university is that you're not there to just get a diploma. You're there to make your life and other people's lives better," said Tom Bolger, one of Ara's Knights.

As I talked to players and coaches who had played for Ara at Miami of Ohio and Northwestern as well as Notre Dame, I began to see a pattern: Ara had a unique drive himself and wanted to surround himself with similar people. They may not have always been the greatest athlete or the smartest person, but they had a hunger and a vision to be successful, and he could recognize that in a person.

You don't have to be a graduate of Notre Dame to be a modern-day knight. It is not necessary to have played for Ara Parseghian. Women as well as men can be knights by following a code of conduct based on integrity and selflessness.

These are some of the virtues that I believe describe a contemporary knight.

1. **Industriousness**—The most worthwhile things are not easy to accomplish. An industrious person works energetically and enthusiastically toward a goal. Having a well-thought-out personal plan will make your efforts productive. When I look back at my football training regimen, it took a lot of weight lifting and running to reach my goal. I also had to work very hard in the classroom. Hard work became a natural thing for me each day on my journey to become one of Ara's Knights.
2. **Teamwork**—Focus on the goals of the team, putting individual pride and accomplishments secondary to the betterment of the team. The end product is a winning culture. There may be things that don't highlight you as an individual, but which are important to overall success. "I have a finance degree, but I tell everybody my most rewarding subject was football because of the teamwork I learned," said Dan Morrin. "I learned to just be ready to be in there, make sure you know everything you need to know, make sure you help other people on the team, and everything is going to turn out."

   In my time playing for Ara, I saw how even the reserves who rarely played in a game helped create this winning culture by consistently being on time, giving their all in practice, and rooting for their teammates instead of creating dissension over issues such as playing time. I witnessed how a club with many individual stars can be beaten by a less talented team that works together to produce a result that is greater than the sum of its parts. Teamwork is just as critical in your job and in your community—when everyone works together to accomplish common goals, everyone achieves more. It's an attitude I brought to my work life in sales, always trying to create a team atmosphere.

3. **Alertness**—If you are going to make a difference in the world, you need to understand what is going on. An informed person can make an educated decision. Ara read two or three newspapers every day. Even long after his careers as a coach and then a broadcaster, he continued to keep up with the world around him. As a coach, he got as much input as possible before making a decision. Every night after practice he would discuss every player with the other coaches, so that if a change needed to be made, it was not done on a whim but with as much information as possible. He wanted others to offer their opinions, but would pull the trigger and take responsibility for his decision. As Harry Truman used to say, "The buck stops here."
4. **Enthusiasm**—Ara always wanted people who had a hunger to compete and learn about life. "We had the word 'enthusiasm' on the board in the locker room," John Huarte said. "I thought that was great. You usually have enthusiasm on game day, but you have to put some zest and spirit into your practice. You get more out of it that way." A knight needs to have passion about daily life, whether it is directed at work, family, or the community. Your technical skills are important, but nothing of value was ever accomplished without passion.
5. **Discipline**—As important as it is to have a plan, a knight needs to have the discipline to see it through. When I was dreaming about becoming a Notre Dame football player for Ara Parseghian, I first thought about how strong I needed to be. My dad and I developed a weight program that took me from a chubby 13-year-old into a strong, hard body after countless weight workouts in my basement. Terry Hanratty said Ara taught him the importance of discipline: "Ara was just so meticulous in how he approached life," he said. "Discipline includes really looking at the details of life. Usually the big things will take care of themselves. It's the little things that will carry you."
6. **Preparedness**—One of the great things I learned around Ara was how to be prepared. Tom Creevey said he thought we were the best prepared team in the country. "Ara always said the game was

incidental. It was the preparation that counts," he said. "Practices were very tough for a purpose, because I think he wanted the game to be easy for us." For me, running and weight lifting wasn't going to get it done by themselves. I learned that I had to love the challenge as much as the thrill of the games at Notre Dame. Every pound I lifted, every mile I ran, I was preparing to be on the battlefield as one of Ara's Knights. Preparation also meant studying film of old games with great players and trying to understand the techniques they used to be successful. I went to summer school three times during my Notre Dame career—not because I needed to, but because it would lighten the load during the academic year and help me graduate with my class in four years.

7. **Generosity**—Being generous does not just mean making financial contributions to a good cause. It also requires sharing your time, wisdom, and energy to help create a stronger family, team, or workplace. Ara wanted his players to be like a family, one in which the upperclassmen welcomed the newcomers and made them feel comfortable rather than taking advantage of them. To haze another player would be like bullying your brother, in Ara's view. He wanted us to hold ourselves to the highest standard of behavior. In my mind, the marriage between Notre Dame and Ara was so good because he was a manifestation of everything for which Notre Dame wanted to be noted: class, character, and integrity. He wanted his Knights to eventually take what they had learned, go out into the world, and be a positive force in the lives of others.
8. **Respect**—It may seem odd, but some of the nastiest on-field competitors are really gentle souls off of it. A knight is respectful to everyone, and never takes advantage of someone who is physically weaker. This includes a deep respect for women. Knights think of all women as if they were their own daughters. I was raised during a time when good manners were taught in the home and at school, and that included gestures such as a man opening a door for a woman, or standing when a woman enters the room. I still do it, and it has nothing to do

with women and men being equal. It is simply an outward expression of respect. I believe that good manners and being polite never go out of style, and the world would be a better place if we regained some sense of civility in how we deal with each other.

9. **Physical Fitness** —Strive to be physically fit, because it will enhance your ability to function in many different kinds of activities. A knight who is physically capable should walk, bike, or swim on a regular schedule at least three times per week in order to maintain cardiovascular health. Ara not only stressed the importance of his players being in good shape, he also wanted his coaches to work out on a regular schedule—playing basketball, handball, running, and lifting on the Nautilus machines a couple of times per week to increase strength and add flexibility. Being physically fit will also add to your confidence.
10. **Spiritual Fitness**—Knights seek a center of peace, based on understanding we were put on this earth for the purpose of making a positive difference in the world. A knight has respect for all living things and does not lie, steal, or kill out of vengeance. Knights do not tell lies. Knights embrace the best of human qualities—justice, compassion, integrity—and understand that they are a beacon light for others to follow. Knights believe that the Kingdom of Heaven is inside of us and all around us. The universal values of love, service to others, and kindness transcend specific religious denominations and they make the world a better place. A Knight realizes God has put an amazing light within him and so he is confident he can be a force for good even in the face of evil and negativity.

Each of these virtues is important by itself. When they all come together in one person, the result is a powerful force for good. Others will regard a person with these qualities as being trustworthy. Of course, we are all human, with weaknesses and frailties common to the human condition. Even some of King Arthur's knights sometimes failed to live up to the code of chivalry. But a modern-day knight humbly strives to live by the code, and to learn from his failures and mistakes.

None of us know what our end will be in this world. But we can determine what our legacy will be. If you love your fellow man, try to make the world a better place and pass your values on to the next generation. Your legacy will be that you were a knight who truly made a difference.

CHAPTER 12

Spring and Summer at Notre Dame

Spring is very much appreciated by everyone who lives and works at the University of Notre Dame. The winter tends to be brutal, then the spring brings a sense of renewal and everyone's attitude changes for the better. Even reaching 50 degrees is enough for some to break out shorts and T-shirts. The sights and sounds of students playing games on the various campus quads begin to fill the days.

There are some planned spring events that give students a chance to interact outside and enjoy themselves. AnTostal (Gaelic for "the festival") is an annual student-organized event that dates back to 1967. It is basically a festival of music, food, and games that vary from year to year but have included events such as volleyball, chariot races, mattress races, flag football games, pig chasing, tug-of-war, pie-throwing, and always plenty of mud. It's a great way to blow off steam before finals.

Another student-organized spring event is the Bookstore Basketball Tournament, so named because it began in 1972 on the outdoor courts behind the old campus bookstore on the South Quad. It is a five-on-five tournament that has grown now to about 700 team entries every year. Some of the teams take winning very seriously, while others put more effort toward coming up with interesting uniforms and creative team names (a few samples: Hoops I Did It Again, Bobby Knight & the Chair Throwers, Weapons of Mass Seduction, and Timeout, I've Lost My Pants). Varsity athletes are allowed to play, though rules limit their number on each squad. Notre Dame attracts a lot of students who played on their high school sports teams, and they seem to enjoy testing their skills against the scholarship athletes.

I also loved to watch the baseball team in the spring, as the ballfield was close to Cartier Field, where the football team practiced. I grew up in New York as a Yankees fan, and guys like Mickey Mantle, Roger Maris, and Whitey Ford were my heroes.

For the players on the football team, in springtime the main focus was practice leading up to the annual spring game. Beginning six weeks before spring practice, the coaches would hold workouts with agility drills, obstacle courses, and basketball games to get us into shape. After agility drills we would run the stadium steps, which was tough on our legs. Years later, the sports medicine people figured out that this wasn't the best thing to do for your knees. But we were doing things as a team, which made us all feel like we were working toward a common goal.

The guys who were really serious about training were already in shape. Gerry DiNardo, Dan Morrin, Gary Potempa, and I lifted regularly to get ready for spring ball. A few of us played handball and basketball to work on movement, because being as strong as a brick building was no benefit if you couldn't move.

A number of us would go to Dave's Gym, a hole-in-the-wall facility in South Bend that had everything you needed to get into lifting shape. Dave Bjoraas, who started his gym in the late '50s, mostly did Olympic-style lifting. The best weight lifters in the area trained at his place, including Winston Bennie, who lifted a phenomenal amount of weight. I was trying to find every possible legal way to get a competitive edge, and Dave introduced us to Nautilus equipment. My workouts consisted of bench pressing, squatting, deadlifting, and Olympic lifting, plus curls, dips, and shoulder work. My total workout could take from 90 minutes up to three hours per day. I was working hard and making gains, but was getting tired.

Then I met Kim Wood, who sold Nautilus machines and had played football at Wisconsin. Kim told me if I cut my workouts to three days per week I would see amazing results. He suggested that I limit bench pressing, squatting, and deadlifting to three times every two weeks. He told me also that the Olympic lifts were dangerous and that there was no need to do them for football. Kim refuted the theory that doing explosive exercises in the weight room would transfer to the football field. He recommended controlled exercises in which your muscles would have to work harder than they do in Olympic lifting, where you throw weights up and down. I followed his advice, and the results started to come. I got stronger and I had a lot more energy.

What I realized was that weight lifting's main benefits were for protecting yourself instead of making you a great football player. Players who didn't lift at all—guys like Greg Marx, Mike Kadish, and Walt Patulski—were knocking me on my tail every day. But lifting did enhance my ability to fire off the line and it made my legs and back stronger. It gave me greater speed when I pulled to block for sweeps and made me stronger for straight-on blocking. My trapezoids and back were getting muscular, my chest was really starting to pop out, and people were noticing the difference.

It was fun working out with teammates because there was always friendly competition in the weight room. Gerry DiNardo was looking strong and was working hard on his speed work. There was a real chance he was going to get to play, maybe even start, as a sophomore.

Ara Parseghian was not a big fan of lifting as a conditioning program. He felt that players got too tight. But he had an open mind and he wanted to know what we were doing down at Dave's Gym on Olive Street. He sent assistant coach Tom Pagna down to Dave's to find out what we were doing. Tom saw the Nautilus machines and Dave explained the benefits to him. Tom liked the idea that the machines helped improve flexibility as well as strength and talked to Ara about getting a line of Nautilus equipment for the school. The seed was planted, and that would happen in a year.

The guys who were training at Dave's Gym were staying healthy and were developing good football strength. Ara appreciated our discipline and hunger to be better. Andy Huff, one of our tough running backs, came to Dave's a couple of times per week. Then some of the younger guys, like Mike Fanning and Greg Collins, began to show up. We wanted to be a good team and this was part of the process.

* * *

The 1972 captains were offensive tackle John Dampeer and defensive tackle Greg Marx. Both were good football players, but their personalities were at different ends of the scale. John was a real thinker who maximized his athletic ability. He had great blocking technique, always got the job done, and was a positive influence on the other guys. Greg Marx was more like a bull in a china shop—very aggressive, which is a positive trait for a guy on defense. He led by example and was an All-American player. Greg was a good guy; you had to get to know him to understand how he channeled his aggressiveness into play on the field.

Greg was named to the *Playboy* preseason All-American team in 1972 and I was picked as an alternate. We traveled together to Chicago for the celebration event and photo shoot, and had a great time. Along with the other players selected, we stayed at the Playboy Towers, a beautiful old hotel on the north side of downtown Chicago. We were allowed to order anything we wanted from room service, and as you can imagine the football players felt like kids in a candy store. Greg and I ordered New York strip steaks, lobster dinners, and shrimp cocktails. The next day we went to a dinner party at Hugh Hefner's Chicago mansion. We bowled in the house, swam in the indoor pool, and got to meet the other All-Americans. I had a great time being around them in that atmosphere. The next year I made the first unit on the *Playboy* All-American team and got to make the trip to Chicago once again.

When spring practice began, the coaches moved Dave Casper into the starting spot at left tackle. Dave had played most of the second half of the 1971 season at tackle and did a great job. His natural position was tight end, but Dave was the best blocker on the team. He could really run, had excellent technique, great balance, and could stay on his block for the interval. He was also very smart about football. He would change the blocking scheme at the line of scrimmage as soon as he recognized a weakness in the defense. Sometimes he was ahead of the coaches, and more than once he bailed me out by helping with assignments. The following year he would be moved to tight end and he would become an All-American at that position, but he was such a good athlete he could have earned that honor at any of about six positions. Dave was a bit of a free spirit and also a solid person who went on to a Hall of Fame NFL career.

The rest of the offensive line included senior Dave Drew at center—not the biggest guy at 225 pounds but a good football player. He was smart, had a good work ethic in practice, and played hard in the games. He was not very talkative but had a good heart, and I really enjoyed playing next to him. John Dampeer was at right tackle, and Mike Creaney was at tight end. And by the end of spring ball, Gerry DiNardo won the right guard spot, beating out some very good players including Tom Bolger and Dan Morrin. All of them had worked very hard in the off-season; Gerry seemed to be a little bit stronger and a little bit faster. In fact, he won the Herring Award as best offensive lineman that spring. So by the end of spring football, our two starting guards were from St. Francis Prep and Our Lady of Grace grade school.

The big competition was at quarterback, between sophomore Tommy Clements and junior Cliff Brown. Tommy was making a big impression, and by the end of spring it looked like he was going to be the leader of Ara's new offense. We had previously been running a power-I offense and some wishbone. After the 1971 season, Ara went to the University of Delaware to talk to head coach Tubby Raymond, who had tweaked and improved the wing-T offense first developed by his predecessor, Dave Nelson. The offensive style, which uses a lot of deception, had helped make Delaware a small college powerhouse. "The secret to the wing-T is that it is sequence football," said Notre Dame assistant coach Bill Hickey. The basic play is a run, and then there is a pass that starts out looking like the run, and then a screen that starts out looking like the run. "You're setting the defense up by running the same look initially but ending up in a run, pass, or screen," he said.

Ara took Tubby Raymond's offense and put his own genius into it. "It played to our strengths as a group," said Tommy Clements. "We had athletic guys up front so we could do a lot of pulling with our guards. We also went with three running backs in the backfield a lot of the time. All of them were good runners," Tommy said. The offensive philosophy also gave the quarterback opportunities to run, something that Tommy was very capable of doing. The offense used a lot of misdirection and sweeps off a fake fullback dive, and a lot of draws and screens, with passes coming off of play action. It was a sophisticated offense to learn, so very few teams ran it. This was an advantage for us because our opponents' defenses weren't that familiar with playing against it.

The success of this offense relied on the ability of the quarterback to recognize where the defense was vulnerable. Ara gave the quarterback the ability to run or pass, and go right or left, just by making a few calls on the line of scrimmage. Ara and Tom Pagna had trained our quarterbacks on how to recognize and attack defenses. It was amazing how Tommy could understand the whole offense, including everyone's blocking assignments, which meant he could really help the offensive linemen get the best angles on their blocks.

Here is an example of what I mean, using one of our basic plays, "fullback trap," which involved the quarterback handing off to the fullback. When that play was called, Tommy would give us our blocking cue after we came to the line of scrimmage. If he called out, "Ready," it meant we would each block straight ahead. "Set" indicated that the center would block the defensive tackle lined up over me in my left guard position, right guard Gerry DiNardo would block the middle linebacker who was over center, and I would pull to the right and block the defensive tackle, who lined up opposite Gerry. "Even" was the call for the center to block the man opposite me and for me to take on the defensive man over center. And "Odd" meant the tight end and tackle would block down while I kicked out to the left to block the defensive end.

Tommy became an on-field extension of Ara Parseghian, someone who could articulate everything the coach wanted to do. That was a tall order, but if Ara was King Arthur, Tommy Clements was truly Sir Lancelot. "We could have lost anyone else on offense and replaced them but there was no way we could have replaced Tom Clements," Dave Casper said. "He didn't say much, but he was probably the smartest guy in three or four states. He was an exceptionally intelligent person." Tommy was not only brilliant, he was also a superb athlete who had been recruited to play point guard for Dean Smith's basketball team at North Carolina. Tommy roomed a couple of doors down from me in Sorin Hall, and I remember him doing a lot of laughing—mostly because he was entertained by his roommate Gerry DiNardo, who kept us all as loose as a goose with his humor.

Among our offensive weapons was speedy wideout Willie Townsend, the older brother of Mike Townsend, the starting safety on defense. The Townsend brothers also played as walk-ons for Digger Phelps' basketball team. As Mike tells it, he and Willie had played high school ball and at Notre Dame they played intramural basketball to stay in shape. They developed a reputation during pickup games, and some students went to Phelps and suggested he give them a tryout. "Coach Parseghian established some guidelines for [Phelps] to even talk to us," including a requirement that the Townsends maintain at least a 2.5 grade point average, according to Mike. The basketball coach brought Willie and Mike in to a closed practice to run some drills and then involved them in a scrimmage. "Digger will never admit this, but we beat his starting five," Mike said. The Townsends ended up playing two seasons on the basketball team.

Sure-handed receiver Pete Demmerle started at split end, and we had a posse of good running backs. Fullbacks included seniors John Cieszkowski and Andy Huff, sophomore Wayne Bullock, and junior John Gambone, another one of those guys who didn't get a lot of playing time but who brought great character and added depth to our team. John Gambone was the first guy I met at Notre Dame as a freshman and we remained good friends throughout college. At halfback we had a lot of guys who contributed. Senior Darryll Dewan was a tough runner, a good blocker, and had good hands as a receiver. Juniors Greg Hill and Gary Diminick were very competitive players who would be used in spot situations. Sophomores Eric Penick, Ron Goodman, and Al Samuel brought speed to the equation. A couple of other sophs, Jim Chauncey and Tom Bake, were solid players who added more character and depth.

Ara had a major rebuilding job to do on defense. The stingy 1971 unit had graduated eight starters. However, that opened up opportunity for a lot of others. The line was anchored by captain Greg Marx, and sophomore Mike Fanning was looking very good in the spring. Mike was 6'7" and 280 pounds, and had been both an All-American football player and an All-State wrestler in high school in Oklahoma. He was heavily recruited, especially by the University of Oklahoma. "One day I just decided that I didn't want to spend the rest of my life wondering if I could play at Notre Dame," he said.

George Hayduk had been a tailback in high school and was an excellent athlete who was moved to defensive end in 1972 and would also play some defensive tackle. The inside tackles along with Greg Marx included Dick Maciag and Kevin Nosbusch, who was an absolute load in the middle. Others that were in the mix at tackle were Denny Lozzi, Larry Susko, Bill Arment, and Greg Szatko, who had a body like Hercules. The 1972 season was the first one in which freshmen were eligible to play football, and freshman Steve Niehaus would end up getting a lot of playing time at defensive tackle.

Our linebackers were some of the best athletes at Notre Dame. The seniors were Jim O'Malley, a hard-hitting middle linebacker from eastern Ohio, and Jim Musuraca, who wasn't very big but wasn't shy about knocking your block off. The juniors were Gary Potempa, a fearless competitor who loved contact, and Tim Sullivan and Tom Devine, both about 6'3" and 220 pounds, with a shared attitude of dominance and intimidation. Three sophomores—Greg Collins, Sherm Smith, and Drew Mahalic—could run, hit, and think fast on the field.

Senior Kenny Schlezes had the most playing experience in the defensive backfield and would serve as the quarterback of the young unit. Junior Mike Townsend was probably the best athlete in the secondary, and he was destined to open a lot of eyes with his play. Another junior, former walk-on Tim Rudnick, showed promise as a very feisty competitor at corner. Two more juniors competing for positions in the defensive backfield were Mike

Naughton and Jim Zloch, while seniors Joe Haggar, Dan O'Toole, and Terry Garner added depth. Sophomore Reggie Barnett, an exceptional student who was majoring in engineering, brought speed and athletic ability to his bid to earn playing time at cornerback.

This defense was young, but hungry to prove itself. After a great spring, we headed into the summer with a commitment to train hard and come back ready for the 1972 season.

Back home, Gerry DiNardo and I planned our workouts and our jobs for the summer. I wouldn't be working as long this year because I had plans to go to summer school. I put in about five weeks as an ironworker with Gerry on 42nd Street in Manhattan. The work was hard, but Gerry was a ball to be around, always joking and finding the lighter side of life to laugh at. We again ran on the Belt Parkway three times per week and lifted three times per week, which helped us get in condition.

When I returned to campus, my mother was happy that the school would be feeding me as I could really put away the groceries. I enjoyed the relaxed atmosphere at Notre Dame during the summer. The professors were usually not as demanding and the weather was hot and humid, so we could work out hard and be ready for those conditions when practice resumed. Notre Dame was a peaceful place in the summer, with sports camps as well as a lot of religious classes, since the university was a center for the Catholic faith.

Brother Owen Justinian, one of the first teachers I had at St. Francis Prep, was there working on his doctorate in theology. Every morning he ran around the lakes, about two miles. I would see him as I was coming back from breakfast. He would have a huge smile on his face, and would ask me if I appreciated the opportunity that I had. I would tell him that I pinched myself and thanked God every day, not just because I was at Notre Dame but also because I played for Ara Parseghian. And it was extra special because I was there with Gerry DiNardo, someone who had come from such a similar background. Brother Owen, a good football player himself at St. Francis Prep, understood what I was saying.

I have tried to always remember where I came from and how special it was to be at Notre Dame at this time in history. We were privileged young men to be around people including Ara Parseghian, Tom Pagna, Father Hesburgh, academic adviser Mike DeCicco, and business professors like John Houck, Sal Bella, and Jerry Sequin. These were unique, classy men who helped groom us from young boys to mature Knights ready to go into the world with a great set of values.

CHAPTER 13

The 1972 Season

Game I: Northwestern

The young, relatively inexperienced Notre Dame team opened the season against Northwestern. The Wildcats were not pushovers, having lost only 7–0 to highly ranked Michigan in their first game. But we came flying out of the gate in this road opener, scoring the first five times we had the ball; the score was 27–0 halfway through the second quarter. The new Irish offense led by Tommy Clements rushed for 386 yards on the way to a 37–0 win.

The revamped defense was led by linebacker Jim O'Malley and freshman defensive tackle Steve Niehaus, each of whom racked up 13 tackles. Jim added an interception. In all, the defense created six turnovers—three interceptions and three fumble recoveries. It was a good sign that the young players had played well and special teams were excellent, as soccer-style kicker Bob Thomas nailed three field goals and Tim Rudnick blocked a field goal attempt.

A lot of players wanted to prove they could contribute. Darryll Dewan, Andy Huff, and John Cieszkowski each ran for a touchdown. The young players got good marks from Ara and the coaching staff. I talked to Gerry DiNardo after the game, his first. He was happy the game was over, but he admitted it was the thrill of a lifetime. It was always good to get the first win. And for Ara, it was the ninth straight year his Irish had come out on top in their first game.

Game 2: Purdue

Purdue had dangerous teams that gave Notre Dame fits during the 1960s and 1970s. The two universities are only 95 miles apart, making for a natural rivalry, and they recruited many of the same players in the Midwest. The 1972 Boilermakers were led on offense by quarterback Gary Danielson, All-American running back Otis Armstrong, and wide receivers Darryl Stingley and Rick Sayers. The top defensive players were linebacker Rick Schavietello as well as linemen Greg Bingham and Dave Butz. Ours was an inexperienced team, and there were concerns about how our young club would do.

It was our first home game of the year and as we stood in the tunnel ready to race onto the field, I grabbed Gerry DiNardo and told him, "This is what it's all about. You are going to have a blast." I remembered how Eddie Gulyas and Rich Thomann had given me words of encouragement before my first home game the year before, and now I wanted to pass that on to my longtime friend.

This was the game when Tommy Clements really arrived on the scene, throwing for 287 yards and two TDs as we beat Purdue 35–14. Tommy's scoring tosses were 39 yards to Mike Creaney and 62 yards to Willie Townsend. Altogether, our offense accounted for 636 yards, showing the great potential for the new wing-T approach. Our defense again played very well, thwarting the Boilermakers twice following fumbles that we committed in our own territory in the first half. We were 2–0, and our young guys were growing up fast.

John Cieszkowski and Andy Huff each scored touchdowns on short runs, and Eric Penick went for 133 yards on only 12 carries, including a 14-yard TD. The newspapers captured a photo of that run, with Gerry DiNardo and me pulling to the left to lead the way. A year later, we would run that same play against USC, and it would become one of the most famous runs during the Era of Ara.

Game 3: Michigan State

After a light workout in South Bend on Friday, we traveled by bus toward East Lansing and stayed about 35 miles away in Jackson, Michigan—a city that would become my home years later. The kids who played for Michigan State were always tough as nails, and you knew you had to tighten your chinstrap when you played them. The 1972 Spartans had some players who went on to have very good NFL careers, including Joe DeLamielleure, a pit bull of a guard; All-American safety Brad Van Pelt, an all-around athlete who also played college baseball and basketball; and tight end Billy Joe DuPree, another tremendous athlete. Their defensive line had players who wanted to mix it up and get physical, and you needed to be ready.

When I came out for warm-ups, I found that their field was as hard as stone, and it reminded me of playing in McCarren Park back in New York City. The stadium seated about 77,000 people, and there was a large smokestack on top of a power plant near the stadium that added to its distinctive feel. The game was televised nationally, and fans were treated to a game that wasn't very pretty, but it had all the excitement of a heavyweight fight. Make that a heavyweight street fight.

Through three quarters, the only scoring came on a couple of Bob Thomas field goals that gave the Irish a 6–0 lead. The Spartans then mounted their best drive and crossed midfield. Quarterback Mark Niesen, a left-hander, tried to pass to DuPree on a third-down play from the ND 44. Defensive back Kenny Schlezes made the play of the game for the Irish, intercepting the throw and returning it to the midfield. We moved the ball from there, with Eric Penick breaking tackles on a 26-yard run. We were using our buck sweep, in which Tommy would fake to the fullback in order to freeze the linebackers and then hand off to a halfback. Our outside guys blocked down, and the guards would pull to lead the sweep. The action would give our blockers angles on the defense. Our drive stalled on the MSU 9-yard line, but another field goal pretty much wrapped up the game.

The Spartans tried desperation passes to catch up, but Reggie Barnett picked off one of them. That set up the game's only touchdown, a seven-yard run by Andy Huff in the last minute. The game was really closer than the final 16–0 score. Ara liked that we won this kind of slugfest. Our defense came to play and proved it had what it took to compete.

Game 4: Pittsburgh

The Pitt Panthers came into Notre Dame Stadium as a heavy underdog. This was a day that both teams played sloppy football, with numerous fumbles and interceptions on both sides. Notre Dame turned it over five times, but Pitt couldn't take advantage and trailed 14–8 midway through the third quarter. With Pitt driving, quarterback John Hogan's pass was intercepted by linebacker Drew Mahalic who raced 56 yards for a score, putting the Irish up 21–8.

That play seemed to take the air out of Pitt's sails, and we added three fourth-quarter touchdowns to come away with a 42–16 win. Andy Huff finished with three TDs on the day. We were rolling up yards with our new offensive scheme, but the turnovers were a concern. We had to eliminate them, or we would pay for it in the future. We did end up winning by a comfortable margin, but if Pittsburgh had brought a little more firepower, it could have been a much different result.

Game 5: Missouri

The toughest thing for a coaching staff to do is to try to get their team up for opponents that aren't supposed to be very good. A few hours after our game against Pittsburgh, we found out that Missouri, our next opponent, had been crushed 62–0 by Nebraska. It's hard to not get overconfident when you hear that. The Tigers had a record of 2–3, and we figured we would breeze through these guys. But that week, Ara kept telling us to look at this team as being as dangerous as a wounded animal. He said they would be playing for their survival and would play their hearts out to avoid getting embarrassed again. Assistant coach Bill Hickey recalled the reaction of our players when they watched film of Missouri's game against Nebraska: "Our kids were snickering," he said. "But when we played them, it was a dogfight."

On a rainy day in South Bend, Mizzou played great ball control, capitalized on Irish mistakes, and took advantage of a controversial call to stun

Notre Dame. The Tigers had some talent on defense, but their best defense was holding on to the ball for 38 minutes. They amassed 223 yards on the ground and 106 in the air on only four pass completions, but the key thing is that they ran 79 plays against our defense, which was weakened somewhat by the loss of defensive tackle Steve Niehaus, who suffered a season-ending knee injury during a practice leading up to the game.

Missouri took advantage of an interception and scored first on a 16-yard end run by Leroy Moss on a fourth-down play. Notre Dame came back quickly as Tommy Clements made some nifty runs and completed a 23-yard pass to halfback Darryll Dewan, setting up Andy Huff's one-yard TD run. Missouri answered with a 67-yard, 11-play drive to take the lead again, 14–7. We were wondering, *Who are these guys?* It was a bitter lesson to learn, that anytime you put on that helmet you have to be ready to *earn* the victory. If you think the other team is going to hand it to you, you're drinking the wrong Kool-Aid.

The Irish put together an 81-yard drive topped off by a one-yard dive by John Cieszkowski for a touchdown to tie the score at 14. Missouri bounced back with a touchdown before half, helped by a fourth-down penalty against the Irish for going offside. But it was tough for us take because it seemed obvious that the Tigers' Don Johnson had fumbled before he started his jump for the end zone, and linebacker Jim Musuraca had recovered the ball for the Irish. However, the officials ruled he lost control of the ball after he was in the end zone. When we looked at film later, it was clear that the running back never had control of the ball. But this was long before the college game included any way to review and reverse calls.

By the second half, the rain was coming down harder, and the Irish found it hard to hang on to the ball. A fumbled punt and a fumbled kickoff led to two field goals by Missouri's Greg Hill. Things got worse with 10 minutes to go when Hill connected on another field goal, boosting the lead to 30–14. The Irish then mounted a desperate comeback attempt. Tommy Clements finished off one drive by running 13 yards for a score. When we got the ball back, we drove 70 yards for another touchdown. The key was a fourth-down play on which Tommy almost slipped dropping back to pass, but managed to sling a 36-yard pass to wideout Jim Roolf, who made a juggling catch on the Tigers 13-yard line. Two plays later, Andy Huff ran 12 yards off the left side for the TD. Unfortunately, we were stopped on two-point conversion tries after both of our late touchdowns, leaving the score at 30–26. After a failed onside kick, we got the ball back deep in our territory with time winding down, but Tommy's long pass was intercepted to seal the biggest upset of the season.

Ara put the blame on himself, which is what he always did. He said that he didn't prepare the team well enough. He also praised Missouri for playing a great football game, doing all the things they need to do to beat the Irish. He didn't raise the issue of the phantom touchdown that Missouri scored in the first half that should have been ruled a fumble. According to Bill Hickey, "Ara said in our staff meeting, 'If I had done that [make an issue of the call], it would look like we were crybabies. Let it be.'" Hickey added, "He had great composure and always thought about whom he was representing."

Game 6: TCU

Now we were the ones licking our wounds. Ara had his work cut out for him in getting us ready for Texas Christian, a team with great personnel, especially on defense. Ara knew our confidence was low and he did a masterful job of getting us ready for the Horned Frogs. All week at practice you could hear the urgency in the voices of Ara and the other coaches. They felt that we were a good team that didn't play with enough focus against Missouri. Ara worked us hard that week and made sure we were physically and mentally ready for TCU.

Ara gave an impassioned talk to us after the pregame warm-ups, just before we left the locker room for the game. This is how I recall it. He said, "All right, everyone up. Today we are going to face a very good football team in TCU. But you know what? These are the kind of games we come to Notre Dame to play. The thing is, men, I wish I was going out there to play. I want to take that kickoff. I want to run with that football. I want to block on those sweeps. I want to make those tackles on defense. I only wish that were possible. You men have that opportunity, so let's go out today and make the most of this opportunity and beat TCU."

At the end of his speech, you could feel that every guy on our team was ready to run through the wall for Ara. We went out and played a great game. A Horned Frogs' halfback, Mike Luttrell, had been quoted in the media saying that the Notre Dame defense wasn't very tough. The Irish defense had something to prove and they did, holding TCU to a game total of 132 yards—and Luttrell got only 26 yards on 13 carries. We pounded out 432 yards on the ground and another 88 yards in the air, 520 yards total. Eric Penick ran for 158 yards on 16 carries, scoring once late in the game. Jim Roolf scored on an 11-yard pass from Tommy Clements, and freshman Art Best scampered 57 yards for our other score in a 21–0 win. Our running game was clicking and we had a number of backs who could carry the load. Ara was happy about the performance—except for the six turnovers that we committed.

Game 7: Navy

Philadelphia is only about 90 miles from New York City, so the Navy game was a great chance for my family to see me play—not just my parents and brother, but also my grandfather, Joseph Gallo. He was a stowaway who came from Italy to the United States when he was 15 and had fought in World War I. He had retired from Con Edison and was in his midseventies at the time. He loved his family and he loved his country, so to see his grandson play in the first college game ever at Veterans Stadium, against a military school like Navy, was very meaningful to him. My mother shared in this pride that her father was feeling. The extended DiNardo family was also at the game, as were our St. Francis Prep coaches Vince O'Connor, Frank Nastro, and Brother Owen Capper. Gerry and I were inspired to play our best for our family and high school coaches and we were proud that two players representing our grade school and high school were the starting guards at the University of Notre Dame.

The game got off to a great start when Gary Diminick took the opening kickoff 84 yards for a touchdown. Gary was only 5'9" and 175 pounds but had great quickness, and he made a couple of nifty moves and followed his blocking on the runback. The Irish played almost a perfect first half, grinding out 282 yards rushing and racing to a 35–0 lead. The best defense is keeping the opponent's offense on the sideline, and that's what happened this day, as we rushed for 526 yards in total and ended with 597 yards in total offense. Andy Huff had his finest game rushing with 121 yards in 16 carries, and Eric Penick had 101 yards in 11 carries and one touchdown—even though he sat out most of the second half with a sore shoulder. Tommy Clements also ran for 95 yards and two touchdowns and directed the offense on several long scoring drives. We pretty much ran inside and outside at will. Navy put up some points in the second half to make the final score 42–23. Meanwhile, our reserves got some valuable experience on both sides of the ball, including sophomore running back Al Samuel, who ran for our last touchdown.

Game 8: Air Force

I enjoyed going to Colorado Springs, Colorado, for the Air Force game. It was the farthest west I had ever been, and I loved the mountains and the dry air. Air Force Academy is beautiful and the players from Air Force were class individuals. They played hard to the whistle, but were clean and showed good sportsmanship. When we came onto the field the air was crisp and snow was piled up against the stadium wall. It had snowed the week before the game and it was cold enough that it was still around. It was my first time playing at high altitude. Luckily, if you are in good shape it doesn't affect you that much, at least as a lineman.

Air Force had a good passing attack and a scrambling defense that caused a lot of havoc with teams. Even though they weren't very big, they had managed a 6–2 record coming into the game. Our defense changed from our usual 4-4-3 to a 4-3-4 to better defend the passing game of Air Force. It worked well, as we held Falcons quarterback Rich Haynie to a total of 99 yards passing, and we intercepted four of his throws. Junior Mike Townsend had three of those interceptions, on his way to leading the country with 10 picks that season and setting a Notre Dame single-season record that still stands.

We incurred quite a few penalties but were still able to successfully run the ball, piling up 294 yards running, which allowed us to control the clock and game on the way to a 21–7 victory. The Irish scored two touchdowns in the second quarter, the first on a seven-yard dash by Gary Diminick, the other on a 13-yard pass from Tommy Clements to Willie Townsend right before the half. After Air Force scored in the third quarter on a run by Joel Carlson, Andy Huff powered into the end zone with about five minutes left to put the game away. With the win, we were 7–1 and had our sights set on a sunny bowl game.

I had an interesting personal experience connected with the Air Force game. One evening, earlier in the season, my phone rang and the caller identified himself as Roxie Pomarico from Denver. He said he regularly watched the Notre Dame replays with Lindsey Nelson and Paul Hornung on Sunday mornings and he was a big Notre Dame fan. He was curious as to whether we were related in some way. He mailed me photos of his family and I shared the pictures with my grandfather, Frank Pomarico. My grandfather didn't know any Pomaricos except the ones in New York, but the Colorado Pomaricos looked very much like the Italians who lived in New York. It is possible they all may have been from the Italian town of Pomarico, and when they arrived as immigrants in New York they may have been given the name Pomarico based on their home.

We kept in touch, and before the Air Force contest Roxie called and said he was going to bring his clan from Denver down to the game. After the game, Roxie grabbed me as I was heading into the locker room and said that his family had planned a reception for me back in Denver. I explained the situation to Ara, who asked if I wanted to go. When I said yes, he replied that it was okay as long as I was back in time for our Sunday night meeting. So I rode back to Denver with a caravan of two busloads of Pomaricos, about 66 of them in all. After a 90-minute drive, we were back in Denver and went to a reception that was like a wedding, with an excellent Frank Sinatra–style singer named Frankie Reno. We stayed up late, and the next morning the family took me to the airport so I could get back to South Bend. I stayed in contact with the Colorado Pomaricos, but never found out for sure if we were related. But I appreciated how they reached out to me, and we became lifetime friends.

Game 9: Miami

Going into the final home game, against the Miami Hurricanes, the word was that a win would get us a bid to the Orange Bowl game on New Year's Day. The Hurricanes had a good defense featuring a strong front line, with Rubin Carter and Tony Cristiani. They also had a set of linebackers who were tough and had the speed to cover a lot of ground.

Our offensive line was fired up for the challenge, and we controlled the ball with drives of 90 and 48 yards. The students were just as excited about the Orange Bowl possibility. They brought oranges to the game and began to toss them around. And because it snowed during the week, they also threw snowballs at each other and at the players as the Irish built a 20–3 lead. Our touchdowns were scored by Willie Townsend on a 10-yard pass from Tommy Clements, and by Tommy and Andy Huff on short runs. The thing is, the lead could have been 21–3. On the extra-point try following our second touchdown, a snowball came close to holder Brian Doherty just as the snap came to him. Brian got distracted, bobbled the ball, and we missed the extra point.

The muff didn't seem to make that much of a difference at the time, but it loomed large when Miami scored two touchdowns in the fourth quarter to make the score 20–17. Late in the game, the Hurricanes got close enough for a 46-yard field goal attempt but missed it wide. The Irish lucked out and we were on our way to the Orange Bowl. It's hard to imagine, but we could have lost that opportunity because of a snowball.

Game 10: USC

At 8–1 going into the nationally televised final regular season game at USC, we still had a chance for a special season. Southern Cal and Alabama were the only undefeated teams left in the country, and USC was ranked No. 1. Assistant coach Bill Hickey said the strong feelings between Notre Dame and USC were enhanced by a certain familiarity. "Every member of the Notre Dame coaching staff knew those Southern Cal kids because we were recruiting them," he said. "We were in the living room with their parents. That's one reason the game was special."

USC had one of the most talented college teams ever in 1972. Its roster included 13 players who would earn All-American status during their careers and 33 who eventually played in the NFL. On offense, the Trojans were led by quarterback Mike Rae, a couple of outstanding running backs in Anthony Davis and Sam Cunningham, and wide receiver Lynn Swann. Linebackers Richard Wood and Charles Anthony were the meat of the defense, and the USC strategy was to funnel everything to them. They were fast, physical, and smart. Our offense was hard to defend because we weren't predictable. But even when we did run a play well, USC had such athletic talent that they recovered quickly and made our gains smaller than they could have been.

It was hard enough to go up against all that talent, but USC also had the backing of a large, crazy crowd in the Coliseum. They had that Trojan horse called Traveler that would run up and down the field when they scored—and in those days they scored a lot. And they always seemed to have the prettiest cheerleaders, who looked like they came off of Hollywood movie sets.

This was the day that Anthony Davis became a USC legend. He began his sensational game by taking the opening kickoff and running 97 yards for a touchdown. Davis was not a very big guy, but had great quickness and could see the field really well. By the end of the game, Davis would tally six TDs, more than any opposing player had ever scored against Notre Dame.

In the first quarter alone, Davis put up three touchdowns, the Trojans led 19–3, and the Irish were reeling. But in the second quarter we drove 77 yards in 10 plays as Tommy Clements threw five yards to Willie Townsend for the score that made it 19–10 at end of the second quarter. I felt that we were in this game, we could play with these guys. During the intermission, we found out that Alabama had lost to Auburn, so we had a legitimate shot at No. 1 if we could win this game.

In the third quarter, Davis got his fourth TD on an 11-yard run following an interception, which put Southern Cal up 25–10. But we still had a lot of fight in us. On the next possession, Tommy Clements threw to Mike Creaney for 36 yards and followed it up with a 20-yard pass to Gary Diminick to get us down to the USC 11-yard line. On fourth-and-2, Art Best drove to the line and fumbled the ball away to the Trojans. That wasn't the end of our comeback, however. Mike Townsend came up with an interception and we were right back in business in Trojans territory. Tommy Clements threw a swing pass to Gary Diminick for an 11-yard touchdown and the score was 25–17.

The momentum had changed. We got the ball back and stayed on the ground, sweeping and driving up the middle against one of the toughest defenses in college football. I loved the challenge of playing against linebacker Richard Wood, one of the best to ever play at USC. Their defensive scheme put the linebackers right up on the line of scrimmage; they just *dared* you to try and run the ball at them. I would fire out and drive into Richard with my face right on his chest and punch my fist on the inside to drive him back. I then would arch my back and keep driving my legs to get him to move back. There were some stalemates, but a few times we were able to get the ball carrier past him for some good yardage. When we got to the 10-yard line, Tommy Clements threw a rocket to Mike Creaney, who made a diving catch for the touchdown. The score at 25–23, we went for the two-point conversion and missed—but the Trojans knew they were in a ballgame.

Then all of our momentum vanished in a matter of seconds. Anthony Davis took the ensuing kickoff and went 96 yards for the touchdown. The Trojans scored twice more and went on to win 45–23. I remember assistant coach Tom Pagna urging us to play as hard as we could, but in the end the day belonged to John McKay's Southern Cal team, which claimed the national championship.

Ara was quoted after the game as saying he was confident we would have won if Davis hadn't returned a second kick for a touchdown. We'll never know. Our 1972 team was good, but not great. There were times when we could have really put our opponent out of the game, but we failed to do so because of turnovers and other mistakes. Still, it was apparent that we had the nucleus for a great ball-control offense that would be tough to stop. We would have to get a stronger defense with more speed, but we had leadership on defense from the juniors who would be coming back as seniors.

First, however, we had an Orange Bowl date with Nebraska, which had won the national championship in 1971. A lot of the same guys were back in 1972.

The Orange Bowl

Cold, snowy weather forced us inside the Athletic and Convocation Center for many of the practices before Christmas. We were allowed to go home for the holiday, but we were to report back for workouts the day after Christmas. We watched a lot of film on Nebraska. They had lost twice (both times by three points) and also tied once, which was hard to believe when you saw them play and the kind of talent they had. The Cornhuskers had extra motivation because this was going to be the last game for retiring head coach Bob Devaney, who had guided Nebraska to two national championships.

They had a great offense, led by Heisman Trophy winner Johnny Rodgers—not only an outstanding runner and pass receiver but also one of the best kick returners ever. Quarterback David Humm and halfback Gary Dixon were good players who benefited from a big, strong, athletic offensive line. It was going to be a challenge for the Fighting Irish. The Cornhuskers defense was led by Rich Glover, the winner of both the Outland Trophy and Lombardi Award as the country's best interior lineman. Tackle John Dutton and end Willie Harper, like Glover, went on to play in the NFL.

We didn't have anything to play for in terms of national rankings, but we wanted to show we could compete with the elite teams in the country. However, things started to go sour two days before the game, when running backs Eric Penick and Art Best made an unscripted cameo appearance in the Orange Bowl Parade. "Art and I went over to the mayor's float, and he was a little tipsy," Eric said. "And he said, 'Come on boys, come on up here.' Art and I were crazy kind of guys. We didn't think anything of it." It was fun until the float went past the grandstand, and Ara caught sight of the players. "Ara was so sore, I thought I was going to die. He put a laser on us with his eyes," Eric said.

No one chastised the players, but when they got to the stadium for the game, their names were not on the depth chart. Ara told the players to stand next to him the whole game. "I felt like poop-a-doop because I let the team down," said Eric, a sophomore who was our leading rusher that year. "But what I really felt bad about is that I embarrassed my mother. She was somebody who was always there for me, who cared for me, who kept me from knowing how tough things really were. Everybody told me how blessed I was to have my mother." As a result of that incident, "I promised myself I would never embarrass my mother like that again," he said.

This was the third straight year that Nebraska was playing in the Orange Bowl, so it was old hat to them. They weren't fazed by all the fuss and the media surrounding the game, they were there to win a football game. We kicked off, and the Cornhuskers came out with a surprise. "Normally, Johnny Rodgers played slot or wide receiver, and our plan was to put Tim Rudnick on him," Gary Potempa said. "But when they broke the huddle on the first series, Rodgers was playing I-back, which he never did before. We almost had to call a timeout because Tim didn't know where to go." Nebraska drove down the field on that opening possession and Rodgers ran eight yards for the game's first score.

On Nebraska's second series, our All-American defensive tackle, Greg Marx, came out of the game with a shoulder injury. In the second quarter, Nebraska lengthened the lead to 14–0 on a one-yard run by Gary Dixon. It seemed like Nebraska was getting faster as we were trying to dig out of the hole. The backbreaker came a little later in the second quarter. Humm, the Nebraska quarterback, threw a lateral to Rodgers in the flat, and when our secondary came up to defend a run, Rodgers stopped and lofted a pass to a wide-open Frosty Anderson for a 52-yard TD and a 20–0 lead.

In the second half, Rodgers scored two more touchdowns on short runs, and then caught a 50-yard scoring pass for good measure. All told, the Heisman Trophy winner scored four touchdowns and threw for another, a spectacular end to his college career. We didn't score until the fourth quarter, on a Tommy Clements throw to Pete Demmerle. The final score was 40–6, the worst loss in Ara's tenure. It was a reminder that no matter how good you think you are, you can still get your ass kicked. And that's just what happened to us that day.

It was a sad way for seniors like Mike Creaney, John Dampeer, Greg Marx, Andy Huff, Jim O'Malley, John Cieszkowski, Jim Musuraca, and others to go out in their last game for Notre Dame. Their four years were full of hard work physically and academically. They had bonds that were like family, and suddenly it was over on a disappointing note. "It was a tough way to leave the football field," said John Cieszkowski. "I remember my dad saying, 'There's a reason for this, and you'll figure it out someday.' My dad and I came to conclusion that, when things are really bad, really ugly, that's when you have to push through. Life goes on."

After the game, I left the locker room feeling terrible. That's when I heard Eddie Broderick, one of our academic advisors, say, "Hey, guys, keep your heads up. You are not dead." It made me think about how Ara always said it is not a shame to get knocked down; the important thing was to get up and keep fighting.

Offensive lineman Max Wasilevich recalled the team meeting we had a couple of weeks after the Orange Bowl: "Everybody is talking, and as soon as Coach Parseghian walks into the room, everybody shuts up. You could hear a pin drop. He goes up to the front, looks at us, and says, 'I just had two weeks of hell. I had to explain to all the alumni why we looked so awful and I guarantee we're never going to play like that again.'" Max said that Ara promised that spring practice would be tough. "We had been humbled, and he laid out the challenge for us: you have to get better," Max said.

The players voted on captains for the next season, and the outcome was so close that Ara did something he had never done before: he went with three captains instead of two. Dave Casper was the team captain, Mike Townsend was defensive captain, and I was named offensive captain. We had a Wisconsin farm kid, a smooth black guy from Ohio, and an Italian from New York. It made for a mix of leadership that was determined to erase the memory of the Nebraska debacle.

"We were embarrassed by Johnny Rodgers and his teammates," Mike said. "We were embarrassed so bad, we knew we had to come up a long way to erase that game." He said being elected a captain was an honor. "It made me realize what I meant to my teammates, and I wanted to lead by example. I wanted to make sure, whether you were on the prep team or the first team, that you felt you were a part of this team."

Dave Casper had broken convention somewhat by telling teammates that he would like to be a captain, but then Dave was an unconventional guy. "Because of all the different positions I played I thought it would not be a bad thing to be captain," he said. "But I have been accused of being different, so I was afraid people might think I didn't want to be captain."

As a 21-year-old, Dave felt that being able to go to a bar was an important part of socializing with friends and he said he resisted a plea from an assistant coach who urged him to persuade our players to abstain from drinking. "The year before we did not have a great year, but having a few beers was not the problem," he said. "We didn't have anyone on the [1973] team that was disruptive. The leadership of the team was still coming from Ara Parseghian, but I knew we had a bunch of good guys. They did not need anyone from within their ranks keeping them in line."

I was very honored to be one of the captains on a Notre Dame team, a feeling made even stronger because my role model, Larry DiNardo, had also been a captain. I was not a rah-rah guy. Instead, I tried to lead by example. I believe leaders should be the hardest workers on any team, and if they are, then their work ethic and attitude become contagious. I worked hard in the weight room, in film study, in practice and in the classroom—everything I could do to be eligible and prepared.

My teammates and I had experienced the ashes of defeat. We were determined to rise again in 1973.

CHAPTER 14

Lessons in Leadership

The results on the field testify to Ara Parseghian's ability to lead. When he took over as head coach at Notre Dame in 1964, the school had gone five straight seasons without a winning record, including a 2–7 mark in 1963. He immediately turned around the program, coming within a whisker of winning the national championship in 1964 with a team that finished 9–1. Over the course of 11 years at Notre Dame, Ara's teams won two national championships and put up a record of 95–17–4, putting him in a pantheon with legendary coaches Knute Rockne and Frank Leahy.

Ara's Knights grew as players and men under his leadership and many were inspired to become leaders in their own right, whether in coaching, business, or in their personal lives. Here are some of the traits they identified as Parseghian's key leadership qualities.

High Expectations: Ara set the national championship as the goal for his teams every season, and he had similarly lofty expectations off the field. Joe Theismann compared Ara to today's top NFL coaches such as Bill Belichick in the way they "create an environment where the expectation is not just success but great success." Joe referred to the fact that the Fighting Irish, when they returned to bowl games after a 45-year absence, could have chosen to go to the Orange Bowl in Miami to play a lesser team in a warmer climate. "But Texas was No. 1 in the nation, and we wanted to play the best," he said of the choice to go to the Cotton Bowl in Dallas instead. As running back Jack Clements put it, "Everything was a search for excellence—academically, athletically, and spiritually."

Dan Morrin, my former roommate, who played offensive line, recalled Ara spelling out his expectations: "Ara said, 'You guys may not be the best football players in the country. But every Saturday, there are millions of people who expect you to be the best. We didn't recruit you because you are great football players, because you can't be as great as everyone thinks. We recruited you because we think you can live up to the expectations of a Notre Dame person. When you get out of here, they're going to expect great things from you guys. And we think you can live up to those expectations."

He continued, "Ara was putting personal responsibility in your corner and it was up to you to live up to it. He was looking at you in that way—you are a great guy, and if you don't do great things, I'm disappointed in you. And he looked at everybody—black, white, big, small—in a way that said he expected a lot out of you." Defensive back Mike Townsend said he has high standards for the people who work for him. "Like Coach Parseghian, I give every tool I possibly can to make sure my people can be successful, because if they are successful, you are successful," said Mike, a supervisor for a pharmaceuticals company in Ohio.

Honesty: "Ara didn't BS us. He was a straight shooter," said linebacker Tim Sullivan, who has always taken the same approach with high school teams he has coached in Texas and with me at Lumen Christi High School in Jackson, Michigan. "If someone is truthful, you can trust them."

Several highly recruited prospects—including Thom Gatewood, Gary Potempa, and Eric Penick—were impressed that Ara simply promised them a chance to compete for a position and to get a great education, while other schools were promising starting positions and even stardom. Terry Hanratty said he went through the same thing: "Some people, you listen to them and you know they're full of crap," he said. "With Ara, you could trust what he told you. Everybody else basically offered me a starting job sophomore year.

Ara said, 'You will have a chance to compete for a starting job at Notre Dame.'" Terry said that made "a lot more sense," and that Ara told him, "'Competition will bring out the best in you. You can't be afraid of it.'"

"Ara always did things the right way," said defensive lineman Mike Fanning. "He walked his talk. A lot of coaches have the gift of gab but the players start to see through them." Former sports information director Roger Valdiserri said you always knew where you stood with Ara. "You would follow him into the front lines. It all goes back to his honesty and sincerity," according to Roger. "I asked him one time, 'Would you ever pay a player to go to Notre Dame?' He said, 'Absolutely not. If I paid one player or two players, how could I tell them what they're doing wrong? How can you lead if on the sideline you're cheating?'"

Communication: The lines of communication ran both ways with Ara. He was very clear about what he expected, but he was also open to hearing what others had to say. Dave Casper compared Ara's communications skills with those of John Madden, his coach with the Oakland Raiders. "Leadership is not something imposed on people. You have to give people some idea of things to do in order to follow you, and Ara set a very clear path of what to do," Dave said. "All the good coaches I've played for had this quality of being easy to follow with clear direction during practice." John Huarte added, "His voice is earnest and clear, and he didn't waste words. You knew what he wanted, now let's go do it."

Sometimes Ara didn't even have to use words to communicate—he just used what we called, "the look." "Head slightly cocked. One black eyebrow arched. An expression that froze you in place," is the way offensive lineman Steve Quehl described it. Linebacker Rich Thomann said, "You knew right where you stood with him by just the way he looked at you. He didn't have to say anything."

Assistant coach Mike Stock said Ara was a good listener. "If you had something you needed to say, he may not have agreed but he listened, whether it was on the field or in meetings." Wally Moore, another assistant, who sadly passed away in 2014, recalled a staff meeting after the Irish had lost a game. "He said to Paul Shoults, 'Paul, why did we lose this game?' Paul gave an idea or two. Then to John Ray. Every man gave their idea as to why we lost the game." After going around the room, Ara summed up the things that had been done poorly. At the end, according to Wally, Ara said, "Now let's work all week to solve these problems."

Great assistants: Joe Theismann compared Ara with Joe Gibbs, Theismann's coach when he guided the Washington Redskins to a Super Bowl win in 1982. "I think one of the greatest qualities of a leader is who you surround yourself with. Both surrounded themselves with great coaches and great teachers of the game of football," Joe said. "Ara knew the way he wanted his football program to be run and he hired the men who ran his football program for him that way. He empowered the people that he hired to teach others."

"People bought into Ara in part because of the assistant coaches who surrounded him," said running back Rocky Bleier. "The loyalty of Ara's staff was not lost on the players." Terry Hanratty added, "Ara was a teacher. And Tom Pagna was the same. If Ara was busy you were with Tom, if Tom was busy you were with Ara."

Ara also empowered sports information director Roger Valdiserri to do his job of handling the press, freeing Ara up to focus on football. "On Sunday, I would write a press release," Roger said. "We thought alike, so I knew what he wanted to say and I quoted him. Ara would come up Sunday night and say, 'Okay, what did I say today?'" Roger came up with the idea of posing three questions in the press release. There was a phone number listed, so the media could call in and hear Ara giving a prerecorded answer. "It saved him time. So many radio reporters wanted to call and talk to him, and he couldn't take that time."

Humility: One reason Ara earned the loyalty of his staff and players is that he deflected accolades away from himself, shining the spotlight on others. He took responsibility for the bad things that happened to the team and he had a policy of never criticizing a player to the media.

Greg Blache tells a story that highlights how Ara shared the rewards with those around him. Greg had been a freshman walk-on whose career was ended by injury, but Ara sensed he had had interest in coaching and brought him on staff, first as an undergrad and then as a graduate assistant. The latter position covered his tuition and books, plus a $1,000 stipend—not much for a guy who was married and had a young boy at home.

"Around Christmas, when the season was finished and before recruiting, I was working construction in Elkhart, which paid four dollars an hour. I had a raggedy old Oldsmobile. At lunch, I'd say, okay that's 16 dollars. If I make it through the afternoon, that's $32. We were so poor, we had this Christmas tree that was about 20 inches tall, set on a table," Greg said.

About that time, Greg was invited to the coaches' Christmas party at Ara's house. During the party, Greg said Ara was handing out envelopes to the assistants. "Ara pulls me aside and says, 'Here, Greg. Here's a little Christmas present for you.' I put the envelope in my pocket. I'm so poor, it's burning in my pocket." Greg went to the bathroom to check out what was inside. "I'm thinking $25. That would be almost a day's work. I open the thing up, and it's $500. My knees got weak. I almost buckled right there." He went back in the party, called his wife aside, and showed her what was in the envelope. "She said, 'Oh, Greg, we can't accept that.'

"I went back to the coach and said, 'Can I talk to you?' He said, 'Sure, Greg, what's the problem?' I looked at the envelope, and he said, 'What, is that not enough?' I said 'No, coach, I can't accept this.' He said 'No, no, no. That's money from the TV show I do. I split it up and give it to you guys for your Christmas present. You've earned every penny of it and more. You take it and you and your family have a great Christmas.'"

Greg said, "I went home and I threw out the little Christmas tree. I said, 'I'm going to get my kid a real Christmas tree.' Certain things like that stand out in your mind forever." Greg went on to have a long, successful coaching career, and he calls Ara "my guardian angel." He said he never made an important career move without asking Ara's advice. "He gave me the opportunity to be a football coach, but more important, he gave me the training, the foundation, and the blueprint to be a good football coach."

Preparedness: "Ara was very well organized, and I think everyone went into each game knowing that we were as prepared as we could possibly be for that particular game," said Tommy Clements, summing up what we all felt.

As Terry Hanratty put it, "We were never surprised by anything the opposing team did. Ara saw their tendencies. We would work on it." Dave Casper said being "fundamentally sound" was a big part of the preparation. "We ran a lot of drills that we didn't really appreciate at the time. But when you get into a game, you go back to the fundamentals," he said.

"He was always prepared," Gary Potempa said. "I never saw him late for anything. The way he talked, it seemed like he had every speech to us prepared. He could be humorous but also serious. As he's gotten older he is still the same person." Roger Valdiserri, sports information director, said Ara's preparation extended to how he handled the media. "He would save one hour every Thursday when he would talk with them," Roger said. After a home game, Ara talked to the press in a small room at the back of the locker room. "He knew what the media was after. He would answer all of their questions, and he was very direct with them."

Dan Morrin said he learned valuable lessons from Ara in the importance of being organized and prepared. Dan runs an electrical construction business with 120 employees. "Like football, life is a game of attrition. People get hurt, get sick, they don't show up, so you have to have replacements," Dan said. "I have a board with a depth chart, which includes where people are on the job, who is the leader, who is the second lead guy, who is my third lead guy," Dan said. "If something happens, everybody knows what to do."

Execution: "Ara wanted you to execute all the time," said defensive back Luther Bradley. "He sat up on that perch and knew what was going on on both sides of the field. I'd hear him say, 'Luther, why did you go over there?' Or, 'Luther, you've got to get deeper.' He was about execution and doing things right."

"The biggest thing I learned is that you have to put the time in," said defensive lineman George Hayduk. "You have to pay attention to the particulars. I was in sales for most of my career. Showing up, being organized, taking care of the little things like Ara did was important in my profession." Mike Townsend said one of the most important lessons he learned from Ara was "No matter what you do, make sure you do it to the best of your capabilities. And if you do that, you can reach achievements that you never thought you could."

Discipline: Ara was a very good golfer who loved the game and played it frequently during the off-season. But according to his son, Mike Parseghian, "He always took pride in the fact that when the fall meetings started, he hung up his clubs and wouldn't play again until the spring." That was part of Ara's self-discipline, and he taught us the need to be disciplined in our own lives.

"It was ingrained in us: in order to be successful, we had to really work at it," said offensive lineman Tom Bolger. "Things don't just happen. You have to put in the time and effort, the planning, and everything around it." Tim Sullivan recalled something that Ara often emphasized: "We are creatures of habit, so you need to work hard to get good habits." Tim said Ara made the point that this would apply as much to our lives after graduation as it did to our college football career.

Gary Potempa got married in 1973, after our last regular season game against Miami, and moved into an apartment in South Bend. The first time he had to go to a meeting to begin preparation for the Sugar Bowl, his car wouldn't start. "I ran about three miles back to the ACC, came walking in, and everybody's already sitting there. I'm still wearing a hat. Ara said to me, 'Potempa, this meeting's for you. Where the hell have you been?' Of course, I know that he doesn't really want an excuse. I just said that I was sorry and went to sit down, and he said, 'What the hell are you doing?' I said, 'What, Coach?' He said, 'Nobody's supposed to wear a hat in the building. Take that hat off.'"

Gary said, "He treated you like a man. You're still kind of a kid, but you start to realize that it's up to you. You have to be responsible for yourself and try to do the right thing, be on time, do all the stuff that's important when you're in the real world."

Positivity: "With Ara, the coaching was not dull or negative. It was a lot of positive influence on the players," John Huarte said. "And I think that's part of leadership. You can't be pounding people down. You have to pick them up and encourage them. People need encouragement. They don't need constant negativity."

Ara's positive attitude built up the confidence and enthusiasm of his players, according to Bill Hickey. "He could get a good college player who could never be considered good enough for the pros and he could make that kid believe he could play better than anyone else on Saturday. The kids were extremely motivated and they wanted to back up his belief in him," Hickey said.

Terry Hanratty recalled his own worst game—throwing five interceptions against USC in 1967: "Monday at practice, Ara called me aside and said, 'What do you think happened Saturday?' I said, 'Coach, sometimes you look out there, and there are 18 defensive backs. Sometimes you look out there, and there's two. And it was just one of those days, I couldn't find the right people.' He said, 'Okay, go out there and work your ass off. We'll be better this week.'"

Flexibility: Ara was flexible enough to adapt to his personnel and the situation. "He was always looking to get the best guys on the field," said linebacker Gary Potempa. During Gary's sophomore year, 1971, a lot of running backs went down to injury, and Ara asked if he could play running back. "I said, 'Hell, yeah, I'll do whatever you need.' Ara asked me if I could catch. And then he said, 'Come on, I want to play catch with you.' He threw some passes to me, and then he said, 'Okay, get over there. You can play running back,'" Gary said. The next season, Ara put Gary on defensive line for the USC game. "The next thing you know, I'm chasing the quarterback in the Coliseum."

Ara's innovative "mirror defense," unveiled against the Texas wishbone offense in the 1971 Cotton Bowl, was an example of how his flexibility enabled him to come up with creative solutions. At different points during his Notre Dame coaching career, he also adapted the offense to fit the skills of his players. Terry Hanratty was a strong-armed quarterback, and the Irish played a pro-style offense with him dropping back into a conventional pocket. With Joe Theismann, there were more unbalanced lines and rollouts where the quarterback could throw or take off and run.

After the 1971 season, Ara changed the offense again, bringing in a wing-T philosophy that took advantage of the ability of our offensive linemen to pull and trap and fit very well with Tommy Clements' gift for carrying out fakes and the fact we had several good running backs. "That is part of what made Ara a great coach," Tommy said. "He took his staff to Delaware, and based on the types of players we had, he determined it would make us better if we ran [their] kind of offense. What he really tried to do was fit our offense to our personnel instead of fitting our personnel to our offense."

Resilience: For all the success that Ara's teams had, there were also lessons to be learned from the defeats. The saying, "We have no breaking point" applied to life as well as football. As John Huarte said, "Anybody who plays football has some bad things happen—injuries, a particular coach doesn't like you, or some other disappointment. Later in life, in business, there are disappointments, and you have to work your way through them."

"The biggest lesson I learned from Ara was how to overcome adversity," said defensive lineman Tom Creevey. "He thought the mark of a good player and a man was to get up after being knocked down. If you were feeling sorry for yourself, he wasn't going to give you a break. You had to fight through it and make your own break."

Eric Penick said he has been through "ups and downs in life," but Ara was always available to counsel him. "He always told me that a man with character is a man who goes through adversity and comes out the other end as good or better than he was before." Eric works in real estate and is also a salesman for an energy company. But his real passion is working as a chaplain with incarcerated young people at the Dallas Youth Village. "It allows me to take all I learned at Notre Dame and show the care and compassion I learned from Ara," Eric said. "I can talk to kids and tell them 'Your life is not over. You can do positive things for yourself, and I'm going to be there with you. If anybody tells you they don't love you, I tell them I love you, and God's love for you will be there forever.'"

Teamwork: Mike Townsend said Ara "routinely placed in your mind that you're only as good as your weakest link." As a result, Mike said, "As a team, we tried to make everybody good whether you were on the prep team or the starting team. Everybody had a sense of worth because Coach saw us the same." Mike noted that Ara wasn't Catholic, "but he had all of us going to Mass. Everyone went because we were part of a team."

Pete Schivarelli was a reserve defensive lineman, but he felt he was an important part of the team. "Ara always said that 'each and every one of you gets reviewed on a daily basis,' and it was true," he said. Offensive lineman Max Wasilevich said Ara drove home the point that "We win as a team and we lose as a team. Everybody had to work together to get to the ultimate pinnacle." As an ophthalmologist, Max has carried that lesson into his practice, citing the example of doing a cataract surgery. "It's a team. You've got the anesthesiologist, the nurse in the room, the scrub techs, the post-op nurses. I learned from my experience with Ara that you're part of a team, and you have to work together to get a job done."

Motivation: Coach Parseghian was "a great motivator" who was skilled at knowing how and when to bring his players to the right emotional state for games, said Gerry DiNardo, who carried what he learned from Ara to his own head coaching jobs at Vanderbilt, LSU, and Indiana. Gerry said Ara gave his best talks before games against the worst teams in order to drive out overconfidence. "Before the big games, he knew we were ready. The big games intensified practice, and a pregame speech before a big game is not all that important," Gerry said. "We needed to see his face. We needed to hear his voice quiver, because then we knew he was ready."

John Cieszkowski recalled how Ara urged us to "strive do something a little better than you think you can do it, because you can always do it a little better. Another big thing, he said, 'You've got to do it with passion.' He passed on a passion for doing things right and trying a little harder each time," John said.

Fairness: Ara and his staff would talk about every player every day. So if they made a decision to move a guy from second team to first team—or to move someone in the other direction—it was not a decision made lightly or hastily. Ara wanted everyone's opinion. He was going to pull the trigger, but his choice would be an educated one.

Jack Clements, who made the team as a walk-on, said he was disappointed in how the movie *Rudy* portrayed the nonscholarship athletes as just cannon fodder for the top units. "The walk-ons on our team had a tremendous opportunity," Jack said. "We were treated no different than scholarship players relative to where we were on the depth chart. "

If a player did something that required discipline, Ara believed in giving a second chance, but he would make it clear what was at stake. "Ara's attitude was that if you were not willing to contribute and be a part of the program, you were making a decision," said assistant coach Greg Blache. "He would give people a second chance. He would say, 'You have options. You can come back here and be a productive player and be part of the community or you can go home and continue to do the things you've done.'"

You could say Ara treated everyone alike, but with one exception. "On the football team, Dad did a good thing. He treated me harder than anybody else," said Ara's son, Mike Parseghian, a high school All-State running back who walked on at Notre Dame "It wasn't favoritism, it was reverse favoritism. I think the rest of the team understood that and realized I wasn't getting any favors, so it probably made it easier for me to make friends with teammates."

In the spring of 1975, Mike suffered an injury that ended his playing career. He went on to coach the Keenan interhall team—and he used his dad as "a sounding board" on how to coach. "Between the two of us, we were pretty good because we won the campus championship two years in a row. My mom was terrified that I was going to drop out of premed and go into coaching," said Mike, who chose the medical path after all and is now an orthopedic surgeon.

Caring: Ara was not buddy-buddy with the players, but you knew he had your best interests in mind as a person, not just a player. "He seemed to distance himself from the players, allowing the assistant coaches to be the go-between," said running back Andy Huff. The attitude was a "professional distance," according to quarterback Bill Etter. "He had to have that so he could stay objective."

Terry Hanratty called Ara the second biggest influence in his life, after his father. "Ara really cared about you. Once I got called in for cutting class, and he chewed my ass off," said Terry, who realized the session was a result of the coach's concern for him as a person. Defensive back Luther Bradley also had a conversation about academics with Ara. "After football season was over, I wanted to run track," Luther said. "He pulled out my grades and said they were not as good as he would like to see. He grilled me to make sure I understood I had to do better in my grades."

George Hayduk said he also saw Ara as a father figure. "One of my most vivid memories is that, after practice, he would get us all together and he knew exactly what to say. If we had a practice where things weren't going good, he knew exactly what to say to get us back up again. He was very insightful about what young people were living through." After the Navy game in George's senior season, Ara awarded him the game ball. "I've told my daughter, you have to sign something, and your heirs have to sign, that you will never get rid of that football. If you do, I'll come back to haunt you. That ball is priceless."

Players saw another side of Ara outside of the football arena. "I'll never forget when my dad came up for a game," Jack Clements said. "We were standing outside the Convo [the Athletic and Convocation Center], and Ara walked out, walked over, and said, 'Hi, Mr. Clements. How's everything in Atchison?'" referring to Jack's home town in Kansas. "That made my dad feel like he was on cloud nine. Here I am, a prep team guy, and to come up to my dad, to know who he was and where he's from was one of the most genuine things I can imagine."

Thom Gatewood was a freshman, walking from campus into town, when someone honked a horn at him. It was Ara, driving a Ford Thunderbird (part of his deal as a commercial spokesman for Ford), and he was offering Tom a ride. Tom said he had broken his finger and was down about not contributing to the team. "You kind of want to run and hide from the coach when you're not doing what you're supposed to be doing," he said. But for the next several minutes, "we were talking about everyday things. The breath was taken away because I was sitting up front with the coach," according to Thom. "He was talking to me like I was a regular guy, and we were on the same plane. He had some things of his kids' in the car, and I could see that he was a real guy."

One time during the summer, Ara invited players over to his house for a barbecue. As he was cooking burgers, I commented about his beautiful home and the swimming pool in the backyard. He told me the whole family enjoyed it but that the main reason for the pool was that it gave his daughter Karen, who suffered from multiple sclerosis, a chance to cool off and exercise in the summer. I realized that this great leader of young men was also a caring father dealing with life's realities, which were not always easy.

Andy Huff summed up the overwhelming sentiment of Ara's Knights. "Overall, Ara has certainly been one of the most key and noteworthy people I've had the pleasure of knowing in my life, perhaps because he was so dedicated and really cared. This certainly came through in his work ethic and focus."

Ara was someone who people wanted to follow. He rallied us to a common purpose and inspired confidence that we could achieve anything we set out to do. Ara made leadership look easy, but of course it never is. His position required him to deal with many different personalities and be able to react to constantly changing situations. In the clutch, we followed him because we trusted him, and we trusted him because of the collection of character traits that we saw in him.

CHAPTER 15

Rising From the Ashes

The end of the 1972 season forced the coaching staff and players to take stock of weaknesses that had been exposed by USC and Nebraska. Each had scored more than 40 points against us. Ara Parseghian was a man on a mission to bring Notre Dame back to a point where it could go toe to toe with the best teams in the country.

"Ara did not want to go through another loss like the one to Nebraska," Tommy Clements said. "That loss was probably the catalyst for the season we had next year. It started in spring practices, which were very difficult and physical, with people competing for positions."

Ara's staff was recruiting more speed on the defensive side of the ball and there were whispers that some top talent would be joining us in the fall. Meanwhile, the returning players were working on drills designed to improve speed and quickness. In addition, some skill-position offensive players were moved to the defensive side of the ball, including Tom Creevey, a former high school quarterback who went from being a reserve back and wideout to defensive end. "I think you build toughness by playing tough every day, and that's why it was such a physical spring," Tom said. "I'm not sure Ara thought toughness was a given with us after the way we played against Nebraska, so in spring practices he instilled in us that we were going to be tough. I think he wanted to get all the cobwebs out from the Nebraska game and get us ready mentally as well as physically for the coming season."

On defense, we needed to replace some very talented players who had graduated, including All-American tackle Greg Marx and linebackers Jim O'Malley and Jim Musuraca. We also had lost safety Kenny Schlezes, who had unofficially served as our defensive quarterback . Fortunately, we had some guys ready to step up. Linebackers who were hungry to show what they could do included senior Gary Potempa and juniors Greg Collins, Sherm Smith, and Drew Mahalic. Two other seniors, Tom Devine and Tim Sullivan, were moved from linebacker to defensive end. Tom had tremendous potential, but four knee operations had slowed him down. Tim had size, speed, and great natural strength, and he added a lot of leadership with his experience and knowledge of football.

Those position shifts coincided with a change from a four-man front to a five-man defensive line that spring. Middle linebacker Gary Potempa, a strong and tenacious player, was moved up to the line to play middle guard. "Our defensive ends were like linebackers. They were fast," Gary said. "We were scrimmaging all the time that spring. I think Ara was testing whether this new idea was going to work."

At defensive tackle, we were looking forward to the return of sophomore Steve Niehaus, who had made a big impression his freshman year until he got hurt before the Missouri game. He was sorely missed the second half of the season. Steve had a gift that made him nearly impossible to block, which forced an offense to do things out of rhythm. He was a quiet guy but spoke volumes with his play. He was held out of spring drills because the coaches already knew what he could do, but Steve lobbied to get back and he returned to the field before the end of spring football. He showed no ill effects of his knee surgery and he was still quick as a cat. Other guys that were looking very good on the defensive line were George Hayduk, Jim Stock, Tom Creevey, Tom Fine, Mike Fanning, and Kevin Nosbusch.

The secondary was going to be led by free safety Mike Townsend, our tri-captain who led the country in interceptions in 1972. Mike said that his experience playing offense in high school helped him anticipate where the ball would go. "I could see a play develop and know who the potential receiver might be if it was a pass play, or if it was a run play where I had to get to the point of attack," he said. On a pass play, Mike would focus on the shoulders of the quarterback, whether they turned left or right. "Then you decide if he has the ball high enough to throw to the deep guy, or low where you know he's going to throw to the short guy. As a free safety, you basically are able to direct yourself to the apex, and hopefully you can get there before the ball gets there and you can steal it."

Also in the defensive backfield was Reggie Barnett, a player with a lot of speed and the smarts to match. Tim Rudnick played safety and returned punts and kickoffs. Other defensive backs were seniors Jim Zlock and Mike Naughton, juniors Mike Parker and Jim Chauncey, and sophomores Bob Zanot and Tom Lopienski. All would get a chance to play for Ara, and they gave our team a lot of depth.

The offensive team had the potential to generate a dominant running attack, starting with a strong offensive line that had a lot of depth. Most of the linemen were guys I would call overachievers. The exception was tri-captain Dave Casper, who was in a league all by himself. He was 6'3" and 245 pounds and could still run a 4.6-second 40-yard dash. Junior Mark Brenneman was moving in at the center position. He could run, had great balance, and had the smarts to help Gerry DiNardo and me figure out which way to go sometimes. As a matter of fact, the coaches developed a play called "opposite pass" because Gerry and I pulled the wrong way once. If the defense was keying on the guards and we pulled one way and the backs went the other way, the linebackers would usually freeze. By that time our backs and receivers had the jump on the defense.

Ara and Tom Pagna were always trying to update our offense so the defense never could really know what they would do. Many times you would see Gerry and me talking to Tommy Clements and people would think we were discussing the play, but in reality we were asking Tommy what count to go on. We had so many things to think about that sometimes we would forget. There were times when Gerry or I would ask Tommy on the line of scrimmage what the count was, and he would tell us loud enough for everyone on both sides of the ball to hear. The other team just thought we were trying to screw them up. They couldn't stop us anyway.

At the tackles were Steve Neece, Steve Sylvester, and a key backup, Steve Quehl, whose journey to become a starter had been slowed by shoulder surgery over the winter. Steve Neece was a 265-pound bull, and you didn't want to get in his way. He had suffered some tough injuries, including a broken ankle, but he came back and played like a man possessed. Steve Sylvester was a good athlete who always got good position to make the block. He went on to play nine years in the NFL.

Gerry DiNardo and I, the boys from Brooklyn, were the starting guards. We were labeled "the Italian Escort" in one news story, because we were always leading the sweeps in Ara's wing-T offense. It was very special to be playing with someone you grew up with from the fifth grade. We knew we could depend on each other and cover for each other on and off the field. The great thing on this team was that we had outstanding players behind us on the depth chart. Seniors Tom Bolger and Dan Morrin were good enough and tough enough to have started at most universities in the country. Senior Joe Alvarado was our long snapper and the backup center. If you didn't know who the long snapper was, then he was doing a good job, because the only way they get their named mentioned is when they have a bad snap. That never happened with Joe; he did a great job all year. John O'Donnell, a St. Francis Prep grad like Gerry and me, was another center who wasn't far behind the group. He didn't get a lot of playing time, but he added great depth to the team and after graduation went on to become an attorney.

The quarterback position was owned by Tommy Clements. He understood what Ara and Tom Pagna wanted and had the physical talent to execute it on the field. He was an extremely bright person, although you wouldn't know it because he only talked when he had things to say. He had ice in his veins and was always cool under pressure. "Tommy Clements was the coolest thing that walked the earth," said running back Eric Penick. "He was so talented and so smart, but he wasn't arrogant." Linebacker Greg Collins added, "You had the feeling that nothing affected Tommy." Cliff Brown and Frank

Allocco were good backups, but Tommy was the man. (Later, I also had the chance to play with Tommy for two years in the Canadian Football League, where he had great success, winning the Grey Cup, the Most Outstanding Player award and also Most Outstanding Rookie.)

The halfbacks for the 1973 team were Eric Penick and Art Best, two explosive runners with the ability to break open a game. Also pitching in at halfback were Ronny Goodman and Al Samuel, both great athletes with good speed. The fullbacks were Wayne Bullock and Russ Kornman. Wayne had become the workhorse who was great around the goal line because he would pound it in there and get the yard you needed. Russ was a ham-and-egger, a guy who would do anything the coaches asked him to do and came up with some big plays during the year. Tom Parise was another fullback who added to our depth.

The leading wide receiver was Pete Demmerle. Pete was about 6'1" and 190 pounds and was not the fastest receiver, but he had the softest hands on the team, ran great routes, and had the knack for making clutch plays. He became both an All-American and Academic All-American player and went on to become an attorney but sadly died of ALS at age 53. Other wide receivers included Willie Townsend, who had a strong year in 1972; Kevin Doherty, who had speed and good hands; and Bobby Washington, a good athlete.

Brian Doherty was the punter, and he doubled as the holder on extra points and field goals. Our place-kicker was Bob Thomas. Bob and Ara would have a field goal contest every week, and I think Ara owed Bob Thomas a lot of milkshakes by the end of the season.

This was the makeup of the team as we finished spring ball. Again, I want to emphasize the important role played by the guys who did not get a lot of game playing time. They were an essential part of whatever success we might have. "We had people on the sideline who could play for a lot of other teams," Mike Townsend said. "We challenged each other every day."

We all had a good feeling about the upcoming season, but knew we couldn't take anything for granted if we were going to get rid of the bad taste left in our mouths from the way 1972 ended. We were a blue-collar squad and we would have to earn every win and so we dedicated our summer to being in the best condition we could be in.

* * *

Late that spring, I was called into the office of athletic director Edward "Moose" Krause. I had never before been asked to go there and I wondered what I might have done wrong. When I got there I was met by Krause and assistant athletic director Colonel John Stephens. They told me the NCAA and the U.S. Defense Department were sponsoring USO trips by football players to the Far East and to Germany to meet with troops and lift their morale. They wanted me to represent the University of Notre Dame on this trip. I remembered that Larry DiNardo and John Dampeer had gone on similar trips in other years, and they said it was an experience they would never forget.

I would be traveling with other college players and a college coach. We would talk with soldiers and show a highlight film on college football to the military personnel. I was humbled to be asked to do such a service for the country and the university. The Vietnam War was just about over, and college players were not being sent there any longer, so my choice came down to the Philippines or Europe. I chose to go to Europe and see Germany, Luxembourg, and Belgium.

The trip was during the summer, and I was going with John Dutton from Nebraska, Steve Craig from Northwestern, Warren Capone from LSU, and John Cappelletti from Penn State. The coach accompanying us was Don Lindsey from USC. We all met in Philadelphia and boarded a plane for Europe.

My roommate for the trip was John Cappelletti, a good guy and a terrific running back who would go on to win the Heisman Trophy that year. John and I were from similar backgrounds with Italian ethnicity and parents who had the same values, and we got along very well. Steve Craig, a tight end, was very bright and thought outside the box. Warren Capone, a linebacker, and John Dutton, a defensive lineman, were two guys I had played against, and their teams had both beaten Notre Dame—Warren's LSU team did it in 1971, and John's Nebraska squad had just killed us in the Orange Bowl. Even so, we all got along well.

Don Lindsey would tease me about how USC had beaten us the last three meetings, but it just gave me more motivation to play well against them that year in South Bend. Don wasn't a bad guy, but he had that attitude that USC was the greatest. I had a hard time arguing with him, since they had just won the national championship. Don was Southern Cal's linebackers coach and they had two of the best in the country at that position, Richard Wood and Charles Anthony, so I just kept my mouth shut and vowed to do my best to help beat them in South Bend in the upcoming season.

The trip was a gratifying experience and I had a ball traveling and visiting air force and army bases. Walking through one air force base, I heard someone call out, "Hey, Pomarico, what the heck are you doing here?" I looked up, and it was a guy from Notre Dame who had been a manager on the football team when I was a freshman. He was now in the air force, and after I told him why I was there, he invited me to go out that night. He took me to several nightclubs and to a little out-of-the-way place that served the best German food I've ever had. He showed me a great time, and it is an example of how Notre Dame people take care of each other around the world. I have forgotten his name, but I will always remember his kindness.

The trip was not at all luxurious. We traveled by buses and trucks to get from place to place. That was fine with me, as I was used to traveling on the 14th Street–Canarsie Line on the New York City subway system. Besides, it was a once-in-a-lifetime experience to travel abroad and help brighten the lives of some soldiers.

After a few weeks home, I headed back to Notre Dame for summer school and the chance to work out before the season started. The campus in summer seemed to operate at a slower pace, which gave me the chance to reflect about my future and my life. I had met a pretty young girl, Aileen Conklin, who had gone to high school with Tom Devine, my roommate for two years in Sorin Hall. Aileen was a very warm person, was sports-minded, and came from an Irish Catholic home in Jackson, Michigan. Her uncle, Hugh, was a priest. She had 10 brothers and sisters and grew up with a bunch of real Notre Dame fans, including Herb Brogan, who was the best friend of Aileen's brother Mike. Aileen's Dad, Mike Conklin, was a Notre Dame fan who loved Ara Parseghian and had attended the classic Notre Dame vs. Michigan State 10–10 tie in 1966.

I first met Aileen when I was a freshman at Notre Dame and she was attending Western Michigan University in Kalamazoo. Aileen would make the 75-mile trip from Kalamazoo to South Bend some weekends to see her good friend, Mary Beth Lafere, a student at St. Mary's College. Aileen and Mary Beth would come over to see Tom Devine, and that's how I met her. We hit it off pretty well, and I started dating her as a junior. By the time I completed my junior year, we were pretty serious. We decided to get married when I graduated.

On my way to South Bend for the summer, I decided to stop and see Aileen and her family. She had told me they were having a party for one of her sisters, who was getting married, so I decided to surprise Aileen by just showing up. We had a great time at the party, and I spent a couple of days with her family. Jackson is just a small town compared to New York, but the people are open and friendly. Being around Aileen's big family was like being in a dorm—there was always something going on.

Aileen and I did get married, two days before my graduation in 1974. The ceremony was in Sacred Heart Church on the Notre Dame campus, and in addition to our families, Ara Parseghian and his wife, Katie, were there to witness it. Aileen and I remain happily married and we have two great kids who are now grown, Tommy and Lisa.

By the end of the summer it hit me that this was going to be the last time I would ever get ready for the football season at Notre Dame. It would be the last time I would go into battle with some of my dearest friends in the world. This *had* to be a big year at Notre Dame; it was the only one I had left.

When all the players returned to campus, we had our fitness test, and everyone was in pretty good shape. "We saw the two teams before us crash and burn. That made us really hungry," Tom Bolger said. "As seniors, we wanted to make sure we went out on all cylinders. We were not going to let things slip through our fingers. And we all got along, which was huge."

Some of our talented incoming freshmen helped stoke our optimism.

Most of the immediate help would be felt on defense, in particular because of Ross Browner and Luther Bradley. Ross was a 6'3", 225-pound defensive end who was a finalist in the Ohio high school 220-yard sprint. He had the quickness of a cat and the strength of an action hero. Ross also came in with an attitude that he was going to play *now*; no one was going to beat him out. There weren't many players who could block him at all and it was obvious he was going to make an impact immediately. Luther was a big defensive back at about 6'2" and 195 pounds. He was extremely smooth and smart and quickly picked up the defensive scheme. Luther had played a lot of offense in high school, but Ara liked to put his best athletes on defense.

On the other side of the ball, a freshman with the chance to make an impact this year was Al Hunter, a running back who had blazing speed for kickoffs and plays out of the backfield. Tommy Clements would be the field general directing a run-oriented offense that had a goal to control the clock. If we did it right, it would frustrate the other teams into taking risks that would lead to mistakes that we could capitalize on.

We would work on special teams every day before the offensive and defensive time-up because Ara wanted the players to be fresh when running kicking drills and to emphasize its importance in making the difference in close games. Our field goal team with Joe Alvarado snapping, Brian Doherty holding, and Bob Thomas kicking was destined to play a significant role in the coming season.

The first scrimmage was on a Saturday, and as usual in the summer it was hot and humid. Early in the scrimmage, we ran a play called fullback trap, which could be blocked four different ways. Quarterback Tommy Clements called for an "odd" block, which meant the tight end and the tackle would block down and the guard would pull out and block the defensive end. As I pulled out to block the end, the linebacker ran in to hit fullback Wayne Bullock. As Wayne spun around trying to get a few yards, he landed on my right ankle and I felt as if it had been ripped in half.

I was down and out for the rest of the scrimmage. By the time I got to the training room, my ankle was swelling fast so the trainers put on ice as soon as they could. When Dr. Leslie Bodnar came in, he ordered X-rays to see if anything was broken. I was lucky; it wasn't broken and my knee was stable. But I would be out for about six weeks while my ligaments healed. That meant I would miss at least the first three or four games.

I was depressed. One minute I was a preseason All-American and one of the captains of a very good Ara Parseghian–coached Notre Dame football team. The next minute I was limping around on crutches, and my ankle was throbbing like a splitting headache.

I went to training table dinner that night and talked with Dan Morrin and Gerry DiNardo about my ankle. It was tough getting injured, but I tried to think about how fast I could come back and help the team. I focused on how much I needed to work out other parts of my body in order to have myself in great condition when I came back from the injury. The good news was that we now had the Nautilus weight system in place at Father Lange's Gym. I could keep in shape with the 10 Nautilus machines we had: hip and back, leg extension, leg curl, leg press, pullover for the back and chest, pec deck for the chest and back, bicep and triceps, and neck machines. I also was very lucky to get advice from Kim Wood, co-owner of Nautilus Midwest along with Pete Brown, the son of coach Paul Brown. Kim would come up from Cincinnati where he was working with the Bengals NFL team on strength conditioning, a job he took on full time with the Bengals in 1975. In 1973, he came regularly to Notre Dame to answer questions about the equipment and training methods and he played a big part in helping me to not only keep in shape, but also get bigger and stronger.

Each week Dr. Bodnar would cut a little window in the cast near the ankle so he could squeeze the cast and make it tighter to reduce the swelling. When he would do that, my ankle would hurt like the dickens for about three days. I had a full cast from my toe to my mid-thigh for about three weeks, then a half cast for a week. After that I would need to rehab my leg for about two weeks before I was ready to return to practice.

At one point, Dr. Bodnar said the ankle was not healing correctly and he raised the possibility of surgery. If he did that, I could say good-bye to the whole season. I didn't want that to happen, so I begged him to stick with the rehab so I could play this year. He still wasn't sure I would be able to do it.

However, after the workouts from Kim Wood and constant rehab, I was given the chance to play after we were four games into the season.

I wanted badly to be back for the Southern California game, which was our sixth game. I wanted the chance to be part of a team that beat USC, which was clearly the most important game on the schedule. They had been the national champions the year before and they had the best talent we would face. It was tough for me to be patient and heal because all my brothers on the team were being productive and I wasn't. I had missed being with them through the rigors of the preseason. Then it was hard to miss the first three games.

I was always proud that the team could count on me to be on the field. In fact, as a sophomore, I had won the Iron Man Award, which went to the player who was on the field for the most time. I logged more than 316 minutes, second most time ever played for an Ara Parseghian team at Notre Dame, behind only lineman Dick Arrington, who played both offense and defense in 1965. Gerry DiNardo won the Iron Man award his sophomore year with more than 307 minutes, fourth-most for one of Ara's Knights at Notre Dame. (Jack Snow was third.) And Larry DiNardo was the Iron Man his junior season, topping 283 minutes. It took a pretty serious injury to sideline any of the guys from Our Lady of Grace and St. Francis Prep.

While I was out, the other linemen, including Tom Bolger and Dan Morrin, did an outstanding job. These guys would have started on 95 percent of the Division I teams in the country. I was finally well enough to dress for the fourth game against Rice in Houston, though I didn't play that day. In that game, Tom was running downfield to cover a punt. "I saw a guy coming out of the corner of my eye," Tom said. "Back then, you could take guys out below the waist. I planted my leg and my knee blew out." Tom suffered a torn ACL, and it was the end of his season.

Dan Morrin did a great job finishing that game. I did prepare and play in the Army game and then played through the rest of the year. However, I did do something on my own that the coaches didn't really catch. I asked Dan to take all the special teams I was scheduled to be on because he could run down field a lot better than I could. He also was a better open-field blocker than

I was because he had more mobility. So Dan played on all kickoff returns, punts, field goals, and extra points. That decision would turn out to be fortunate when Dan made one of the key blocks of the season. And what a season it was.

CHAPTER 16

Fall Brings the Driven Spirit

The fall season at Notre Dame is special, and not just because of football. The uncomfortable heat and humidity of the summer have gone away, replaced with something cooler and crisper that is invigorating to the body and spirit. On the best of autumn days, the mornings are golden, and you might need a sweatshirt or light jacket heading to the dining hall or class. By afternoon, it can be warm enough to go with just shirtsleeves. Every week, on a Midwest campus like Notre Dame with its thousands of trees, you can watch the turning of colors, from green to a palette that includes multiple shades of red, yellow, and orange. It as if God, the great artist, had been saving up all year for a grand finale.

Many times in the fall I would walk around the lakes behind the Golden Dome, stopping first to say a prayer at the Grotto, which sits between St. Mary's Lake to the west and St. Joseph's Lake to the east. Heading west from the Grotto, I pass Old College, the oldest building on campus dating back to 1843 when it was built by the university's founder, Edward Sorin. Now it houses undergraduates who are considering joining the Holy Cross religious order. Old College sits next to the Log Chapel, a replica of one built by Stephen Badin in 1831 as a missionary headquarters, 11 years before the founding of Notre Dame.

Still going west, I pass Morrissey Manor, named after Andrew Morrissey, the seventh president of Notre Dame. Morrissey and Lyons, two adjacent dorms, were built in 1925 and feature the sort of Tudor style and impressive brickwork that were popular just before the Great Depression. I lived in Lyons one summer; it's a great dorm with a distinctive arch at the entrance. In 1974, it became a women's dorm.

On my walk, I can feel the cool breeze as I make the turn near the Old Security building that is now called the West Lake Hall and is used by the graphic arts department. Then the path starts to turn as I pass Carroll Hall, another building that formerly housed young men studying for the religious life. I then approach the old tennis courts that were closest to Business US 31, a road that divided St. Mary's and Notre Dame. I can see the cars passing as I walk north toward Our Lady of Fatima House, which is used for retreats. Close to St. Mary's Road, which runs between St. Mary's College and Notre Dame, there used to be a dorm called Holy Cross on a hill overlooking the lake. It was a great old place that had awesome parties—sort of the "animal house" of the time.

This was close to where the lakes intersected, and usually I would "figure eight" my route and go on the west side of St. Joseph's Lake toward Columbia Hall, a residence hall for the Holy Cross brothers. Staying along the lake path, I pass Sacred Heart Parish Center. The trees surrounding the lake path in this area sometimes make me think I am in the middle of some English forest, sometimes not being able to see anything but trees and foliage. One of my favorite sections of this walk is going past the front of Moreau Seminary, which provides a beautiful view across the lake of the Golden Dome and Sacred Heart Basilica. It is a terrific spot for photographs in any season.

Past Moreau, I head east to Holy Cross House, a residence for older priests. The path then leads to the Boat House, where sailing boats are housed and where students enjoy St. Joseph's Beach during warm weather. Moving south, I pass the campus power plant. Notre Dame is really its own city, with a fire department, security/police department and the power plant. Past the power plant, I come to a set of stairs that could bring you to Holy Cross Drive, or I could stay on the path past Lewis Hall, formerly housing for nuns and now a dorm for female undergrads. My daughter lived in Lewis for a couple of years, and I had the notion that maybe it would be a nice quiet place because it used to be a convent, but I found out different when I visited there on a Friday night and saw that their parties rivaled those in any men's dorm. So much for my idea that the building's history as a convent would make a difference.

The last stop around the lakes is a building that houses the Sara Bea Learning Center for Students with Disabilities, the campus post office, and the laundry distribution. Of course, football practice and games kept me pretty busy during the fall when I was a student. When I began returning after graduation, I got to appreciate even more the bursts of beauty that made this season so special.

Walking along the campus at Notre Dame, I would think of how special it was and how driven I had to be to make it as a player at Notre Dame. As mountain climber Peter Habeler writes in *The Lonely Victory*, you had to love the journey as much as reaching the summit. This Driven Spirit is a quality that goes beyond the natural gifts we are born with. Underlining everything is a burning desire to achieve and be successful. Part spiritual, part physical, the Driven Spirit is inside of every champion, I believe. Being a champion doesn't mean that you win all the time, but it denotes an attitude of competing for everything you determine is worth striving to achieve.

These are the characteristics that I identify as part of the Driven Spirit.

1. **Focus**. The Driven Spirit requires a singleness of purpose that blocks out everything that isn't connected to attaining your goals. For me with football, it meant training as hard as I could with weights and running to become the starting guard for the University of Notre Dame. My focus also involved staying out of trouble and working hard in the classroom to be eligible academically.
2. **Unselfishness.** In a team situation, you can't care who gets the credit as long as you win. You can really make a difference if you can put the needs of the team or your organization ahead of your personal need for recognition.

3. **Toughness.** The Driven Spirit requires you to be tough both physically and mentally. Ara Parseghian wanted players who were not only good athletes, but also were hungry for success. He wanted people that understood that they weren't guaranteed a starting position, only an opportunity to earn one. Ara wanted us to be honest with our effort, in preparation, and in leaving everything on the field.
4. **Intelligence.** Champions who have the Driven Spirit are street smart as well as IQ smart. They have the discipline to learn everything they can to help them in the pursuit of their goals. I tried to find out the most effective ways to train and I also spent hours studying top players in order to learn their techniques.
5. **Relentlessness.** One of Ara's favorite sayings was, "We have no breaking point." You have to have an attitude of continuing to drive toward your goal, no matter what the score or the obstacle. You never really lose, it's just that the clock ran out. You might think the person who will fight to the death is nuts, but you have to be a little nuts to be a champion—not just in athletics, but in all things you believe are worth fighting for.
6. **Resilience.** You may need to regroup after a setback. But you need to learn from your mistakes in order to come back stronger and smarter. Marv Levy, a coach that I played for in the Canadian Football League, once recited to us some lines from a Scottish ballad about a sailor:

"Fight on, my men," says Sir Andrew Barton,
"I am hurt, but I am not slain;
I'll lay me down and bleed a while,
And then I'll rise and fight again."

7. **Hunger.** The Driven Spirit has no room for arrogance. You need to think and compete like an underdog, understanding that the victory does not always go to the biggest, strongest, or fastest. An individual or team with the intense hunger to win will often overcome one that has more talent and potential.

8. **Courage.** It is important that you have the guts to risk failure in the pursuit of something great. More than a century ago, Theodore Roosevelt said,

   > It is not the critic who counts; not the man who points out how the strong man stumbles, or where the doer of deeds could have done them better. The credit belongs to the man who is actually in the arena, whose face is marred by dust and sweat and blood; who strives valiantly; who errs, who comes short again and again, because there is no effort without error and shortcoming; but who does actually strive to do the deeds; who knows great enthusiasms, the great devotions; who spends himself in a worthy cause; who at the best knows in the end the triumph of high achievement, and who at the worst, if he fails, at least fails while daring greatly, so that his place shall never be with those cold and timid souls who neither know victory nor defeat.

9. **Character.** If you have the Driven Spirit, you focus on who you really are rather than on how others perceive you to be. You can't buy character; it is a learned behavior based on the patterns of thinking, speaking, and acting that you develop through life. You will form a strong character if you choose habits based on virtues such as helpfulness, caring, loyalty, self-discipline, understanding, forgiveness, sharing, responsibility, courteousness, fairness, honesty, thankfulness, kindness, self-respect, and trustworthiness.
10. **The Light Within.** The world is full of darkness and confusion, but there are people in the world who will not be brought to their knees or submit to the dark side. These people will never give up, never stop trying—even when all seems to be lost. The source of their light is love: love for themselves, love for others in this world, love for the journey, and love for God. This light is what makes them whole and gives them peace.

Ara Parseghian always challenged us players to look at ourselves honestly to assess whether we really gave our all. He urged us to ask ourselves if we could have done better. If we had not done our best, we had cheated ourselves and our teammates.

When I was a freshman, Notre Dame went to the Cotton Bowl and upset the No. 1 team, Texas. The players on the team received a meaningful gift after that game. There was a frame with a small mirror on one side, and on the other side was a poem entitled "The Man in the Glass," written in 1934 by Peter Dale Wimbrow Sr.:

When you get what you want in your struggle for self,
And the whole world makes you King for the day.
Just go to the mirror and look at yourself,
And see what the man has to say.

For it isn't your mother or father or wife,
Who judgment upon you must pass.
The fellow whose verdict counts the most in your life
Is the one staring you back from the glass.

Some people may say you're a straight shooting chum,
And call you a wonderful guy,
But, the man in the glass says you're only a bum
If you can't look him straight in the eye.

He's the fellow to please never mind the rest,
For he's with you clear to the end.
And you passed your most dangerous difficult test.
If the man in the glass is your friend.

You may fool the whole world down the pathway of years,
And get pats on the back as you pass.
But, your final reward will be heart aches and tears,
If you cheat the man in the glass.

Ara Parseghian had the Driven Spirit, and beyond his role as a football coach he held deep ideals that he tried to pass on to each and every player he had. The 1973 team would be made up of players who strived to never cheat the man in the glass.

CHAPTER 17

The Special 1973 Season

Game 1: Northwestern

Northwestern had opened its season a week before we did in 1973 by beating Michigan State 14–10. We had a young team overall, and in fact two freshmen were starting. One was strong safety Luther Bradley, who was so nervous he threw up his pregame meal. "Ara comes over to my locker about an hour before the game, and I'm shaking in my boots," Luther said. "I had never played before a crowd that large. And he says to me, 'How do you feel?' I said I was really nervous. And he says to me, 'If I didn't think you were good enough, I wouldn't put you out there.' He said, 'You'll be fine, you just watch.'"

The other starting freshman was Ross Browner, who was part of an inexperienced front four. Ross and sophomore Jim Stock were the ends, and sophomore Steve Niehaus and junior Mike Fanning were the tackles. It didn't take long for Ross to make an impact. With the Wildcats punting from deep in their own territory, Ross flew in from the line of scrimmage, soared like Batman, and blocked the kick. The ball went through the end zone for a safety, the first two points of the year for the Fighting Irish. It was part of a great first half for our defense. The defensive line kept alternating between a four-man and a five-man front line, which wreaked havoc with the Wildcats offense. In the first half, Northwestern was able to gain only a measly nine yards total.

Meanwhile, the Irish offense had rolled up 279 yards and five touchdowns in the first half. Art Best ran one in from the 2-yard line, and Tommy Clements connected with Pete Demmerle on a nine-yard score in the first quarter. The second quarter again belonged to the Irish. Ron Goodman took a pitch and raced two yards around left end for a TD, Tommy Clements leaped into the end zone from the 1-yard line for the next score, and then Tommy ran one in, untouched, over the left side from the 3-yard line.

That made it 37–0 at the half. Cliff Brown came in at quarterback for the second half and did a solid job, directing the Irish on a scoring drive that ended with a 21-yard scamper by Gary Diminick. Northwestern threatened a couple of times to break the shutout. The first time, Mike Townsend stopped the drive with an end zone interception. On the second occasion, Ross Browner sacked the Northwestern quarterback and caused a fumble that the Irish recovered, preserving the 44–0 opening-game shutout. Linebacker Greg Collins led the defense with two solo tackles and 16 assists.

Tom Bolger, who replaced me at left guard, had an excellent game. Dan Morrin also played in the second half, and we were as solid as we could be on the offensive line. Both of them typified the strong character that our seniors brought to the team.

"Our senior class wasn't the most talented class, but we were living proof of the whole being greater than the sum of the parts," said defensive lineman Tom Creevey. "We fed off of each other and didn't want to let each other down." Like many of our seniors, Tom primarily played as a backup. "There's nothing worse than having some of your older players with negative attitudes. Most of our seniors kept a positive attitude throughout because Ara kept everyone in play and made everyone feel important."

All in all, the Northwestern game was a very good start. But there was an extremely sad note to the day as we found out that Tommy Clements' 14-year-old sister, Alice, had been killed in a car crash. Tommy came from a close-knit family and he took the loss hard. The tragedy put things in perspective. There I was, upset about my injury, which in reality was a just a temporary setback compared with a young girl losing her life. It makes one sit back and realize that life just doesn't stop for anyone. We have to hold on to the good things as much as we can and learn from the bad things, and most of all we have to live in the now and be as productive and helpful as we can.

Game 2: Purdue

Tommy Clements didn't get back from his sister's funeral until Wednesday, but he still wanted to play the upcoming game against Purdue. Perhaps the game preparation helped keep his mind occupied. Cliff Brown was preparing to run the ship if Tommy couldn't play, and we were confident in him, but with Tommy at the helm, the ship had been running very smoothly.

Ross-Ade Stadium in West Lafayette is a tough place to play—especially when the crowd smells an upset. Early in the game, Art Best ran 64 yards to the Boilermakers 11, setting up a Bob Thomas field goal to get the Irish on the board first. Purdue responded in the second quarter when Olympic sprinter Larry Burton beat defensive back Tim Rudnick on a 53-yard touchdown reception, putting the home team up 7–3. We got the ball on the 10-yard line, and with strong running by Art Best and Eric Penick and pass receptions by Wayne Bullock, took the lead, 10–7, with Art going the final nine yards.

At the start of the second half, the teams traded fumbles. Finally, the Irish put together a scoring drive, with Tommy Clements running for good yardage and completing passes and Wayne Bullock running hard. Wayne crashed over from the 1-yard line to up the Irish lead to 17–7. We tacked on a 42-yard-field goal by Bob Thomas following a 52-yard drive that featured runs by Gary Diminick, Art Best, Wayne Bullock, and Al Hunter. Art had an outstanding game, rushing for 125 yards on 16 attempts. We outgained the Boilermakers 290 yards to 33 yards on the ground on the way to the 20–7 victory.

The Irish defense was strong and Alex Agase, who had left Northwestern to take over as the Purdue head coach, said he was very impressed with Ross Browner's speed and quickness and Luther Bradley's anticipation as he broke up two passes and also picked up his first collegiate interception, falling to the ground after picking off a deep pass. "I was so excited just to catch the ball," Luther said. "When I ran off the field, [defensive coach] Paul Shoults came over and said, 'Luther, it's okay to catch the ball and stay on your feet and run with it.'"

I was glad to say good-bye to Ross-Ade Stadium. The Boilermakers always had great linebackers and strong, quick defensive linemen. It was the second game that I missed in 1973, but Dr. Leslie Bodnar said the ankle was starting to heal. In the coming week my cast would be cut in half, and I could start training to strengthen my thigh.

Game 3: Michigan State

After 19 seasons, Duffy Daugherty retired as head coach at Michigan State and his replacement, Denny Stolz, was off to a 1–2 start. But that didn't lessen the intensity of the feeling between these two rivals. "I think Michigan State hit harder than any team we played in the years I was on the field," said linebacker/nose guard Gary Potempa. "If you weren't ready, you would get outhit by those guys."

The Spartans offense revolved around their running game, but our defense had held our first two opponents combined to less than 100 yards, so we were going to be matching strength against strength. In the first quarter, a couple of Irish drives stalled, and Bob Thomas missed field goal tries of 49 and 52 yards. The Spartans didn't even get one first down in the first quarter, and after a Notre Dame fumble, MSU also missed a field goal. The Irish finally got rolling in the second quarter. After taking over on our own 20-yard line, Eric Penick ran around left end for 16 yards, and then Tommy Clements went 19 yards on a keeper. The drive ended when Wayne Bullock busted in from the 1-yard-line and the Irish went up 7–0.

Later in the quarter, Tommy took to the air. He hit tight end Dave Casper on a screen, and with some great downfield blocking Dave rumbled for 30 yards, running through a couple of defenders to get the final yards. Three plays later, from the State 30-yard line, Tommy threw to Pete Demmerle, who caught the ball at the 15, shook off a defender, and went in for the score that made it 14–0. The Irish finally looked like they were on track to take control.

But on the next possession, Tommy was belted hard on a sack and he may have suffered a slight concussion. (In those days, there had been no research on the permanent effects of concussions and there was no set protocol for determining on the sideline if a concussion had occurred.) Cliff Brown finished the half at quarterback, and Tommy returned in the second half, which is when a couple of Irish mistakes enabled the Spartans to get back in the game.

In the third quarter, the Spartans again were stopped by the Irish defense and had to punt. Bob Zanot, usually a sure-handed punt returner, fumbled at the Irish 18-yard line. Our defense held there, but Dirk Kryt came on to kick a field goal that brought the score to 14–3. Then, early in the fourth quarter, MSU linebacker Ray Nester intercepted one of Tommy's passes and ran it back 22 yards for a touchdown to bring the score to 14–10. Things were getting tight, and got even tighter on Michigan State's next possession when quarterback Charlie Baggett threw a bomb to Dane Fortney for 40 yards before Tim Rudnick ran him down on the Irish 24-yard line.

With the game on the line, Baggett rolled to his right and Gary Potempa hit him just as he threw. Mike Townsend stepped in front of a Baggett pass on the 16-yard line and ran it back 47 yards. "I had seen that play in practice all week. The quarterback threw it to the guy I was on," Mike said. When his interception run ended, he was mobbed his defensive teammates. "All the guys jumped on me and I was down on the bottom of the pile. I was worn out. I was so tired. I said, 'Would you please get off me?' I could hardly talk."

The Spartans did get the ball back in the game's waning seconds, but Baggett's desperation heave was intercepted at the MSU 43-yard line by Tim Rudnick, who ran it back 30 yards as time ran out. We survived, but had not executed well on offense—especially in the second half, when turnovers were a big problem. "I think it was an eye-opener for the team. We didn't play well but we won," said Tom Bolger. "We figured out that we had to play our best game all the time, and I think without a question that carried over to the rest of the season. We grew up a lot in that game."

Game 4: Rice

My cast had come off and I had been riding a bike to get my ankle ready to handle running. It was very sore, but nothing worse, and I was able to dress and make the trip for the Rice game. During the week of practice leading up to the game, our coaches plastered the locker room walls with newspaper clippings in which the Rice team and their supporters took shots at us. "They were saying we were fat, they would run us to the ground because we were used to the cool air up north and the heat would get to us," Mike Townsend said. "All we wanted to do was go down to Houston and lay leather on them to a level they had never seen."

Rice coach Al Conover wanted to fight fire with fire, so he had invited every Catholic priest in Houston to sit behind his team's bench and he made all of the Catholics on the team cocaptains for the game. He even started a freshman quarterback who was Catholic—Tommy Kramer, who went on play in the NFL and was elected to the College Football Hall of Fame.

In our locker room, Ara Parseghian brought the emotion of the week to a crescendo with a pregame speech that was short but impactful, recalled Mike Townsend. "He point blank said, 'I want you to take those Riddell helmets, shoulder pads, thigh pads, kneepads, and Riddell shoes and I want you to run right through Rice so that they understand that we came down and we are Notre Dame.' And that was it," Mike remembered.

We went out and dominated the game, although two early drives were stymied by fumbles. Late in the first quarter, the Irish put together a nine-play, 51-yard drive, with Wayne Bullock going over left tackle from the 1-yard line for the score. In the second quarter, Tommy Clements found Dave Casper on the goal line for a 21-yard TD, making it 14–0. Owls quarterback Tommy Kramer went to the air and completed passes of 13 and 33 yards, but Reggie Barnett put an end to the threat with an interception. During the first half, the Irish gained 271 yards, but 70 yards in penalties kept us from scoring more than the two TDs.

The second half began with Gary Diminick running the kickoff back 39 yards, and we moved quickly down the field. Art Best ran 31 yards down the right sideline, Tommy Clements hit Wayne Bullock with an eight-yard pass to get it to the 1-yard line, and then Wayne blasted over left tackle for the score. In the fourth quarter, Brian Doherty pinned Rice deep with a 62-yard punt that was downed on the 2-yard line. Cliff Brown came in and did a good job of leading the Irish offense to its final score. Al Samuel ran for 15 yards and caught a pass for 10 yards, and Cliff ran 38 yards on a keeper for the touchdown that made the final score 28–0.

The Irish defense mauled the Owls in the second half, holding them to three first downs and 30 yards total offense. For the game, we put up 536 yards of offense to 142 yards for the home team. The game really wasn't as close as the final score. "We came in at the end of the game, and the whole locker room was quiet," Mike Townsend said. "When Coach Parseghian came in, he was mad because there was all this quietness. He said, 'What's wrong with you guys?' But we didn't feel we had beaten them bad enough because they had said all that stuff about us."

I got into the game for an extra point, my first action of the year, and it felt great to run on the field. I don't know how much I could have played, but I was confident I would be ready for the next week. The Rice game, unfortunately, was the one in which Tom Bolger, who had moved into the starting position at left guard, suffered a torn knee ligament that knocked him out for the year. Tom did a great job in the time he started, and quite honestly we didn't miss a beat with him in there. He was an awesome athlete who was quick, tough, and had good natural strength; more important, he was smart and a great teammate. He was truly one of Ara's Knights and a credit to Notre Dame. I could say that about dozens of guys each year who played for Ara Parseghian, but a lot of them were on that 1973 team. We had great depth on this team and a lot of the depth came from seniors.

Game 5: Army

As a high school student in 1969, I had a chance to watch Notre Dame play Army at Yankee Stadium. It was a thrill because I was a huge Yankees fan and to this day still have a soft spot in my heart for that baseball team. Back then, I looked at the upcoming schedule and thought if I made it at Notre Dame that the team would be back playing in Yankee Stadium in 1973 and I would have the chance to play on the same field on which my heroes had competed. But as I got closer to the game, I realized that the Army contest had been switched to Michie Stadium at West Point. Although I was disappointed by the change of venue, West Point was a beautiful place to visit in the fall, set on the Hudson River amidst the trees and mountains. It was a big game for all of us from the East Coast. Gerry DiNardo, Dan Morrin, and I knew that our parents, families, and friends would all be there, along with some of our old coaches and teachers. Tickets in those days were about $8.

We stayed in a hotel not far from West Point and went through the same ritual we always did before games. Ara liked consistency. We had prime rib for Friday night dinner, then attended team meetings, followed by a trip to the movies. Dan Morrin and I always hung out together and sat next to each other during the bus rides and movies. We also roomed together until he got married to his wife, Linda, in our senior year, and we have stayed lifelong friends. Dan is another one of Ara's Knights who refused to do anything that wasn't the right thing to do for the team. He loved Notre Dame, he loved Ara Parseghian, and loved being part of this special team at this special school that stood for so many values that he believed in as well. We were living history and we knew it.

Army had a scrambling type of team with a lot of overachievers. They had the discipline, courage, and smarts that would be needed to protect our country in the years to come, but realistically they were short on football talent. The Cadets actually scored first, with a field goal, and they held that 3–0 lead going into the second quarter. But as the game went into the second quarter, Army never really had a chance. We controlled the tempo and clock on offense while our defense crushed Army's attack on the way to a 62–3 romp. Ara was playing reserves and telling them to just run the ball up the middle in an effort to hold down the score, but Army still couldn't stop us.

It was my first game back as a starter, and I was very excited to play. I didn't have the speed I had before the ankle injury, but I was determined to get a game under my belt before the Southern California game. We scored over left guard on one play, and it was a great feeling to drive the defender back and see our running back go into the end zone next to me.

It was a good win for the Irish because it put everyone in a very positive mood. "We got in the locker room after the game, and our guys were really fired up because that's when USC Week began," Tommy Clements said. We felt at this point that we could beat anyone. We would have a chance to prove it the following week when we played last year's national champions and our big rival.

Game 6: Southern California

The anticipation for the 1973 Southern Cal contest was unlike anything I had been part of. USC boasted a 23-game unbeaten streak, the longest in the country. They were the defending national champions and had beaten us in 1972 with Anthony Davis running wild for six touchdowns in the Los Angeles Coliseum. We had not beaten USC in the last six tries. We tied twice, but the other four games were losses, including the one in 1970 in a West Coast monsoon that cost us a national title.

If we could win this game, we had a shot at an undefeated season and very good bowl game. Ara told us that if we kept winning, the polls would take care of themselves. We would need some help to leapfrog some teams, but none of that made any difference if we didn't beat USC. It was everything to our season. There is no doubt that Southern Cal also regarded it as a huge game, too, in their effort to repeat as national champions. In fact, for the first time since 1927, they were bringing their entire marching band into South Bend—all 175 members. And you knew it was the Game of the Week because the Goodyear blimp was coming.

Everyone on the Notre Dame campus was going nuts. Instant pep rallies erupted all week in the dining halls. Every day, students cheered and encouraged us players as we walked to class. There were impromptu rallies in the Huddle food court and in the bookstore. Students took the *Sports Illustrated* cover featuring Anthony Davis from the year before and taped it on the sidewalks around campus so people could walk on it. Someone even hung a Davis dummy outside of a Sorin Hall window, and students threw stuff at it as they went past.

Even members of the faculty took notice. Business school professor John Houck told us that the energy being generated for this game could run a whole General Motors plant. John was one of my favorite professors at Notre Dame. He really cared about the students and was a leading advocate for business ethics, something that he helped instill in the young men and women who took his business courses at the Dome.

When we came in to start our practice week, each of us found a letter from the Phantom posted on our locker.

"The Phantom Speaks"

In the early season I stated a truth "ALL ENERGY FOLLOWS THOUGHT." Before anything ever comes to a reality, it must form a thought first. Prayer works. This may also—it is a thought—projected along with work toward a goal. I don't feel the need of getting an upset stomach for 5 days before we play Southern Cal. I see it differently—we must approach the preparation and the game with one united thought. If we put all our minds into a single-minded thought—and we work hard—and we play with emotion—united—I hold we will win!

I choose not to see it any other way—because any other way is not positive. Positive will be our strength. We are going to do it! Start Monday we—are—going after Southern Cal. We have to prepare with a full attentive mind. We have to hustle and perform and execute at our best. Let's project the thought of a sound game—no turnovers—no miscues or missed assignments, no let ups emotionally and physically. They can be had—and we can and will do it.

Against Army we worried the worry of all teams. When exactly the same number of players are pitted against the same number, when they have relative size and speed—when they have similar backgrounds in tradition and coaching. What is the difference? The difference is strictly in the "desire" one group has over the other. Notice I said "one group," not one individual. Take the greatest player who ever played—allow me to pick eleven interhall players and eleven to one I'll win. When we take the field versus Southern Cal—If we are of one mind and have one goal, and play a full 60 minutes with a full Notre Dame heart—we have got to emerge the victor! Southern Cal has had one coming for a long, long time. They've out sized and out individualized many—but we will out team them. We will be the Giant killers—if we go after it. No game is as important as the game you are playing.

Time has come to quit thinking about it—quit talking about it (words are empty) and go out and do it!!!!!!!!!!!!!!! Beat Southern Cal !!!!!!!!!!!!!!!!

The Monday practice at Cartier Field was a very special one for me. Ara gave me the game ball for the Army game. There were a lot of players who were deserving of the honor, but since it was my first game back, he decided that it should be me. I loved that ball for what it represented, which was four years of very hard work for a program that I believed in with all my heart.

Every practice that week was like the buildup for a heavyweight championship fight. Former greats, including Paul Hornung, visited us at practice, and one day the band came out and played the "Victory March" and a couple of other pep songs for us at practice. We got the feeling the entire student body was funneling its energy our way. I remarked to Dan Morrin, "USC is a very good football team, but can they beat our whole campus?"

USC had great offensive weapons, such as quarterback Pat Haden and wide receivers Lynn Swann and J.K. McKay, the son of head coach John McKay. But stopping All-American running back Anthony Davis was job No. 1. It was personal—not just because of the six touchdowns in the previous year's contest, but also because of the way he showboated. "We remembered Anthony Davis doing his dance in the end zone. One thing we wanted to do was stop that S.O.B.," said defensive lineman George Hayduk. Linebacker Gary Potempa recalled that TV coverage of the upcoming game invariably seemed to show a clip in which Davis ran over Gary's roommate, corner Tim Rudnick. "My roommate was pretty pissed about it," Gary said.

The coaches selected Greg Hill, one of our reserve running backs, to wear a Davis jersey and imitate his running style in practice all week. "We were amazed. Greg Hill gave us a run for our money on defense," said linebacker Tim Sullivan. "He wasn't just slash and dash; he did a zone-type read and he could dance and make his own holes. He did a fantastic job of imitating Anthony Davis and helping us get ready for him." Gary Potempa also gave Greg Hill a lot of credit for his work that week. "He had moves and he played great," Greg said. "That was what made our team great: it was all these guys who just busted their ass."

Our offensive game plan emphasized controlling the ball because Ara wanted to limit the opportunities for the explosive Southern Cal offense that could hurt you from anywhere on the field. It was going to be a big task as the Trojans had a great defense anchored by two awesome linebackers, Richard Wood and Charles Anthony. Richard Wood was about 6'3", 235 pounds and could run like a deer. It was almost impossible to block him, and you had to catch him first. Charles Anthony was a little smaller at 6'1" and 225 pounds, but he could hit like you'd run against a brick wall and had good speed. These guys were physical, smart, and well coached. Ray Rodriguez was the third linebacker, complementing Wood and Anthony. The rest of the defense was also very athletic. The front line was big and could move. It was made up of captain Monte Doris, freshman Gary Jeter, Dale Mitchell, and Art Riley. In the defensive backfield were Marvin Cobb, Charles Phillips, Danny Reece, and Artimus Parker. Because of their speed and ability to pressure, the Trojans had already recorded 17 interceptions in their first six games.

By the end of the week, we were all jacked up for the game, and Ara knew it. He was trying to keep our enthusiasm controlled and not leave the game on the practice field. Ara would always have the offense, defense, prep team, and freshmen concoct humorous cheers for Thursday and Friday at the end of practice, and this was no exception. During USC Week, the offense won with a jingle set to the tune of a well-known Texaco commercial, which ended with "You can trust your car to the man who wears the star—the big, bright Texaco star!" But ours went like this:

A.D. he ran for six.
plus his mouth that makes us sick,
but the times they are a'changing
and his tail will be a hanging
on 400 hundred TV stations
clear across the nation.
You can see ND

kick the shit out of SC
at the great big Golden Dome.

After practice on Friday, Ara would typically give us a few words to think about before we went to dinner and meetings. As Ara spoke this week, you could feel the team being lifted off the ground. This was the gist of his message:

> Notre Dame has great tradition, a tradition founded on a desire to excel in everything we do in our life. We now have a great opportunity to add to the tradition of Notre Dame. USC is going to try to keep its winning streak going, and we are going to stop it. We are going to play as hard as we can for 60 minutes and never give up trying to win this game, no matter what the score is. The whole country will be watching as this game will be on national TV. Let's go out and show the country the type of solid character we have here at Notre Dame and let's win this one for ourselves—you, me, and all the other coaches and people in this program.

The Friday night pep rally was even more raucous than usual, and the crowd went wild when Ara implored them, "I want to be able to count on the Notre Dame spirit tomorrow afternoon!" Afterward, Dan Morrin and I stopped at the Grotto to say our prayer and then we went to Moreau Seminary for our movie, fruit snack, and a good night's sleep away from the campus festivities across the lake. The night went quickly, and then we were up for Mass in Moreau Seminary. We received our religious medals, the ones we got for every game and which I put in my kneepad for the game. Then we went over to the North Dinning Hall for our pregame meal and final meetings before heading to our dorms to see our families. My dad and Gerry DiNardo's father were coming in for the game, as were Dan Morrin's father and uncles.

As we walked from Sorin Hall to the stadium, fans had their programs and were trying to spot players to get autographs. It was a thrill to be asked to sign your name because you were a player, but I was glad to finally get to the stadium. As we prepared to head out for the game, Ara really didn't have to say much. He knew we were ready. He basically said, "All right, men, this is it. We are prepared. Play 60 minutes, play the interval, and we will win this game."

With that, the locker room erupted. I felt three feet off the ground going down the stairs to the tunnel. There was that little old man, he had to be 85 years old, waiting with a big smile at the end of the stairs to tell us to go out there and do our best. As we approached the opening of the tunnel, you could sense the enormous anticipation building in the stadium. I looked at Gerry DiNardo and Dan Morrin and said, "This is it, guys. Let's get them."

It was a gray, cloudy day, with the threat of rain. The Irish ran out of the tunnel onto the field, led by Ara and the three captains. I was so glad to be in the game and to have one more chance to beat the Trojans. We won the toss and elected to receive the ball, and Southern Cal chose to defend the south end zone. Ronny Goodman took the opening kickoff to the Irish 26-yard line and our offense took the field. We ran for one first down, showing off the bat that we could more than hold our own in the trenches. "We felt we could knock them off the ball at the line of scrimmage," said assistant coach Mike Stock. "We felt very strongly about that. We were stronger and tougher." We picked up another first down when Tommy Clements connected with Dave Casper for a 16-yard gain and although the drive stalled we were filled with confidence that we could move the ball. Brian Doherty punted the ball out of bounds at the Trojans 8-yard line and our defense took the field.

According to Mike Townsend, ND assistant coach Paul Shoults told our defense before the game about a boast that USC Coach John McKay had made. "Coach Shoults told us that McKay said if USC gets seven, eight yards on the first play, maybe a first down, the game is over. Southern Cal wins. No sense in Notre Dame playing."

The defense was pumped up for that first play, which turned out to be a quick screen pass in the right flat to All-American receiver Lynn Swann. Freshman defensive back Luther Bradley came up and hammered Swann so hard that the pass went incomplete and Swann's helmet went flying. "I'm just an 18-year-old guy who sees this superstar crossing me and all I wanted to do was make sure he didn't make me look bad," Luther said. "And so I read the play, I go and hit him, and his helmet falls off. People are going nuts. I remember Gary Potempa hitting me on my head, almost hurting me, to congratulate me."

Gary Potempa recalled, "Luther would make those great plays and he would just smile. I said, 'Man, I'm happy you're here.' And I remember running up to Lynn Swann saying, 'We just won the game.' I think they were shocked we had this attitude."

Mike Townsend said the play set the tone for our defense. "After that, it was all our game," he said. Two plays later, our other freshman starter, Ross Browner, nearly sacked Haden in the end zone, but the QB threw away the ball at the last moment. The guys on our defense were playing like they were possessed, and the front line of Mike Fanning, Gary Potempa, George Hayduk, Jim Stock, and Ross Browner had Haden running for his life for much of the game.

On fourth down, USC's Jim Lucas lined up in his own end zone to punt. Tim Rudnick fired in and tipped the kick, which went out of bounds on the Trojans 28-yard line. The pressure on the punt was the result of a scheme suggested by graduate assistant Mike Creaney, who had played tight end for ND the previous three seasons. That summer, Mike had played in the annual All-Star Game in which top college players competed against the defending NFL champion (a tradition that ended in 1976). USC's staff was tapped to coach the college team because the Trojans had won the national championship. Mike played on offense and on special teams, where he noticed a flaw in the punt protection.

"To Ara's credit, here's this snot-nosed assistant in graduate school coming to him with my [play]book from the summer, telling him there's an opportunity to give USC a problem in the kicking game," Creaney said. "He didn't tell me to sit down or shut up." Instead, Ara grilled Mike for about 20 minutes on what he knew. Mike said Ara then went and designed a specific punt rush to attack the Trojans. Indeed, it would continue to pay dividends as the game went on.

Following the tipped punt, from the 28, Tommy Clements hit Pete Demmerle for 16 yards and one first down, but then the USC defense stiffened. Bob Thomas came on to boot a 32-yard field goal, and we had taken a 3–0 lead.

Following the kickoff, Anthony Davis carried for a couple of short gains. After Gary Potempa brought down Davis on the second run, Tim Rudnick was penalized for a late hit, giving USC its first first down of the game. "Timmy hit him and said, 'Hey, pal, this is not the damn Coliseum,'" Gary said.

A little later, Haden hit Swann for a 26-yard pass to the 12-yard line. It took five plays, but USC finally scored when Davis took a pitch sweep to the right and raced one yard for the TD that put Southern Cal on top 7–3. Davis did his little dance in the end zone, and our guys screamed at him, "We don't do that here at Notre Dame." But Davis was making a career against us, having scored his seventh touchdown in five quarters.

After the teams traded punts in the ensuing two possessions, we took over on our own 41-yard line. Tommy Clements pitched one to Pete Demmerle for 14 yards and one first down, Art Best moved the chains again on a fourth-down plunge, and Eric Penick ran for another first down before the drive stalled. Bob Thomas kicked another 32-yard field to bring us to within one point 7–6, with 5:26 left in the half.

USC kept trying to establish a consistent running game with Davis, but the Irish defense was making every yard tough to gain and forced a three-and-out. After another short punt, we started a drive on the Southern Cal 47-yard line. Tommy Clements threw to Pete Demmerle for 13 yards and again connected for 10 yards, with Pete making a terrific catch by stepping in front of two defenders. We were on the USC 13-yard line and in front of the boisterous student section on the north end as a light rain began to fall and time clicked down toward halftime. From the 3-yard line, Wayne Bullock was stopped on his run inches short of the goal line. On fourth down, Tommy dove over the left side for the score. On the play, I pushed Charles Anthony to the right and left tackle Steve Neece drove his man into the end zone, giving Tommy a path to get in. That put the Irish up 13–7, with 30 seconds to go in the half. When the Trojans got the ball back, Luther Bradley intercepted a long pass, and the score held as we went into the break.

At halftime there was a lot of excitement in the locker room. Our ball-possession strategy was working, and Southern Cal had picked up only three first downs in the half, none of them in the second quarter. But our coaches urged us to remember that USC could come back in a flash with their big-play capability.

USC took the second half kickoff and moved past midfield, but that was it. After a punt, we took over on our own 15-yard line. The Trojans were supposed to be the team that could break things open on a single play, but it was our turn to show that we could also play that game. Ara called for a buck sweep. It was our signature play, much like the sweep that the Green Bay Packers used in the Vince Lombardi era. Ara had us repeat that play over and over until we had it perfect in practice, and now we were going to spring it on Southern Cal.

Clements scores against USC

We lined up in a balanced look, with two tight ends and double wingbacks, one to each side. When we came to the line of scrimmage, Tommy Clements had the choice to run the play right or left, depending on the defensive look. He opted to call the sweep going to the left. Right wingback Eric Penick went in motion, Tommy faked a fullback dive to the right and then handed off to Eric who headed around left end. Gerry DiNardo and I, the guards, had pulled to lead him around the corner. I got into my defensive back and pushed him into the guy Gerry was blocking, which opened an alley that Eric rushed into. Art Best came screaming in from his left wingback position and knocked two guys over. Steve Neece and Robin Weber blocked down and got their guys. Dave Casper came across the field and crushed an USC defender who could have tackled Eric.

As I got up from my block, I heard a roar starting and saw Eric's No. 44 racing ahead of three defenders. "The people in the stadium saw it faster than we did on the sidelines, and you could just hear the roar erupt, because everyone knew no one was going to catch him," said assistant coach Bill Hickey. "That was the loudest I ever heard Notre Dame Stadium," said Tommy Clements, who played three years and also served four years as an assistant coach for the Fighting Irish. Eric's legs were moving like two pistons, and after 85 yards he was in the end zone. It seemed like the earth was shaking as our team rushed to mob him in the end zone.

Eric said he didn't hear anything while he ran downfield. "But I did hear it when we got to the end zone, with everybody screaming and yelling," he said. "I was really happy that Ara was happy. He hugged me, and I was happy that I could do what I needed to do for my team. It wasn't about me. I wanted us to be the team that beat USC after seven years. I wanted to be part of that team."

Indeed, it was one of the great runs in Notre Dame history, but Eric said it was all about the team effort. "Ara always told me to make sure I let the guys know how much I appreciate that they're blocking for me," he said. "I can run the ball as hard as I can, with every ounce of power I have, but if they don't put a hole there, it doesn't matter."

We had done to USC what they had done to us the year before—spring the big play—and we were up 20–7. But Southern Cal had too much pride and too much talent to just pack it in. Lynn Swann snagged three passes on the subsequent drive, the last one a 27-yard pass that he caught in the end zone thrown by Haden under pressure, and our lead was cut to 20–14.

After an exchange of punts, the Irish drove back into USC territory, a key play being a fourth-down run by Russ Kornman for six yards. Tommy Clements actually fumbled the snap, but Russ alertly grabbed it in midair without breaking stride and rumbled ahead, enabling us to continue the drive. With the third quarter winding down, Bob Thomas nailed another field goal—from 32 yards out, just like the first two—giving us a little cushion at 23–14.

In the fourth quarter, USC moved the ball to the ND 20-yard line mostly on Haden's passing, then Davis fumbled during a run up the middle, and Greg Collins recovered for the Irish. Later in the quarter, Haden completed a pass to J.K. McKay, but he got popped by Luther Bradley, and Greg again covered the fumble.

USC got one more chance with less than three minutes to go, but Luther picked off a Haden pass to seal the 23–14 win. It was a coming-out party for the freshman defensive back, as he had two interceptions, caused a fumble, broke up a couple of other passes, and laid that crushing hit on Lynn Swann on USC's first play of the game. "I went through the whole game not really knowing where I was. It was a spiritual thing for me," Luther said. "I didn't even remember it until the next day, when I saw the film."

Our entire defense played out of their minds in this game, holding Anthony Davis to 55 yards rushing on 19 carries and zero receptions. We dominated the game, holding the ball for more than 39 minutes. "It felt like a triumph of good over evil, sweet revenge for losing all those years," said offensive lineman Steve Quehl. "We came together as a team and began to believe in ourselves as contenders."

When the game ended, the student body poured onto the field to celebrate with us. I looked for Don Lindsey, the USC assistant coach with whom I'd traveled to Europe that summer. He also came looking for me, and when we met he looked me in the eye and said, "Great game. You guys deserved to win. Good luck the rest of the year." It was a class thing to do, and I thanked Don and wished his team luck as well.

Mike Creaney, the graduate assistant who had helped draw up the effective punt rush after playing for USC coaches in the preseason College All-Star Game, encountered USC assistant coach Craig Fertig. "He looked me up," Creaney said, "shook my hand, and said, 'Kept the book, huh?'" Fertig, by the way, was the 1964 Southern Cal quarterback who had dashed Notre Dame's national championship aspirations by throwing a touchdown pass in the waning moments of the season's final game. This day he saw the Fighting

Irish doom his own team's chances to finish No. 1.

The game was meaningful to Notre Dame fans all around the country—especially in Southern California. where USC fans had held bragging rights for several years. Tom Chitwood was at a viewing party where only he and one other person, his friend Ronnie, rooted for the Irish. "When Eric Penick was running the fly sweep, Ronnie and I were screaming at the top of our lungs, 'Go! Go! Go!' When he scored, we went nuts. The rest of the room was stunned."

Michael Amodei was in school in Southern California taking the PSAT college preparatory test but left before finishing the last section so he could see the kickoff. Michael is now executive editor at Ave Maria Press, a publisher of Catholic books located on the Notre Dame campus. He is also the top usher at Notre Dame Stadium. He remembers when our 1973 team came back for a 40-year reunion and we were honored on the field. Eric Penick was experiencing some health problems and had a hard time walking back to our seats up in the stands, so Michael began to lead him to some bleachers right on the field in the north end zone. Eric, out of breath, asked Michael where they were going. "'Where you scored the touchdown,' I said. From there, the walk seemed easier," Michael said.

I really celebrated that night with family and friends. It was the greatest victory of my athletic life, because USC was such a mountain to climb. You feel good about yourself when you know you have triumphed against great competition. Notre Dame vs. USC was like Muhammad Ali vs. Joe Frazier: it brought out the best in both of us. And it seemed like the national championship was potentially on the line whenever we played during those days.

Some moments will always be embedded in our memories. I believe Eric Penick's run is one of those moments that will always be remembered by me, my teammates, and every Notre Dame fan. And this game was one of the greatest in the long rivalry between two schools with great histories.

Game 7: Navy

The win over Southern Cal moved us up to fifth in the polls, behind Ohio State, Alabama, Oklahoma, and Michigan, in that order. We had hard evidence that we could beat anybody. "It was the first time we had beaten our big rival in a long time, and it gave us the confidence that allowed us to continue on our roll," Tommy Clements said.

Next up was Navy in South Bend. As I have said before, playing against Navy and the other academies was special because their young men had a never-say-die attitude. We could have had a letdown after the emotion of the previous week, but we were on a mission to crush every opponent in our quest for the Holy Grail of college football: an undefeated season. Navy had bombed Air Force 42–6 and only lost 14–0 to Michigan, so we knew they could play with elite teams.

The Middies played us tough until late in the first quarter when Tommy directed a 61-yard scoring drive, ending with a 20-yard sweep by Eric Penick for the score. In the second quarter, we drove 78 yards for another TD, with Al Hunter going the last three yards behind a great block by Gerry DiNardo. Our defense kept shutting down Navy, with Gary Potempa, Greg Collins, Mike Fanning, and Ross Browner all over the Middies and their quarterback, Al Glenny. We went into halftime leading 14–0.

The second half was more productive for our offense. We got to the end zone twice early in the third quarter. After a Greg Collins interception and then a tremendous diving catch by Pete Demmerle that brought the ball to the 1-yard line, Tommy Clements scored over right guard following blocks by Gerry DiNardo and Steve Sylvester. The defense again set up a score as Reggie Barnett recovered a fumble on the Navy 30. Al Samuel finished the drive with a seven-yard run around left end thanks to a great block by Dave Casper.

Jim Stock recorded a safety for us, chasing down Glenny in the end zone. Glenny later connected on 25-yard pass following a recovered fumble. Our reserves scored the last two touchdowns in the fourth quarter. The first one was set up by a 74-yard kickoff return by Al Hunter, a foreshadowing of a crucial play the speedy freshman would make in a later game. Cliff Brown finished the drive by passing to Willie Townsend for nine yards. Then, with Frank Allocco at quarterback, Tommy Parise ran in for the TD that made the final score 44–7.

Twelve Irish players ran for a total of 447 yards in the game, though none of them for more than 66 yards. It was Ara's philosophy to use a lot of running backs instead of just featuring one. He believed it kept his backs fresh, and it also made it more difficult for the defense to key on a single player. Perhaps most of all, Ara loved that this system emphasized victory as a team rather than individual accolades.

Game 8: Pittsburgh

Pittsburgh's new coach Johnny Majors had begun to build a major power. He already had a terrific tailback, freshman Tony Dorsett, and the previous week Pitt had rushed for 455 yards and put up 576 yards in total offense in a win against Syracuse that had brought the Panthers' record to 5–2–1. Dorsett had rushed for 1,139 in his first eight games—an average of 142 yards per game. Of course, Dorsett was a special back, one who went on to win a Heisman Trophy and earn induction to both the College and Pro Football Halls of Fame. It would be a big challenge on the road for the Irish, coming into the game with the top-ranked defense in the country.

Dorsett showed his talent, running for 209 yards in 29 carries. However, he never scored in the game, and the Irish forced key turnovers throughout—seven in total. Tommy Clements had a modest day statistically for us because of a pulled groin, but his leadership and knowledge of how to run the offense was apparent. Wayne Bullock had a big game for us on a day that was blustery with snow showers, running for 167 yards in 27 carries. He ran for three scores and caught a TD pass from Tommy to account for all of our touchdowns. The final score was 31–10.

After the game, Ara singled out Mike Townsend for making crucial tackles downfield that prevented scores, along with breaking up a couple of passes and intercepting another. On one play, Dorsett cut against the grain and got into the secondary. "He was five or six yards in front of me but I had the angle," Mike said. "I caught him around the 20-yard line, and they didn't score." Dorsett had gained 65 yards on the play, but Mike's determination to track him down paid off.

We were 8–0, with two regular season games to go.

Game 9: Air Force

After Pitt, we had the following Saturday off, and the next game was going to be on a Thursday—a Thanksgiving Day game against Air Force to be nationally televised by ABC. The Falcons, coached by Ben Martin, were coming in with a 6–3 record and a four-game winning streak.

It was the last game I would be playing in Notre Dame Stadium. I couldn't believe this was all coming to an end—the practices, the workouts, the chance to run out of the tunnel and onto the home field. Finally I knew why so many players before me got sentimental about this time at Notre Dame. It was truly a great program. Even players who might not get off the bench a lot had the chance to learn from Ara and from Notre Dame how to be successful in life. It had been such a great experience that all the seniors felt sad to see it end. However, there was still football to be played.

Air Force was fighting to play in a bowl game, but it wasn't a great day for the Falcons. We scored four times in the first quarter to take a 28–0 lead. Tommy Clements opened the scoring with a 14-yard pass to All American David Casper, who made an awesome catch in traffic for the touchdown. Eric Penick tallied twice, on a great 6-yard run and a four-yard sweep to the left. The other touchdown was an eight-yard run by Wayne Bullock up the middle.

The Falcons got on the board in the second quarter with a 21-yard pass play from Rich Haynie to Alvin Bready. But Art Best's 69-yard run set up the first of two field goals by Bob Thomas and we took a 34–6 lead at the half. Air Force got a 51-yard field goal by Dave Lawson to make it 34–9, but the Irish kept control otherwise. Senior Notre Dame quarterback Cliff Brown opened the fourth quarter with a 22-yard touchdown pass to Pete Demmerle and Al Samuel added a five-yard scoring run after taking a pitch from Frank Allocco. Air Force picked up another score in the fourth quarter to make the final 48–15 in the last home game for me and the other seniors.

Game 10: Miami

We had gone into the Thanksgiving Day game against Air Force still ranked No. 5. Two days later, No. 1 Ohio State was set to play at No. 4 Michigan. "Ara said, 'Let's hope that Michigan and Ohio State tie. That's what we need,'" Gerry DiNardo recalled. Improbably, that's exactly what happened: those two teams battled to a 10–10 tie. "We're watching this game and we look at each other. We think Ara saying that had something to do with the result of the game. That's how crazy it was," Gerry said.

This opened up the door for us to climb to the top, because we would be playing Alabama in the Sugar Bowl. Oklahoma was on probation and would not be playing any bowl games. But we still had a job to do, finishing up the regular season in the Sunshine State against the University of Miami. The Hurricanes came in 5–5, but they had played a brutal schedule. They had beaten Texas and lost by only four points to unbeaten Oklahoma. Plus, they had some NFL-caliber talent that was big, strong, and quick. I would be playing opposite Tony Cristiani, a very good football player and one of their key seniors. Also on that defensive line was Rubin Carter, who went on to play more than a decade in the NFL.

It was a hot and humid night, and some in the press thought the big Irish linemen would melt in the tropical weather. But we were in good shape and we stuck to the game plan of controlling the ball through the running game and mixing in play-action passes to keep the opponent guessing. Everything was clicking. "I felt the closeness of our team that fall, and as we played each week we got stronger and stronger," Mike Townsend said. "When someone went out, we said 'It doesn't matter.' We plugged somebody else in and just carried on."

We showed how far we had come that season by totally dominating Miami 44–0. The first Notre Dame scoring drive featured a 40-yard run by Art Best, with Wayne Bullock carrying in from the 2-yard line. With that, the rout was on. It was 24–0 by halftime, by which time the Irish had gained 291 yards in offense. The score climbed to 38–0 by the end of the third quarter, and then in the final stanza backup QB Cliff Brown ran six yards to cap a 44–0 win. "That score was amazing because Miami wasn't that bad. We were on fire," said assistant coach Bill Hickey.

Ara readily went to his offensive substitutes in games like this but was more reluctant to make wholesale substitutions on defense, according to Gary Potempa. "He really wanted shutouts," Gary said. "I don't think he ever said it, but every player on the team knew it. If our opponent got a field goal, then the reserves could play." With the game in hand against Miami, Gary told one of the little-used reserves to go in for him. "My coach, George Kelly, said to me, 'You can't do that.' I said that I was going to do it, that we were seniors, and he's a great guy and great player. George said, 'Okay, but if Ara asks, you have to tell him you're hurt.'"

We were the first Notre Dame team in 24 years to go unbeaten and untied in the regular schedule. The Irish were rated No. 3 in the AP poll, which would hold another vote after the bowl games. UPI did not vote after the bowls and named Alabama as its national champion. The Irish had been invited to play in the Sugar Bowl against Alabama. This set up the dream matchup for the AP national championship.

The calendar year had begun on January 1 with our team getting thrashed by Nebraska. We had risen like a phoenix from the ashes of defeat and on December 31 we would have a chance for total redemption.

We came into that year with no expectations, but the ultimate goal of winning a national championship was within reach. We weren't even that good at the beginning. We just got better and better. And at the end of the year, we were playing pretty good football.

The Sweep

CHAPTER 18

The Sugar Bowl

Every few years it seems, a college football contest is labeled the "Game of the Century." Many times the action does not live up to the hype. But the Sugar Bowl on December 31, 1973, turned out to be a true epic. No. 1 Alabama was taking on Notre Dame, ranked No. 3 by the AP, which would vote again after the bowl games. No. 2 Oklahoma, which was unbeaten but had tied Southern Cal, was on probation and ineligible to play in a bowl. So there was little question that the winner of this game between two unbeaten teams would claim the national title.

Most people considered Alabama the favorite because of their great speed and vast number of weapons. This game was to be played in New Orleans at Tulane Stadium, much closer to Bama's home turf. The game would be played outdoors, which meant the weather could become a factor.

There were a lot of intriguing aspects to the matchup. Regional pride was on the line, North against South. Notre Dame was a Catholic university playing a school that came from the heart of Baptist territory. The head coaches, Ara Parseghian and Paul "Bear" Bryant, were extremely successful and highly respected, both destined for the College Hall of Fame. And it matched up Notre Dame and Alabama—two illustrious college football programs that had never before met on the gridiron.

After our final regular-season game against Miami, we took time out for final exams then were able to go home for a few days. Around December

22 we came back to campus to get ready for the game. "The coaches had used that time from the end of the season until we started preparation to develop the game plan," Tommy Clements said. Our quarterback had grown up a big fan of Alabama QB Joe Namath, so he was aware of the history of Alabama under Bear Bryant. "We were playing a great opponent and a great coach," Tommy said. "I came to Notre Dame to play in big games, like against Southern Cal, or to play for a chance to win a national championship."

Because of the cold weather in Indiana, we held most of our practices in the Athletic and Convocation Center (ACC), which didn't have an artificial turf surface. To simulate sultry conditions in Louisiana, "They turned up the heat in the ACC and they had us wear sweats underneath our equipment," Gary Potempa recalled.

As we studied tape on Alabama, it was easy to see why they were so highly ranked. They had an awesome defense and an offense that could run and score from anywhere on the field. The offense featured a pair of gifted quarterbacks. One was Gary Rutledge, a double threat who had passed for 897 yards and eight touchdowns and had rushed for 253 yards and six TDs that season. Richard Todd, who would go on to play about a decade in the NFL, had rushed for 560 yards and two TDs and passed for 325 yards and four scores. Alabama's leading rusher was Wilbur Jackson, the first African American to get a football scholarship to the school. Jackson had rushed for 752 yards and eight touchdowns that season, and he eventually played eight years in the NFL.

The Crimson Tide offensive line was led by tackle Buddy Brown, a consensus All-American, and Sylvester Croom at center, who later became the first black head coach in the SEC when he took over at Mississippi State in 2004. Alabama's offense averaged 366 yards rushing per game and passed for 115—481 combined yards, which was good enough for second in the country. Bama scored more than 60 points twice and overall averaged 41.3 points per game.

The Alabama defense was eighth in the country in points allowed (8.1 per game) and shut out four of its opponents. It was led by sophomore linebacker Woodrow Lowe, who had 134 tackles and was named an All-American.

Other leaders on defense were linemen Mike Raines and John Croyle as well as Mike DuBose, who later served as head coach at Alabama.

"Roll Tide Roll" was the rallying cry for Alabama, and they had indeed rolled over all 11 of their regular-season opponents. None of them came closer than 14 points. They were very quick but also very tough on the line of scrimmage. It was going to be a dogfight. It was once the case that Northern teams were much bigger than their Southern counterparts, but that was no longer reality—they were big and tough. They carried themselves like champions and they even had great uniforms—simple like ours with just two colors, crimson and white. Both programs were familiar with winning national championships, and their fans were itching to claim another one.

The two teams were similar in that they liked to control the ball by running it and owning the clock, though they did it different ways. Alabama ran the wishbone to perfection, and the Tide had two backfield sets that they would interchange with confidence. A lot of times, the other team's defense would just get worn down and run out of gas before the end of the game. The Irish, on the other hand, primarily ran the wing-T offense, which used the power running game as well as a lot of misdirection to keep opponents off balance. Play-action passes came out of the same looks, adding to the defense's difficulty in determining where the play was heading.

The Big Easy was a festive setting for the game. Alabama and Notre Dame fans packed the French Quarter, and in the bars on Bourbon Street, boisterous partisans sang their schools' fight songs. Restaurants were packed, and the week from Christmas to New Year's was one big party. Our families were having a great time, going to Brennan's for breakfast and Pat O'Brien's for drinks. My family stayed at the same hotel as the team. The DiNardos also stayed there, including Larry (who was then in law school at Notre Dame) and his wife, Paula. My fiancée, Aileen Conklin; her mother, Irene; father, Mike; and her sister, Cindy, came down for the festivities as well. Aileen and I were going to get married a few months later and this was a great way to spend the holidays. I received a Sugar Bowl watch, but I requested a woman's watch; I asked my mother if she minded if I gave it to Aileen. Bless her soul, my mother said, "Frankie, she is going to be your wife. Of course I don't mind." Aileen really enjoyed the present.

There were events nightly that both teams would participate in. Max Wasilevich recalled a banquet that both teams attended: "Bear Bryant gets up. He has that hat on. He looks at the audience and with his drawl he says, 'I want to welcome the people from Notre Dame and the North.' I thought, *Oh my God, are we still waging the Civil War?*"

But there was no trash talking between the teams. "These were two class coaches who really required that their players be respectful of their opponents," Tom Creevey said. Assistant coach Bill Hickey added, "It was fun to play Alabama because they reflected Bear Bryant, which meant there would be tremendous hitting and effort. But when the whistle blew, we walked back to our huddles. Bear made them play hard but also made them play legally."

In the days before the game, we had a chance to get around New Orleans, learn about the history, and enjoy some of the unique food, like gumbo and the beignets at Café du Monde. They love their food spicy and their coffee strong in that city, and so do I.

But we were really there for one reason: to win the game. We practiced hard. The winner would be national champion, something that would stay with players for the rest of their lives. It would mean that for one time in their lives, they could say they were the best. We were chasing a Holy Grail, but there was another team that wanted it as much as we did.

Tulane Stadium was built on a former plantation where sugar had been granulated, and it looked like an old battleship. It served as the site of the Sugar Bowl from 1935 to 1974, so we were the next-to-last ones to play the bowl there. A crowd of more than 85,000 packed the stadium, and ABC covered the game with Chris Schenkel, Howard Cosell, and Bud Wilkinson—truly the "A Team." This game would draw a huge TV audience, with a 25.3 Nielsen rating. (To put it in perspective, the highest Nielsen-rated championship game in the BCS era was 21.7 for the 2006 Texas-USC game.)

Luther Bradley, a freshman at the time, said he was nervous before the game: "The thing that cooled my nerves, I was on the elevator to go down to the game. Tom Clements was on the elevator, and I asked him if he was nervous and he said no. He said being nervous is self-inflicted and that he was just going to go out there and have fun. That was enough to get me to think I was going to be all right."

During the bus ride to the stadium, George Hayduk reflected on the path that had brought him to this moment: "I thought to myself, *Here you are, a kid from Factoryville, Pennsylvania, population 1,000. You're really fortunate to be in this situation, playing for the national championship in front of 80,000 fans and millions watching on TV.*"

For this game, we wore our white jerseys with gold pants and gold helmets. We also had special shoes that were gold, with a blue stripe. They looked cool. The problem was, it had rained earlier that night, and players were slipping all over the place in warm-ups. "You'd go to cut and you'd end up right on your butt," Gary Potempa said. The coaches were able to find other shoes, maybe from Tulane or the Saints, and we changed when we got back to the locker room. "They had a bank of shoes. It was like going bowling. You know: 'Give me size 13s.' And those are the shoes we wore in the game," Gary said.

Ara knew we were ready. He simply reminded us to play the full 60 minutes no matter the score, to play the interval and we would be all right. The Tide came on-field first, and then we came out into the open air, thick with humidity and anticipation.

The game opened with Alabama kicking deep into our end zone, where Gary Diminick took a knee, so we would start from the 20. The first play was double tight ends, with double wings and a fullback. This is a play we ran all year that put Tommy Clements in control of the blocking scheme, which could go any of four different ways. Tommy called "even," which meant that we blocked straight ahead. I fired out as fast as I could into linebacker Woodrow Lowe and tried to blast him as hard as possible. I got into him and occupied him for a second as Wayne Bullock ran past us for seven yards before Lowe slipped off me to make the tackle. It was a good start to our running game. I knew we were in for a tough battle, but my attitude was "let's get it on." No matter what, I knew I needed to keep firing out, blasting into anything that moved.

The next few plays saw Wayne go up the middle again, this time for 15 yards, and then Eric Penick over the left side for six yards. In the huddle, the guys were jacked up with enthusiasm because we knew we could move the ball. After a couple of first downs the drive stalled, and Brian Doherty came in and punted out of bounds at the Alabama 16-yard line.

Our defense totally stonewalled the Tide in the first quarter, holding them to zero first downs and zero total yardage. "Ara had the defensive tackles playing on the outside shoulders of the guards," George Hayduk said. "We were responsible for taking away the fullback dive. I remember Ara telling us to not let the offensive guard hook us to the inside, make sure we play his outside shoulder. It worked for the first quarter. They had a hard time running against us with their option." On the option, our linebackers and ends were responsible for the quarterback and the safety had responsibility for the pitch man. With the option shut down, Alabama was not a team that was comfortable relying on its passing game.

Our defense gave us good field position, and late in the quarter, we started a drive on our own 36, mixing passing and running. On play-action, Tommy Clements passed to Pete Demmerle, who made a terrific catch spinning and holding on to the ball for a 19-yard gain. Wayne Bullock went over the right side for five yards, then Tommy hit Pete two more times, once for 26 yards and then for 14. Wayne finished the drive with a one-yard plunge over the left side into the end zone. Unfortunately, holder Brian Doherty fumbled the wet ball on a snap that was a little high and to the right, so Bob Thomas never got to kick the extra point, leaving the score at 6–0. In a game like this, every point could be critical.

The Alabama offense finally began to move the ball downfield in the second quarter. But after reaching the Irish 17-yard line, Rutledge fumbled a planned pitch to Randy Billingsley and Jim Stock recovered for us on our 36. Tommy Clements threw to Dave Casper on a screen pass and the big tight end rumbled for big yards, but the play was called back because of a clip. Then Wayne Bullock did something he hardly ever did: he fumbled and the Tide recovered on their own 48-yard line. From there, Rutledge guided them to a score in seven plays with Billingsley going the last 6 yards. When Bill

Davis made the extra point, Bama took the lead 7–6, exactly halfway through the second quarter.

Senior Gary Diminick and freshman Al Hunter were back to receive the ensuing kickoff. Al took the kick on the 7-yard line and went right up the middle. He got key blocks from Gary and from Dan Morrin—when I came back from injury earlier in the season, I had asked Dan to take my place on special teams because of my limited mobility. Dan stayed on his block up the middle, helping spring Al, who broke through the pack at about the 30-yard line and was off to the races, simply outrunning every defender all the way to the end zone for a 93-yard touchdown return. The stadium erupted, and every player on the Notre Dame bench ran onto the field to congratulate Al on his Sugar Bowl record-breaking kickoff return. (There were no penalties for those kinds of celebrations in the 1973 college game.)

Ara decided to go for the two-point conversion. The play call was for a tackle trap pass out of a double tight end set, with Dave Casper on the right side and Pete Demmerle on the left. The formation was a power-I right. Tommy Clements faked a handoff to Eric Penick, and the Alabama defense froze just long enough for Tommy to loft a perfect pass over a defender to Pete. It was good for two points that put us ahead 14–7. Tommy's throw showed he had ice water in his veins, and that was going to be needed if we were going to pull this one out.

The teams exchanged punts on the next two possessions. Richard Todd came in at QB for the Crimson Tide and he worked the option to perfection to move his team down the field. When the Irish defense stiffened, Davis came in to kick a 39-yard field goal, narrowing the Notre Dame lead to 14–10.

With time running out in the second quarter, we were able to move to Alabama 31-yard line in four plays, including two runs by Tommy Clements totaling 27 yards. As time ran out, Bob Thomas came up short on a 48-yard field goal try and we went to the locker room with the four-point lead. Although we were ahead, Alabama had come on strong in the second quarter, amassing 154 total yards in offense after being completely shut down in the first quarter. The game felt like two heavyweight boxers throwing haymakers, but neither one was going to stay down for the count.

The hitting was fierce, and if you had a bad play you just had to forget it and focus on making the next play better. Defensive end Jim Stock got hurt, and backup Tom Creevey ended up playing considerable time. "It was a long way from being a high school quarterback to being a defensive end playing for the national championship," Tom said. "Ara had taught us about being persistent—never give up, you never know when your number is going to be called. So here I was, the last game of my career, and my number was called."

The second half began with Cliff Brown kicking to Alabama, which continued the momentum it had built in the previous quarter. Rutledge moved the ball down the field, mixing a perfect option run offense with passing. Finally, Jackson ran five yards into the end zone to cap an 11-play, 88-yard drive that put the Crimson Tide on top 17–14 with 11:10 to go in the third quarter. The cries of "Roll Tide Roll" seemed to be getting louder.

We were unable to do much on the next series, and Bama took over on the Irish 48 after a punt. Richard Todd was back at quarterback and he ran the ball 16 yards on the option for a first down at the ND 32. But our defense dug in, and on fourth down, Davis was wide right on a 45-yard field-goal try. On our next drive, Tommy Clements and Dave Casper hooked up on a 28-yard pass that brought us into Alabama territory, but Bob Thomas was unable to convert on a 54-yard field goal attempt, leaving Alabama to take over on its 20-yard line.

On third-and-9, the defense created the turnover we needed when Willie Shelby fumbled and linebacker Drew Mahalic recovered it in midair and ran it back to the Alabama 12-yard line. We were on the left hash mark, and our coaches had noticed an Alabama defensive tendency. "If we had the ball on the left hash and we put the left halfback in motion, they would double rotate their secondary," said assistant coach Mike Stock. "It meant there would be no backside coverage in the flat. So we ran the crisscross counter."

The play was a handoff to Eric Penick, coming from the right wing position and running to the left side. The left side of our line blocked to the inside, which got the Alabama defense leaning out of position to the right. Right guard Gerry DiNardo and right end Dave Casper pulled to lead the blocking on the left side. Gerry kicked out the end, and Dave flattened two guys down the field, and Eric ran untouched into the end zone. It was the perfect play and it was perfectly executed. Bob Thomas added the extra point, and with 2:30 remaining in the third quarter, the Irish were back on top, 21–17.

Momentum was back on our side, and after forcing an Alabama punt, we took over on our own 25. By the time the third quarter was over, we had driven into Alabama territory with hopes of driving into the end zone and getting some breathing room. We were 15 minutes away from a national championship, but miles to go before we could sleep on that claim.

From the 39, Art Best ran 14 yards to the Alabama 25. But on the next play, Art got popped hard and fumbled, and the Tide recovered on the 22. Rutledge came back in at QB and moved the Tide for one first down, but when he tried to throw downfield to Johnny Sharpless, the receiver bobbled the ball, and Reggie Barnett intercepted on the ND 32. But we were only back in business temporarily, as Wayne Bullock fumbled on our second play, and Bama got the ball back on the Irish 39. The teams were slugging it out toe to toe, and momentum was shifting like a roller coaster.

Tide running back Paul Spivey ran up the middle for two yards, and then Billingsley swept around left end for nine yards and a first down. Rutledge gained only one yard on an option keeper to the right and then passed to Billingsley in the flat for two yards. At that point, Bear Bryant pulled Rutledge and put in Todd for a play call that took the Irish by surprise.

"They didn't run counters. I couldn't believe they didn't run any misdirection stuff. They were really set on the option," Gary Potempa said. "So as soon as they started running it one way, I was just flying in there." But the misdirection came on this play. Todd handed off to running back Mike Stock who began heading around right end. As the defense flowed to that side, Stock suddenly stopped and fired the ball down the left sideline to Todd, who had leaked out of the backfield after handing the ball off. Todd was all alone, and he sprinted into the end zone for the touchdown that put the Crimson Tide ahead 23–21 with 9:39 left in the game. But this time it was Alabama that missed the extra point, leaving the margin at two points.

We knew then that we would not have many more opportunities to score. Gary Diminick returned the kickoff to the 19-yard line, and we started from there. The first play was a counter in which Dave Casper and I pulled to the right and Al Hunter cut inside of our blocks, good for a 15-yard gain. Then we ran the same play to the other side with Eric Penick going for four yards behind a pull block by Gerry DiNardo. On the next play, Tommy Clements faked another counter to the left and rolled right looking for a pass. With no one open, he took off and ran for a first down. Wayne Bullock gained only a yard on first down, and on the next play, Tommy rolled left again planning to throw, but under heavy pressure, he pulled down the ball and ran 8 yards to the Alabama 45 yard line. Tommy was taking control against one of the finest defenses in the country.

On third-and-1, Tommy faked to the fullback, rolled right, and threw it deep. Dave Casper muscled the ball away from two Alabama defenders, a tremendous catch that put us on the 15-yard line of the Tide.

From there, Al Hunter ran right on a counter for three yards. Then Tommy went around left end for eight yards and a first down on the 4. We were knocking on the door for a touchdown, but the proud Bama defense dug in and got tough. Eric Penick took a pitch and went left for one yard, then Art Best gained another hard-to-come-by yard on a counter to the right. An incomplete pass on third down left it fourth-and-goal at the 2-yard line. Ara sent in Bob Thomas for the field goal try—only 19 yards, but with the season on the line. It was not what you would call a dead-solid, perfect kick, but Bob put it inside the right upright. It was as beautiful as any 50-yard field goal, and the three points gave us a 24–23 lead with 4:26 remaining, as Alabama's missed extra point loomed large.

Emotions on the field were running high. Alabama brought the kickoff all the way to their own 39, giving them good field position with plenty of time to get close enough for a field goal. On first down, Rutledge ran the option to the right, but Luther Bradley, who mirrored the quarterback on the play, dropped him for a four-yard loss. On second down, Rutledge threw incomplete to Sharpless on the right sideline. The Tide needed 14 yards on third down to keep the drive alive, but as Rutledge rolled to the left, he was sacked by Ross Browner for a loss of five yards. I don't know how Rutledge held on to the ball—he was really blasted by Ross.

With fourth-and-19, the Bear decided to punt and see if his defense could get the ball back or pin Notre Dame near its own end zone and force a mistake. Greg Gantt got off a great punt that sailed over Tim Rudnick's head, hit around the 20, and started rolling toward the end zone. A host of Alabama players surrounded the ball until it got to the 1-yard line, where they killed it.

However, on the punt, Ross Browner had run into Gantt. Bryant had a decision to make. He could take the 15-yard penalty, which would leave his team with fourth down and four yards to go at their own 45, or he could decline the penalty and rely on his defense to get the ball back in good field position. One thing about great coaches is they are not afraid to make decisions and take the heat if they don't work out. Bear declined the penalty, and with three minutes to go, we took over on our own 1-yard line.

There was an unusual aspect to the field at that end of Tulane Stadium. As you went from the field into the end zone, the ground sloped down noticeably, perhaps for drainage reasons. We noticed that before the game, and Ara had our long snapper, Joe Alvarado, practice snapping the ball toward the knees of our punter, Brian Doherty, so that the ball would actually arrive waist-high, given the slope. But you had to hope the different routine wouldn't cause a mistake and you had to worry about the pressure on a punter kicking uphill from his own end zone. This added to our urgency to make a first down. Otherwise, Alabama would very likely end up with the ball in prime position to kick a game-winning field goal.

Wayne Bullock went straight ahead for three yards on the first play, then plunged for another yard on second down. At third and about six, Alabama called timeout with 2:12 to go.

Tommy Clements went to the sideline during the timeout. "I was standing there with Ara and he said, 'Let's go with power-I right, tackle trap, pass left.' And I said, 'Are you sure about that?' And he said, 'Yeah.' So I said, 'Okay.' And it was a great call on his part," Tommy remembered. It was a pass play designed to look like a run, coming out of an I-formation with an additional back set in the backfield to the right. The primary target was Dave Casper, our All-American tight end, who was going to line up on the right side. But to help sell the idea that it really was a run, Ara inserted Robin Weber into the game at tight end on the left side. Robin had only caught one pass all season.

"Alabama had two guys on Casper all game. It took a tremendous amount of faith and guts by Ara to call that play," said assistant coach Bill Hickey.

"Robin Weber was like a tackle—big guy, big hands," said linebacker Tim Sullivan. "He was a heck of a blocker. But a lot of times in practice, we didn't cover Robin because he wasn't that good at catching the ball."

The Notre Dame defensive unit was rallying on the sideline in case it had to go back into the game. "I went up to every single guy saying, 'We've got to stop them. Let's go!'" Gary Potempa said.

Tommy Clements gave us the play in the huddle and then called for a long snap count to try to draw the defense offside. Before we broke the huddle, Dave Casper reminded everyone not to move early. But when we lined up, some of the Alabama players shifted a little, and it was Dave who went offside. The penalty made it third-and-8 from our own 3-yard line.

From the sideline, Ara signaled to Tommy to run the same play that had been called. This was the moment of truth. In the broadcast booth, Chris Schenkel told viewers, "This is the dream match. The most important game of the year." Howard Cosell, who never understated anything, added, "Notre Dame and Alabama. At Notre Dame, football is a religion. At Alabama, it's a way of life."

My assignment was to check the linebacker and block down on the middle guard. Steve Sylvester pulled from his right tackle spot to execute a trap block, again suggesting to the defense that the play would be a run, and Tommy faked a handoff to Eric Penick.

As Tommy dropped back into the end zone about five yards, Dave Casper was having a hard time getting open. "They tackled Casper. He was on the ground," said assistant coach Mike Stock. "And here goes Weber up the field, doing exactly what he was supposed to do. We told him if the corner comes up to support against the run, angle away from the safety behind the corner, and you'll have a chance to be open. We taught that the whole season."

That's exactly what happened. The cornerback on Robin's side bit on the run fake, and Robin ran right past him, then began angling toward the left sideline. "I looked in the direction of where Weber was supposed to be coming to, and saw how the defense reacted," Tommy said. He was under pressure, but he lofted the ball over a leaping rusher and down the field toward Robin as he approached the 30-yard line.

As I went through my blocking scheme, I heard a roar from the crowd. I looked up, and all the Irish players on the field and sideline were jumping up and down, so I knew something good had happened. And it was Robin catching Tommy's pass over his left shoulder before running out of bounds at the 38-yard line, right at the Alabama bench. "Robin caught it, and we ran across the field and kissed him," Tim Sullivan said. "It was one of the greatest catches in my football experience. And the poise that Tommy had was just unbelievable."

We no longer had our backs against the wall, but we needed another first down to avoid having to punt it back to Alabama. On third down, Tommy took care of that with a seven-yard run around right end. A couple of plays later, time expired. Notre Dame players and fans all poured onto the field to celebrate. Ara's Knights had won the national championship, the Holy Grail of college football.

Ara gave a classy speech to the Sugar Bowl crowd after the game. "I would like to pay tribute to the Alabama team, one of the finest football teams we've ever played. One of the best-coached football teams we've ever played. We're thrilled. It was a great game for college football," he said.

Tommy Clements was selected MVP of the game and deserved it. He ran for 74 yards on 15 carries and completed 7-of-12 passes for 169 yards and no interceptions. He directed Ara's offense to perfection and was as cool as a player could be under pressure.

The locker room was jammed afterward. Some of the guys said that Bear Bryant came in to congratulate Ara and Tommy.

I was almost in a state of shock. It had been such a long journey to get there—years of working on strength and speed just to get a chance to play at Notre Dame, then four years of total commitment to improving myself mentally and physically. I almost felt as if there must be more to do. *This moment,* I wondered, *can it really be true?*

Perhaps I'm not the only one who had those feelings. After the Sugar Bowl, Dave Casper went directly from New Orleans to a college All-Star Game in Hawaii. When he got back to Notre Dame several days later, he went into the coaches' offices to get his car keys, as we had all left our cars under the stadium when we traveled to the Sugar Bowl. "Coach Parseghian was there," Dave said. "When I walked in, the first thing he said to me was, 'Why did you jump offside?' I actually think he was serious. If he was like me, he probably can't believe we won and he's still afraid any mistake we made will come back to get us, just in case someone said we had to replay the game."

But no one asked us to play it again. It was a game with excitement to provide memories for a lifetime. And when you look it up in the books, it still says we reached the summit—we were national champs in 1973.

Epilogue

Playing for Ara Parseghian was a little like trying to hold water in your hands. You know it is precious and you don't want to let it get away. You want to record every moment because it is so meaningful. We wanted to be around him as much as we could so we could learn as much about life that he knew. But no matter how hard you try to hold on, water will slip through the slivers of space between your fingers. "All things must pass," as George Harrison said.

But it was a shock that Ara Parseghian's coaching career lasted only one more season after that epic win over Alabama for the 1973 national championship. And it is a shame that not one of Ara's assistant coaches or players ever got a chance to be head coach of the Fighting Irish and pass on the lessons learned from the master. I can't help but think Notre Dame would have fared far better over the years if one or more of Ara's Knights had been given the reins.

In mid-December, 1974, Ara announced he would leave coaching for at least a year because he was "physically exhausted and mentally drained" from 24 years of coaching football. Looking back, some of Ara's Knights had seen the telltale signs. "When Ara came to Notre Dame he was 40 years old, but he looked like he was 30 and acted like he was 20," said Jim Lynch, captain of the 1966 national championship team. "Ten years later they honored him at a reception and now Ara was 50, but looked like he was 60 and acted like he was 70. The difference in those 10 years was amazing."

Ara's health concerns were partly based on the deaths of three of his friends, which occurred within a few months of each other. Additionally, his sister and his daughter, Karan, were battling multiple sclerosis, and Ara served as chairman of the National Multiple Sclerosis Society in 1974. His wife, Katie, was worried about his health.

There is no question that the pressure of coaching at Notre Dame took a physical toll on a coach as intense as Ara. Frank Leahy, like Ara, coached 11 seasons at Notre Dame. In his final season, in 1953, Leahy collapsed at halftime during a game and was actually given Catholic last rites. Frank Leahy's son, offensive lineman Jim Leahy, recalled a time during 1968 or 1969 when his father became ill. During practice, Ara called Jim aside. "He asked how my father was doing." Jim said. "And he also asked, 'How old was he when he left here?' I told him he had been 44. 'My God, that's how old I am,' Ara said."

The 1974 team was favored to repeat as national champions, but several preseason events derailed the team. Running back Eric Penick suffered a broken ankle before the spring game. In the summer, Tim Simon, a defensive back and kick-return specialist, incurred a season-ending eye injury in an accident at home. Steve Quehl was in line to take over left guard in 1974 until an incident during his summer construction job. "An explosion of the transmission in the truck I was driving nearly severed my leg," Steve said. It took reconstruction of bone and tissue to save the limb so he could walk again. "I remember lying in the hospital, feeling pain and self-pity in contending waves, and reckoning from all reports that my college career, along with any hopes of a shot at the pros, was dead." But Steve courageously worked his way back to play again in 1975.

Then there was the episode involving six players attending summer school. An 18-year-old woman went to police and accused them of raping her in a dorm room. The involved players—Ross Browner, Luther Bradley, Willie Fry, Al Hunter, Roy Henry, and Dan Knott—denied the allegation, and the woman eventually decided to not press charges. Because it involved a high-profile program like Notre Dame, the story got a lot of coverage around the country. The accused players were going into their sophomore year, and several of them had played a big role as freshmen. They all strenuously denied the allegation of rape. From the stories I have heard from people with more direct knowledge of the incident, I will say that I believe the players' denials. But there was a lot of pressure on the Notre Dame administration to expel the students, who had violated a school rule by having a woman in the dormitory after approved hours. Ara went to bat for the players in meetings with university officials.

"Ara begged and pleaded to give those kids a chance because he didn't want them to be ostracized," said Greg Blache, an assistant coach who attended meetings on the issue with Ara, Notre Dame president Theodore Hesburgh, and executive vice-president Edmund Joyce, who was in charge of athletics. In one of those meetings, "Ara said to Hesburgh, 'I've never asked you for anything for me. I've asked you for things for the team, for the players, for the university.' He said, 'But on behalf of these kids, if you can't do it for them, could you do it for me on their behalf? Because I think it's important that we save these guys. The media is going to kill them enough. We have to give them a lifeline.'"

Ara's efforts eventually did succeed in getting their punishment reduced to a one-year suspension instead of expulsion. If they stayed away from campus and stayed out of trouble for the year, the university would consider bringing them back. Another assistant coach, Bill Hickey, said Ara's "whole purpose was to make the administration understand these guys were really a victim of circumstance." According to Bill, "Only one person at Notre Dame at the time could have helped those players, and it was Ara."

Luther Bradley, one of the six suspended players, called it "one of the darkest times of my life." He recalled his conversation with Ara regarding the suspension: "He said, 'It's hard right now. You guys are getting a lot of press.' He said, 'Time is going to heal. You are going to be okay. You are going to be fine.'" Luther continued, "With him just saying that, I knew that even if I didn't have an opportunity to come back to Notre Dame that it was going to be okay. He provided me the fortitude and the stamina to forge ahead and say, 'Okay, I think I can make it through and be a better person for it.'"

Luther did return to Notre Dame, earned All-American honors as part of the 1977 national championship team, and went on to play in both the NFL and USFL. Today he is a senior market relations representative for a major health insurer and gives inspirational speeches to church youth groups. "I talk about how I failed," he said. "I tell them that when I went to Notre Dame, I had these goals in mind: to be a starter, to get good grades, to graduate from ND, and to be on the cover of a national magazine. After that incident, one of my goals came through—we were on Page 1 of the *New York Times*." He added, "It was very painful. But I endured and learned some tremendous lessons. I even said that I'm glad I went through it because it made me a much better person for it."

Greg Blache saw the strain the incident put on the coach: "He was hurt for the kids and afraid they would not be able to overcome what had happened." Greg Collins, starting linebacker in 1974, said he believed the dormitory incident and its aftermath were big factors in Ara's eventual resignation. "I didn't think it was the football that got him," Collins said. "I think that summer really took it out of him."

Mike Parseghian also said the battle to help the players took a lot out of his dad. "He was very distraught," Mike said. "The university wanted to expel the guys with no recourse to coming back, and he individually worked very hard to make it an option at the end of the year to see how the guys were doing and get them back in school."

After that one year, five of the six players (all but Roy Henry) returned to the university. I can't help but wonder how many national championships Notre Dame might have won if the dormitory incident had never happened and if Ara had remained coach. With all of those talented players and under the direction of senior QB Tom Clements, the Irish would have been a big favorite to repeat in 1974. Additionally, that fall, a freshman named Joe Montana arrived at Notre Dame. I can only imagine how he would have realized his potential sooner under the guidance of Ara and his great staff.

The 1974 season began with impressive wins over Georgia Tech and Northwestern. But in the season's third game an old nemesis, Purdue, upset the Irish, putting a damper on the quest to repeat as national champions.

By this time, high blood pressure was becoming a real concern for the Notre Dame head coach, according to assistant Mike Stock. "A doctor would come in every Wednesday to closely monitor how he was," Mike said. Bill Hickey, another assistant coach, added, "The doctor said, 'Ara, if you keep this up, you will be a dead man. Step away from this for a year and you can get back on track if you want to, but you are a walking time bomb, and it's going to kill you.'"

At Notre Dame, the pressure to win is constant. The more you win, the more expectations rise until there is less joy in victories and defeats became bitterer. With Ara's great success, alumni and fans expected so much that he began hearing criticism even in victory if the wins were not convincing enough. In November at Veterans Stadium in Philadelphia, the heavily favored Irish narrowly beat Navy, 14–6. "The Navy game was real close, and we barely won, and he took a lot of heat for that. I thought he was thinking, *I've had enough*," said Mike Fanning, an All-American defensive tackle for the Irish in 1974.

Mike Stock said he vividly remembered the Navy game and its aftermath. "I saw Ara on the plane ride back and he looked tired and drained." Mike added, "The pressure at Notre Dame is hard to explain. Only the people who sit there can tell you about it. There is so much expectation. It didn't take long for him to go from savior to 'What are you going to do next?'" It was on that plane ride back from the Navy game that Ara reportedly told Edmund Joyce of his intention to resign when the season ended.

Four weeks later, the Irish were 9–1 and ranked No. 5 when they went to the Los Angeles Coliseum to play No. 6 USC. Ara's last regular-season game turned out to be one of the strangest games ever in the long intersectional series.

Twenty-nine minutes into the game, Notre Dame had amassed a 24–0 lead, totally dominating its rival. Greg Collins said USC players were complaining and pointing fingers at each other. "I've never seen anything like it," Greg said. "I'm looking at them and I know that team is beaten." With 10 seconds left in the half, Southern Cal finally got on the board when Anthony Davis caught a seven-yard TD pass from Pat Haden. The Irish took what appeared to be a comfortable lead, 24–6, into halftime.

Then, as Greg put it, "everything went goofy." Davis took the second-half kickoff and ran it back 102 yards for a score, and then the floodgates opened. Davis scored two more TDs before the quarter was half over. The Trojans capitalized on every Notre Dame miscue and put up 35 points in the third quarter. After being down 24–0, USC rallied to claim a 55–24 victory, the final 28 points coming as the result of Irish turnovers. After that game, USC went on to win the Rose Bowl and claim a national championship—although they needed some help from Ara's team to make that possible. But I'm getting ahead of myself.

A few weeks after the season ended, Ara turned in his "resignation." I put that in quotation marks, because more than one of Ara's Knights said the coach was really hoping for a sabbatical. This is how the *Chicago Tribune* reported it on Monday, Dec. 16, 1974:

> Ara Parseghian, emotionally and physically exhausted, has resigned at Notre Dame to take at least a one-year rest from football coaching.
>
> The 51-year-old coach said he will remain at the university, at least during the sabbatical, and does not now contemplate a jump into the pro coaching ranks.

Just one day later, the *Tribune* reported that beleaguered coach of the Green Bay Packers Dan Devine—who had been a runner-up for the Notre Dame job when Ara was hired—had quit the NFL and had accepted the head-coaching job at Notre Dame. The *Tribune* reported:

> Two sources said Devine, who received a five-year contract, actually signed with Notre Dame on Friday.

Mike Parseghian, who was a sophomore in 1974, said he didn't find out his father was leaving until a day or two before the announcement. "I knew the stresses he was going through," Mike said. "His original goal had been to continue coaching until I graduated."

Offensive lineman Steve Quehl had been rehabbing from the accident that had sidelined him for the season when he heard the news that Ara was leaving. "I was crushed," Steve said. "I had desperately wanted to come back and play a senior season under Coach, who was the main reason I had come to Notre Dame." Gerry DiNardo, a starting guard in 1974, was on Christmas break back in Queens when the news broke. "I was upset that Ara was leaving and I was mad that he didn't tell us," Gerry said. But after the players returned from break, "He got us together and explained that he wanted to tell us personally." The problem was, Devine's camp had leaked the story early, Gerry said. Perhaps they wanted the story of the new job out before Devine got fired at Green Bay.

"Then when we find out Ara asked for a sabbatical, we even got madder," Gerry said. Four assistant coaches had agreed to take the job on an interim basis—Tom Pagna, Paul Shoults, Joe Yonto, and George Kelly. "This is about [Ara's] genius," said Gerry, who said the sabbatical idea was a new idea on the coaching scene. He described Ara's thinking as "If this is a great academic institution and faculty members benefit from a break, and their students benefit from them taking a break, why wouldn't I be a better coach when I come back?" Gerry said, "I know I got mad at the university for not letting him take a sabbatical."

Tom Pagna would have been a great coach, Terry Hanratty said. "Tom was Ara's almost son. Ara wanted to take one year off. Fr. Joyce had told Dan Devine's mother that if the job opened, Dan would be the next coach." No one but Devine was ever interviewed for the job, as Hesburgh confirmed in his autobiography, *God, Country, Notre Dame.*

Roger Valdiserri, the former sports information director at Notre Dame, said Ara had written out his thinking about the transition on a legal sheet of paper before he went to see Fr. Joyce. "He summarized all the qualities of each assistant that could take over," Roger said. "The first thing Fr. Joyce said was, 'Ara, never mind. I've got your replacement.' So Ara never got to discuss any of the things he had on the sheet.'"

"Ara was heartbroken when he had to come in and tell us they had already given a contract to Dan Devine," Bill Hickey said. "He stepped down with the idea that either Tom Pagna or Paul Shoults would become head coach, like most orderly transitions at most colleges." Dan Devine coached six seasons at Notre Dame, winning a national championship in 1977. His record at Notre Dame was 53–16–1, for a .764 winning percentage. That didn't measure up to the .836 winning percentage that Ara produced at Notre Dame, but it is admittedly difficult to follow a legend.

It wasn't the only time that Notre Dame had the opportunity to hire one of Ara's Knights as head football coach. When Devine retired at the end of the 1980 season, Pagna was not even 50 years old. But the school hired Gerry Faust, a very successful high school coach and a man who loved Notre Dame, but whose lack of any college coaching experience doomed his tenure.

When Lou Holtz resigned at the end of the 1996 season, Gerry DiNardo was just coming off a 10–2 season as the head coach at LSU. He never got an interview for the Notre Dame job. Tommy Clements, who had worked as quarterbacks coach for four seasons under Holtz, did get interviewed, but the job went to Irish defensive coordinator Bob Davie. When Ty Willingham was fired after the 2004 regular season, Tommy was again a candidate for the position. By this time, he had worked as an assistant coach with several NFL teams and had been offensive coordinator for the Buffalo Bills. Greg Blache, an assistant under Ara, was defensive coordinator for the Washington Redskins at that time and was also interviewed for the job. But both Tommy and Greg lost out to Charlie Weis, a Notre Dame grad and offensive coordinator for the New England Patriots.

In 2009, the job opened up again. Tommy was the quarterbacks coach for the Green Bay Packers, but he got passed over once more, as Notre Dame hired Brian Kelly. "I called Tommy and asked him if he wanted the job. He said he would love to do it," Terry Hanratty said. "I said, 'I'll make a call right now.' Even Aaron Rodgers put in a good word for him." Terry added, "Tommy should have had a shot along the way. He is a bright guy, articulate, and he would have been a great recruiter."

* * *

After Notre Dame announced the hiring of Dan Devine, Ara's Knights had one last game—against Alabama in the Orange Bowl in Miami. It was a rematch of the classic Sugar Bowl played the season before, in which the Irish claimed a national championship with a 24–23 win. The Crimson Tide was once again unbeaten and playing for a national championship.

In his autobiography *Bear*, Alabama head coach Bear Bryant reveals that Ara wrote to him after the 1973 Sugar Bowl:

> I got a letter from Ara Parseghian shortly afterward, the only one I ever received from a coach who beat me. He said how much his group had enjoyed playing us, how wrong the impressions were beforehand. (They pictured us as a bunch of rednecks, and we had some thoughts about them, too.) He said how much everybody got out of the game, and how great it was for college football that we now had a series going. It was very gracious, Ara's letter. One I'd loved to have written him.

For the rematch, Notre Dame players were inspired to send Ara out a winner. "I don't know that I ever felt more confident in a big game as a player than I felt in that one," Gerry DiNardo said. "Because we'd be damned if we were going to lose his last game."

The Irish came into the game as a 12-point underdog. But on New Year's night 1975, they came out with poise and determination. Following a Crimson Tide fumble, Wayne Bullock crossed the goal line on a short burst to make it 7–0. A little later, Tommy Clements directed a 77-yard drive, capped off by a Mark McLane eight-yard run that made the score 13–0 after the missed extra point. The Tide hit a field goal in the second quarter to make the score 13–3, and it held until the fourth quarter.

The Irish defense had stymied Bama's wishbone running attack, and the Crimson Tide was forced to take to the air. Quarterback Richard Todd connected with Russ Schamun on a 48-yard scoring play, and with a successful two-point conversion, the Irish lead was cut to 13–11 with 3:13 left in the game. The Tide got the ball back once more, but Todd threw a pass that was picked off by Reggie Barnett to seal the upset victory and ruin Alabama's perfect season. (Again, unbeaten Oklahoma had not played in a bowl game because of recruiting violations, and so UPI voted Rose Bowl winner Southern Cal as national champs.)

For the Irish players, it was one last chance to hoist Ara on their shoulders. "I remember feeling very emotional about it," Gerry DiNardo said. "I felt great about the win and then, selfishly, I felt so glad it was over for me. I didn't want to continue without Ara."

Ara Parseghian never returned to coaching. But he did return to the game. Beginning in 1975, he worked as a color analyst on college football games, and continued for 14 seasons. "When he went into broadcasting, he was able to go onsite, meet with the coaches, meet with the players, and watch and analyze the games," Mike Parseghian said. "It kept him involved not just with football but with the people and the camaraderie and teamwork. If he tried to stay home and do nothing but play golf, I think he would have gone crazy and would have ended up going back into coaching."

In 1980, he was inducted into the College Football Hall of Fame. Ara also became increasingly involved with medical causes. Besides his work for the National Multiple Sclerosis Society, he joined with son, Mike, and Mike's wife, Cindy, to found the Ara Parseghian Medical Research Foundation in 1994. The foundation is seeking a cure for Niemann-Pick Disease Type C. Three of Mike and Cindy's children died from the disease, a genetic disorder that damages the nervous system.

Roger Valdiserri remains close with Ara, meeting him weekly for lunch. "He is not even an alumnus, but he loved Notre Dame. He still does," Roger said. He and Ara sometimes discuss the state of Notre Dame football, but Ara will never criticize another coach. "He'll say, 'They do what they have to do.' That's him." Roger concluded, "When you look at all his qualities, he was the perfect fit for Notre Dame."

At Notre Dame, Ara Parseghian orchestrated something powerful, precise, and magical. It almost seemed as if the music died when he left, but it was up to Ara's Knights to extend his message and example of courage, commitment, and integrity. Ara kept a professional distance from players while he coached them, but many of us got to experience his warmth after our college playing time was over. "That role of player-coach needs to exist all the way through," said Rocky Bleier, but "once you leave, he becomes a different person."

Former players are full of stories about personal notes from him and phone conversations that they have enjoyed with him over the years. "It has been a real treat to get to know him after we played football," said Dan Morrin, my former roommate. "It's nice to know that that steely eyed guy who was so precise was such a nice guy who was always looking out for us. I've called him up a few times, and he would talk to me for 45 minutes."

After Notre Dame, Tommy Clements joined the Ottawa Rough Riders of the Canadian Football League, beginning a very successful 14-year career that resulted in his induction into the Canadian Football Hall of Fame. "During my first year playing up in Canada, I got a call from Ara as I was getting ready to go to practice. He was just calling to see how I was doing and how the team was doing. And that is how Ara is. He is a great guy, and for him to take the time out to do that, it meant a lot to me," Clements said.

When Gerry DiNardo became a college head coach, he would sometimes get a note from Ara congratulating him on a win. "I couldn't have been happier," said Gerry, who kept all of the notes. "When I got the Indiana [head coaching] job, he sent me a note saying that I sure had bad timing because Antwaan Randle El had graduated the year before."

"I've had my ups and downs in life, but Ara was always there for me," Eric Penick said. He summed up his experience this way: "All over the world people wanted to do what I did, and yet at one time I didn't appreciate it. I realize now how blessed I really am. Ara taught me and Notre Dame taught me and the people around me taught me I can accomplish anything in this world I want to accomplish."

In one conversation that I had with Ara, he told me that the best way to approach being a football coach is to motivate the individuals on your team as people, not as football players. And I believe he always tried to look at us that way. In some ways we were his children, and he had a masterful way of motivating us. We wanted to perform for him because we held him in such high esteem. We wanted to be like him.

We get together as a team every five years to celebrate the 1973 national championship. At the 40-year reunion in 2013, Ara walked with a cane, and his charcoal-black hair had become silver. But his mind was sharp and so was his humor. He kept us laughing, teasing us that "When you get older, you have a tendency to think the run was longer, the pass was longer, the tackle was harder." I'm sure there is more than a grain of truth in that. And so, dear reader, you are free to take that into account as you read our stories of those days.

I loved the guys on that 1973 team. We were very much like a family, and it was all because of Ara's program. When we gathered for that 40th reunion, we reminisced about the funny things that happened back when we were in school. We talked about our brothers who have passed on, and the ones who couldn't be with us because of illness. We traded stories about our families, our gray hair or lack of it, our knee and hip replacements, and all the other medical issues that come with getting older.

And at the Notre Dame football game that Saturday, we went on the playing field, and the announcer introduced us as the 1973 national champions. Whether you were a starter or a reserve, all the members of the Notre Dame 1973 team coached by Ara Parseghian stood a little taller, and our chests expanded a little broader as we remembered that once we were the finest team in the country. For that one shining moment in New Orleans, we were at the summit of our sport.

"Don't let it be forgot that once there was a spot, for one brief shining moment, that was known as Camelot." Those words come from the Broadway musical *Camelot*, which debuted in 1960. It was the same year that John F. Kennedy was elected president. Since the president's death, his era has often been referred to as a Camelot, a time when a dynamic young leader led a great nation.

I have compared playing for Ara Parseghian at Notre Dame to Camelot under King Arthur, a place of high ideals and purpose. The difference is that Camelot is a myth. The Era of Ara was real, with a leader who challenged us to strive for important goals on the field and in life. As one of Ara's Knights, I am forever grateful to have had the chance to be part of it.

Sorin Hall

Acknowledgments

This book was years in the making. The idea for it began at a time when I sometimes made presentations to clubs including the Knights of Columbus, Rotary, and Kiwanis. When I was asked what it was like to play for Ara Parseghian, I said that it was like playing for royalty. More than one person suggested to me that the inside story of that period would make for a great book. In fact, while other books have been published about the remarkable Ara Parseghian era at Notre Dame, none had been written primarily from the viewpoint of the many players who experienced it I worked with journalist Pete Sampson in gathering some initial interviews, but after a while lost focus as other things came along in life.

I put the project aside for several years until 2013, when I contacted fellow Notre Dame graduate Ray Serafin, a former journalist and now a speechwriter. Ray was unsure at first, but his lovely wife, Ann Kastrantas Serafin, urged him to take it on, believing it would be a project that would be good for his spirit. She was right, and Ray and I worked together to bring this book to life. My beautiful wife, Aileen, also provided steadfast support and encouragement that was important in seeing the project through.

The authors could not have put together this book without the assistance of many people. John Heisler, the sports information director at Notre Dame, made a number of valuable suggestions about how to gather information and get the interest of a publisher. He provided the annual football reviews published by the Notre Dame *Scholastic*, the nation's oldest continuously running collegiate publication. We want to express our thanks to all of the student editors and writers who worked on those yearly football publications, which provide a vivid chronicle of what transpired during the entire Ara Parseghian era. In addition, we made use of many Notre Dame football game highlights that have been uploaded to YouTube over the years. We also wish to extend our appreciation to some folks who gave us excellent counsel and support, in particular Michael Amodei, executive editor at Ave Maria Press on the Notre Dame campus and Bill Haney, a veteran author, editor, and publisher, who suggested that our book would fit in "the sweet spot" at Triumph Books in Chicago.

It turned out that Tom Bast, editorial director at Triumph Books, was someone whom I had gotten to know and played handball with when I traveled the Midwest representing Nautilus some years before. This was one of several moments of serendipity that came into play for us. We provided Tom some initial chapters, and he supported our project, while also giving us some frank feedback on how we could make it better. We also had the pleasure to work with Jeff Fedotin, who took on the role of editing and guiding us through the process for Triumph Books. The sketches in this book were created by my talented artist son, Thomas Pomarico.

The authors also wish to acknowledge other material that we drew from in writing this book:

The Lonely Victory, Peter Habeler (Simon & Schuster, 1979)

Resurrection: The Miracle Season That Saved Notre Dame, Jim Dent (Thomas Dunne Books, 2009)

The Phantom Letters: Motivation at Notre Dame in the Parseghian Era, Tom Pagna (St. Augustine's Press, 2005)

God, Country, Notre Dame: The Autobiography of Theodore M. Hesburgh, Theodore M. Hesburgh with Jerry Reedy (University of Notre Dame Press, 1990)

"Epic Battle of Opposites: Irish vs. Tide in 1973," Bill Pennington, *New York Times,* December 8, 2012

Ara Parseghian: 1956–1963, Northwestern University Library, University Archives

"Parseghian Quits Irish Grid Post," David Condon, *Chicago Tribune*, December 16, 1974

"Dan Devine Gets Notre Dame Job," Cooper Rollow, *Chicago Tribune*, December 17, 1974

Camelot, book and lyrics by Alan Jay Lerner, music by Frederick Loewe

Finally, the authors want to thank the dozens of former players, coaches, and friends who shared their memories. Just listening to these individuals made the project worthwhile. The amazing thing is how willingly they shared their memories of those years and their reflections on how their association with their coaches and teammates influenced their lives. Here is a list of those who gave their time (all were Notre Dame players or coaches unless otherwise noted; years and positions based on the online University of Notre Dame Football Archives).

Denny Allan, running back, 1968–1970; Greg Blache, assistant coach, 1972–1975; Rocky Bleier, running back, 1965–1967; Tom Bolger, offensive lineman, 1971–1973; Luther Bradley, defensive back, 1973, 1975–1977; Tirrel Burton, running back, Miami (Ohio) University, 1953–1955; Jack Cahill, friend from St. Francis Prep and Notre Dame; Jim Carroll, linebacker, 1962–64; Dave Casper, offensive lineman and tight end, 1971–1973; John Cieszkowski, fullback, 1969–1972; Jack Clements, running back, 1971; Tom Clements, quarterback, 1972–1974; Greg Collins, linebacker, 1972–1974; Mike Creaney, tight end, 1970–1972; Tom Creevey, defensive lineman, 1973; John Dampeer, offensive lineman, 1970–1972; Gerry DiNardo, offensive lineman, 1972–1974; Pete Duranko, fullback, defensive lineman, 1963–1966; Bill Etter, quarterback, 1969, 1971–1972; Mike Fanning, defensive lineman, 1972–1974; Thom Gatewood, split end, 1969–1971; Terry Hanratty, quarterback, 1966–1968; George Hayduk, defensive lineman, 1971–1973; Bill Hickey, assistant coach, 1969–1974; John Huarte, quarterback, 1962–1964; Andy Huff, fullback, 1969, 1971–1972; Jim Leahy, offensive lineman,

1968; Jim Lynch, linebacker, 1964–1966; Mike McCoy, defensive lineman, 1967–1969; Wally Moore, assistant coach, 1966–1974; Dan Morrin, offensive lineman, 1971–1973; Bob Neidert, defensive lineman, 1968–1970; Mike Oriard, offensive lineman, 1968–1969; Tom Pagna, running back, Miami (Ohio), 1950–53, assistant coach, Northwestern 1959–1963 and Notre Dame, 1964–1974; Mike Parseghian, running back, 1974; Eric Penick, running back, 1972–1974; Gary Potempa, linebacker, 1971–1973; Steve Quehl, offensive lineman, 1972–1973, 1975; Pat Sarb, defensive back, 1974; Pete Schivarelli, defensive lineman, 1969–1970; Tim Simon, split end, 1973, defensive back, 1975; Pat Steenberge, quarterback, 1970–1971; Mike Stock, fullback, Northwestern, 1958–1960, assistant coach, Notre Dame, 1969–1974; Tim Sullivan, linebacker 1971–1973; Joe Theismann, quarterback, 1968–1970; Rich Thomann, linebacker, 1969–1971; Mike Townsend, defensive back, 1971–1973; Roger Valdiserri, sports information director, 1966–1995; Max Wasilevich, offensive lineman, 1973.